The Grief Survival Guide

Navigating Loss and All That Comes With It

Jeff Brazier

HODDER &
STOUGHTON

First published in Great Britain in 2017 by Hodder & Stoughton
An Hachette UK company

This book is a work of non-fiction based on the life, experiences and
recollections of the author. In some cases names of people, places and
certain details have been changed to protect the privacy of others.

A CIP catalogue record for this title is available from the British Library

Hardback ISBN 978 1 473 66025 0
Trade paperback ISBN 978 1 473 66026 7
Ebook ISBN 978 1 473 66027 4

Typeset in Celeste by Hewer Text UK Ltd, Edinburgh
Printed and bound by Clays Ltd, St Ives plc

Hodder & Stoughton policy is to use papers that are natural, renewable
and recyclable products and made from wood grown in sustainable
forests. The logging and manufacturing processes are expected to
conform to the environmental regulations of the country of origin.

Hodder & Stoughton Ltd
Carmelite House
50 Victoria Embankment
London EC4Y 0DZ

www.hodder.co.uk

To my beautiful sons, Bobby and Freddy, whose lives have given me purpose, fulfillment and an unequivocal love. Your futures will forever be my greatest pleasure, honour and achievement. I write this book predominantly for you, to inspire and comfort you and others, in the hope that by sharing our story, the successes and the failures, we may benefit others around the world; those who are also experiencing the darkness, loneliness and desperation created by the indisputable effects of grief.

Contents

Introduction

'If you're not living then you're dying, no matter your age or health' – Mary Turner, 69, died from ovarian cancer on 12 April 2017 shortly after generously sharing her wisdom and wit for the good of others in this book.

Our personal relationship with grief is unique. You as a person are different to every other human being on the planet, so it makes perfect sense that no two people would grieve identically.

You may have lost someone from your life without the opportunity to say goodbye, or at the end of a struggle with a long-term illness. You may have to deal with losing someone and feeling that you could have done more to help them. The variations of the end-of-life scenario are limitless, so bear this in mind when searching for answers and meaning behind bereavement, because nobody can decide how you cope but yourself.

The way you feel in grief is dependent upon many factors and it's impossible to second-guess how you will process those feelings. Will you give yourself permission to cry? Will you load yourself with feelings of blame and guilt? Will you hide your emotions from the kids to protect them? Will you pretend to feel nothing?

The point is, you're not alone. But what I aim to show you in this book is that there are ways to make grief less harsh and eventually become manageable, and there are almost as many ways to unwittingly make bereavement harder and let it go from being an excruciatingly tough experience to a constant source of difficulty.

Grief is bloody good at hide-and-seek and will pretty much find you each and every time, no matter how long it took you to cram yourself into the washing basket while expertly putting some dirty underwear on your head for cover. You have no choice but to sit down nicely and play Scrabble with it.

Why you, Brazier?

Because I am the teenager whose mother sat him down to tell him that the biological father he had not known about, let alone met, had drowned in a riverboat accident four years before that day. I am the 22-year-old sobbing uncontrollably outside the church after the sharp introduction to death that only your first funeral can deliver.

I am the 29-year-old receiving the phone call that made me drop to my knees and changed my world forever. I'm the same 29-year-old who had six months to prepare two young children for the inconceivable while coming to terms with an unimaginable change of reality.

'How will I cope? I still feel like a child myself. How do I compensate for the irreplaceable? How? What? Why? When?'

You and I are more alike than you might think.

I've been the person who visits you and talks to you about the loss of your wife, hoping that my experience up to then might serve in some way useful. I'm the student who qualifies as a life coach and NLP practitioner so I can accelerate the process for people coming to terms with a number of issues, including death. I am the talking therapist who learns more about bereavement through my clients than I could have ever known through personal experience.

I am a man writing a book about our relationship with grief so that

I might shine a light on your path and help you find what you need – your navigational companion on life's inevitable yet thoroughly unpredictable, unwanted and uncertain adventure.

What is grief?

Before you begin, to get you started it's important that I share with you some of the perspective I have gained through this writing process. What do you think grief is? If you closed your eyes and imagined a picture of grief, what would it look like? Is it the grim reaper? A black cloud? An aggressive-looking monster?

We feel like a victim of grief sometimes. We wish it would leave us alone, let us get on with our day without dictating our weary emotions and making us cry or feel profoundly sad. Why can't we grieve at our own pace, in our own time? Why does it have to be so engulfing and downright inconvenient? We see grief as the enemy, the reason everything is up in the air, meaning we can't think straight or see any further than what we're doing right now.

Now let me just ask you, what would happen if grief didn't exist? If we didn't look back, because it didn't hurt to see people die? What would remind us to think of that person? Would we need to set alarms on our calendar to remember them? If grief didn't exist, how would that impact on how close we got to people, seeing as it didn't emotionally come at a cost when they died? How would we show how valuable they were to us in life and after their life had ended?

I'm not trying to tell you how you should feel about grief; my main intention is to get you *thinking* about it. As you read through the chapters of this book, you will gain so much perspective, insight that will challenge what you know about loss, so it would be useful for you to keep a journal throughout each chapter, so you can record and re-use the subtle differences to the way that you think.

Here's how I see grief

I see him as a man called Jeffrey, Jeffrey Grief. A short, quiet, rose-cheeked and inconspicuous middle-aged man with a little moustache, wearing braces, a pin-stripe shirt and a green tie. His trousers have a very strong crease in the front and while he is anything but fashionable he is meticulous in his appearance and wears well-shined shoes with an outfit that never alters.

He strikes me as the kind of guy who probably still lives with his mum, Mrs Grief. He is socially awkward but very into his work. He is a freelancer so he has many clients who require his services. He has no fixed office, which saves him on the overheads, and he personally likes the fact that he can work remotely, contacting his clients any place at any time.

He doesn't take a day off, he is never late and never bends the rules. His attention to detail is staggering and his thorough approach has won him many efficiency-in-the-workplace awards, which he keeps on a shelf in his bedroom, at his mum's.

His role at work is to tap you, his employer, on the shoulder. His job is to remind you of the person who has died. He doesn't take it personally when you curse his existence; he knows it's part of the job and that one day you'll have a much more amicable working relationship.

Within that working relationship he guides his clients expertly through a series of thoughts and emotions that are absolutely necessary to their overall well-being. He holds their hands through a lot of rough times, and sure, he is the one who triggers the thought that brings about the feelings, but he is a professional and always stays around long enough to ensure that his client has got exactly what they need from it.

If his job is going well, the time he spends with that client reduces until the client has accepted their working relationship and has even started to invite Jeffrey into their home and on outings, particularly on special occasions.

Mr Grief always feels happy knowing his work is appreciated by his client but he never goes beyond the protocol and maintains a dignified distance. This is business, not personal, you see. There comes a time when Jeffrey shakes hands with his client and leaves them with their memories. He sends cards and the odd email from time to time, just to ensure that relationship is never forgotten, but the end of one client's journey heralds the beginning of another's.

Jeffrey loves the variation in his clients, remarking that 'You never really know what you're going to get.' Some clients learn that they have to work with him a lot sooner than others; either way, he loves the challenge.

Some clients make a very bad habit of running from him, but little do they know, he won the Sussex School Inter-district Cross-country Championship five years in a row. Although he's in his early forties, Jeffrey is one of those wiry-looking runners who don't look fit, but boy does he have an engine on him!

He is a regular attendant at the Hove Park Run, for which he regularly chalks up 5k in a time of 16 minutes and 38 seconds. Very competitive! There really is no hope of outwitting or outmanoeuvring this fellow, so until his clients realise this he just sees it as extra fitness for him.

Jeffrey once had a date through Plenty of Fish and on his profile he put that his biggest quality was his patience. He needed to have lots – living with his mother wasn't easy and also many of his clients were very skilled at denying his existence.

Work policy states that although he can tap someone on the shoulder an unlimited number of times every day, a tap on the shoulder is all that he can administer, so if that isn't enough to grab their attention he simply has to persist, over and over again, until he is acknowledged.

Jeffrey also added on his application that he liked playing

Scrabble, baking cakes and collects rare birds' eggs as his listed hobbies. Grief isn't really scary in this context, is he? Just a guy doing his job. I could carry on the description forever, but for the sake of your sanity and before you change your mind about reading the rest of this book, I'll leave it there.

The point of sharing my elaborate metaphor for the actual role that grief plays in our life is that reducing something that we could potentially be scared of to something that we understand and do not fear is of great benefit.

We can't understand something that we are not willing to observe, and only those who face grief, whatever shape and size it is for you, can actually start to understand what it looks like and how it works. Scary as it might be, you wouldn't walk down a dark alley with your eyes closed, would you? Well, the same applies to grief. You'd be taking a common yet unnecessary risk by refusing to watch where you were going.

The biggest lie we are told in grief

There's no better place to start this book than by tackling the biggest misconception I hear in grief. So often people are told to 'be strong', a phrase or decision that can be taken two ways. Sadly, the typical interpretation of what it is to be strong in grief is the complete opposite to the actual truth.

The root of this sentiment – being strong in the face of adversity – may well have become popular since it chimed with what our parents or grandparents experienced in their childhoods during and after the Second World War. In the forties and fifties there were so many immi-nent dangers to actual life and real concerns about keeping safe, or worrying about loved ones fighting for the country, that you had to set aside what could be seen as 'petty or selfish worries' when so much physical suffering was going on around you. These ingrained sensibilities may well have contributed to the repression of some of our true feelings.

I'm always interested to know what my clients think strength is in the context of suffering or grief – 'Putting everyone else first, keeping it together, carrying on' would represent a typical response, often followed by a list of reasons they felt they had to stay strong. One client told me: 'My younger sister needs me, she lost her husband. I have to be strong for my mum because I don't want to add to her problems. I've got two teenagers who are going through a tough time and I can't crumble in front of them.' Like many of us, she had compiled a long list of reasons not to grieve openly.

Weakness in the face of suffering or grief can often be perceived as crying, burdening others or not getting as much done because you're too upset. And if you do allow yourself to be weak? Some feel that they would 'probably sob all day'. Another suggestion is that you might store your unspent tears in boxes that you can't open because you're scared it will flood out and you will drown in them.

Boxing up your tears or emotions is never helpful in the long run, and if you find yourself doing this or something similar you will be in danger of storing up so many boxes that you will risk damaging your health and mental well-being. Piling new boxes on top of existing ones doesn't mean the tears in the older boxes aren't still there.

Your family can all see that you're boxing things up and it's only really you who thinks it's a secret. Your partner and family won't think it's a secret because they have to deal with the floods of tears when you break down at night. The kids know you have boxes whenever they see how stressed they make you. Some secret!

By 'being strong' you may be reducing your ability to support your family effectively. In harbouring such a stack of negativity and sadness, the boxes will inevitably fall over, spilling all the contents everywhere. Which your family, who you're trying to protect in the first place, will have to mop up.

Suppressing all your emotions is perceived by some as the strong thing to do. But it isn't, and nowadays we recognise that sharing our feelings and distress is a sign of strength. Of course we have the right to hold on to our baggage, or boxes created by the suppression of grief. There is, however, another option, and it is better to give the contents of those boxes to the 'charity shop' than it is to hang on to them all in storage, which is very costly. (Yes, we are still talking about emotional baggage!)

If you 'hoard' grief, one day you will not be able to move. Every room and available space in your front and back garden will be occupied with 'worthless toot'. Instead, keep your memories in the loft and on your walls, put your emotions out with the trash once a week, and see how they're recycled into the fuel that inspires an honest journey through grief. Can you picture your house of grief? Is it clean and tidy, or cluttered and unkept?

Strength is allowing yourself to be vulnerable, to be real and to answer honestly any questions you are posed on a daily basis on your emotional state. To be able to live in the moment, no matter how unappealing that truth is, is to show great courage and kindness to yourself. Even if your physical appearance may suggest you are going through tremendous stress, tiredness and great upset, that's exactly how we should feel after a big loss, isn't it? Grief is meant to hurt. It would be unrealistic to expect anything else. That's the overriding point here. If you continue fostering an outdated approach by hiding the reality, keeping it all locked away, showing the world a very different story to the emotional rollercoaster rocketing around within you, you are being weak. Strength is the ability to do what's best for you, to allow what is natural and to keep expressing your emotions, no matter how ugly, challenging or desperate that becomes.

This is the guide that nobody wants but that everybody needs. I hope – in some small way – it helps you.

1

The Worst News Imaginable

A terminal prognosis.

There is no right or wrong way to react when you are told your illness is too advanced to cure and there will be different responses for different people. For most, however, this is unbelievable, shocking news. Even if you knew there was an outside chance it might happen, hearing it from your doctor will be devastating.

You may fall silent. You may not be able to believe what you're hearing and not know what to say or do. You may start to cry and feel as though you won't be able to stop. You may feel numb, as though you have no emotion. You may become very irate and scared.

The likely questions that will rush through your mind are:

Why me?

Have I done something to deserve this?

Why can't you find a treatment to help me?

It is natural to feel desperate, upset, angry or disbelieving. Be sure to give yourself the time and space to take in what is happening. You might want to be on your own. Or you may need to spend time with your partner, family or friends to help you deal with the news; and then, of course, there is the matter of how you break it to others, given that you hardly want to accept it yourself.

When you do find the words for others they will also be very upset and feel that they don't know what to say. Even if all you can do at first is get upset together, that can be a huge help. There really are no words at this point, just feeling.

If you don't feel like talking straight away, don't. Just let the people around you know that's what you need. However, you shouldn't push your emotions aside completely. It's always better to express how you feel and allow your emotions to come to the surface – even if that is uncomfortable and hard to cope with. Has my body let me down? Have I let my body down? What if I hadn't been so careless with my health? But I've always taken such good care of myself. We look for a logical reason, a 'thing' to blame our life sentence on. Sometimes a lack of an explanation makes it worse. Questions everywhere and very little by way of a solid answer. I'd always assumed life ends when you're old. Suddenly we imagine what it feels like to die. I begrudge the thought even entering my mind. Is it worse to know we're going to die or to realise we haven't sufficiently lived? How silly do we feel for assuming life was a 'given'?

2

Breaking the News

Telling family and friends will be a particularly daunting task; in fact it will be the hardest sentence you'll ever have had to deliver. If you don't give your loved ones the benefit of your new reality, then they won't be able to start adjusting to the facts. The pain of finding out will never compare to the pain of losing you. One you can keep from them until you're ready; the latter is quite uncontainable. The truth and facts are not pleasant, but it's the reality, so let them have that at least.

I very clearly remember the conversation that I had with Jade in the Royal Marsden. She didn't want to tell the boys, who were four and five at the time, that she would now definitely be saying goodbye to them at some near point. We had told them a story up until then that Mummy might have to go to heaven because of how ill she felt, but that she was doing everything she could to feel better.

In that period there was still hope for the children and they were always very eager to know if Mummy was going to be OK, when Mummy would be coming home, etc. When she received the final prognosis and knew she was going to die, we had to discuss when the right time to tell them would be.

She knew she had to do it because she wanted them to know the truth. They needed to adjust to what their soon-to-be sabotaged future held and they needed to be able to ask all of the questions that would infest their poor minds on learning about the tragic news.

She decided the time had to be now. I brought them into the room and at her request left them in privacy, waiting silently outside the door. She bravely told them the story that we had agreed was best for them to hear – that God wanted Mummy to be an angel and that soon he would send for her and she would become a big, bright star that they would be able to see in the sky on its way to heaven. It's heartbreaking that she had to say goodbye to her young children – or that anyone ever needs to do the same – and the thought of that conversation always reduces me to tears. Our poor boys, poor Jade.

They soon burst out of the room and continued to play with the toys in the waiting area, almost as though they hadn't heard anything. It wasn't the reaction I was expecting – there were no tears – and I realise now, of course, that they were simply in shock, refusing to acknowledge the devastating piece of information that Mummy had just given them. Why would they?

I had to ask them if they had understood what Mummy had told them just so they didn't completely suppress the moment, but they didn't want to deal with it and all I could do was hold them as tight as I could and tell them that I would always be there for them. It wasn't until later that evening, when we returned to Glasgow to rejoin the *X Factor* tour that I was hosting, that the questions began.

Knowing the truth meant that they could spend the following six weeks venting their disapproval, resenting the cancer that was going to take their mummy away. We talked at length about where she was going, what she would be doing and how she would get all of her hair back and be able to wear all her nice dresses. It never took the pain and apprehension away, but it gave them answers.

When Jade died on 22 March 2009, I broke the news to them that evening after taking a few hours to compose myself. They weren't with her when she died. We had been on the tour up until that point, keeping busy, benefitting from the safety that the tour bubble afforded us, being around lots of caring and considerate individuals who wrapped us up in their warmth. As soon as I woke up that morning I knew; a look at my phone confirmed it – lots of missed calls and messages telling me what had happened. I immediately booked flights for us to return home. Jade and I had agreed that it would be better for the boys this way. We didn't feel that they should be present leading up to the moment she died. They had said goodbye and they had been waiting for me to confirm days later that she was finally on her way to heaven.

While travelling back I thought about telling them. It was going to be an impossible task and I had no idea of the words to use. Just before sitting them down, I walked out into the garden for some air and to my complete surprise there she was, one solitary shining star in the clear night sky.

I walked the boys outside and there were few words required – they knew who the star was and we sat gazing up at her for a while before blowing kisses and getting into bed to face the unknown together.

Feelings you may have when you are the one receiving the diagnosis

My experiences aside, over the first few days, you can go through a range of emotions. They may change very quickly and sometimes you might feel numb or as though you're having some kind of out-of-body experience.

Some people describe how they felt very calm and detached when they were first told they didn't have long to live. That's adrenalin kicking in and it gives us short, sharp clarity but it runs out eventually and leaves us to deal with the emotions it was masking.

At different times, you will probably feel shock, anger and sadness. These emotions can feel overwhelming. This news will mean that you can't plan your future in the way you had hoped. Dying may mean leaving behind a partner, children and other important people in your life. You may wonder how they will cope and not want to see them upset, and feelings of guilt can arise as a consequence.

You may find it difficult to look around and see life going on as normal for most people. It can feel very strange to watch others appearing carefree or complaining about things that you, with your new perspective on the value of life, may find hard to hear.

Coping with this rollercoaster of feelings can be absolutely exhausting. You may feel as if you are stuck under a huge black cloud and that there is no point in doing anything.

Most people will have some or all of these emotions. This usually changes gradually. Many people say that the intensity and distress lessens in time. This doesn't mean that you stop worrying or feeling upset. But the feelings get more bearable. You will most likely be able to think about your situation a little more calmly and plan what you want to do.

Sharing your emotions

Sharing your fears and sadness with people you love and trust is vital, because talking about your feelings helps you to cope. It also helps your friends and family to understand more about your situation. In turn, this will help them to assist and support you.

Working on the assumptions of what others want you to do and feel, or others assuming what you might not want to talk about, does nothing to help the situation. Clear communication of fears, struggles, complications and desires means you're all on the same page and no time or effort is wasted on 'guessing' how everyone feels.

However, some people find sharing their thoughts and emotions too difficult, and would rather keep things to themselves. It is important to do whatever feels best for you. Whether we choose to do what's for the best or what feels easiest is up to us, and usually we slide from one to the other.

That said, this needs to happen in your own time, so don't let other people pressure you into talking straight away if you don't feel ready. This is a very personal, emotional time. You can choose how you handle things. If you would like to talk, make sure you choose people you can talk to easily, who will understand how you feel and be able to support you. If, after a while, you still feel overwhelmed and that you can't cope, try speaking to someone outside your immediate family and friends, someone with no connection whatsoever.

Some perspective

Throughout my personal experience of having four relatives go through the process of learning they will die and seeing a number of clients in various stages of their diagnosis, one thing becomes abundantly obvious: some of the most alive people in our society are somewhat surprisingly those who have been given a length of time to live. This also gives an interesting perspective on what it means to be 'alive' and in contrast what 'dying' actually means too.

Is it a moment or a process? Are we alive right up to the second that we make our transition or do you consider yourself dying when you receive a terminal prognosis? I think we're all dying if you consider we are nearer our death each passing moment of our lives.

Some have a tendency to take a term given by doctors very literally, and sadly exhaust or reduce their efforts immediately, but others take it as a challenge, creating an act of defiance that gives a life new purpose and, very often, more time.

Something that really jumps out is how significant our mindset is to our chances of a prolonged life, if that's what we want.

3
Four Women

An Introduction

Mary, Heidi, Dawn and Andrea: four women of different ages who shared their experiences with me. I was able to explore a range of issues with them, and their thoughtful responses to my questions are given in the following chapters. Here is a quick introduction to them.

Mary Turner, aged 68. Diagnosed with ovarian cancer in March 2011, leading to a terminal diagnosis in April 2014 when she was given eighteen months to live. Mary gave me her interview two years and seven months after that date and remained positive and upbeat until the moment she confidently told her family she was 'going' on 12 April 2017.

Heidi Loughlin, aged 34, mother of two beautiful boys, Tait, age 2 and Noah, age three. Heidi initially mistook inflammatory breast cancer for mastitis in September 2015 while pregnant with her daughter Alley Louise, who sadly died from a bleed on the brain eight days after birth. Inflammatory breast cancer is rare – only 500 women in the UK currently have it. IBC differs from other types of breast cancer in its symptoms, outlook and treatment. Symptoms include breast swelling, redness of the skin and pitting or ridging of the skin of the breast so that it may have a texture like orange peel. Heidi was given a term of two and a half years from September

2016, after starting the drug Kadcyla.

Dawn Sharpe, aged 50, mother of two, Jaimie, 29 and Conor, 21. Diagnosed with cancer in 2004, told she was terminal in 2009 and given two years to live. Eight years later Dawn has been nicknamed 'the miracle' by her doctors.

Aundrea Bannatyne, aged 42. Single mother of two boys, Jack, 14 and James, 10. Diagnosed with pancreatic cancer on 13 July 2016 and given a prognosis four weeks later of six to twelve months' life expectancy.

A terminal illness is a disease that cannot be cured or adequately treated and that is reasonably expected to result in the death of the patient within a short period of time. This term is more commonly used for progressive diseases such as cancer or advanced heart disease.

Irrespective of its literal or medical definitions, some people feel that the title isn't a true reflection of their current reality, refusing to be defined this way and preferring to use different language to describe themselves.

What does your terminal diagnosis mean to you?
Heidi: 'I understand the need to describe the fact that we have a "term" to see out, but isn't that true for all of us, ill or not? I'm alive and will be right up until these drugs I'm on stop working and there aren't any others to replace them.'

Regardless of your attitude towards the terminology, having a life-limiting illness such as cancer can also be a catalyst for the most inspirational behaviour. It has always struck me that in the face of death, those who have learned of their imminent fate often suddenly burst into life – the very opposite of what those around them might have expected or be comfortable seeing.

Heidi: 'I've never been more alive than I am today. It's the most refreshing perspective on all the things that matter. It's given me the tools to appreciate and respect the things that are not worth worrying about.'

There is a lot to do in terms of concluding personal affairs and arranging other people's futures. Preparation for all involved can follow a similar path, although there is a huge difference between the person who is in a place of acceptance of their fate and the one who is absolutely refusing to accept the outcome. As Mary Turner, my first interviewee for the book, professed: 'At a point, it becomes less about the person who is leaving and more about those that are being left behind.'

That was just one statement of true acceptance and courage of the many that Mary and my other kind contributors offered in conversation about the key considerations in preparation for death.

If you're enduring a diagnosis with a term and feel like you have a reasonable level of acceptance, then the areas below may steer you in the right direction or at least start prompting you to ask yourself and others the right questions.

Alternatively, you may feel this is all too painful to face, or, like Aundrea Bannatyne, you simply do not accept the prognosis: 'I loathe the words "terminal diagnosis". They don't know me, they've literally written me off and told me to go home and make memories, but I'm too headstrong and too determined. Right now I'm only taking two paracetamol a day for the pain and I'm proving them wrong already.'

How did you break the news to loved ones?
There's no right or wrong here but it's a tough secret to keep, so while you might feel like you would be protecting your loved ones by not telling them, what you are actually doing is restricting their chance to make the very most of the time they have left with you. Time is precious as you know, so don't waste any.

Mary: 'I told my daughter in the car park of a golf club and she ran off crying. It was hard for her to accept at the time.'

Heidi: 'I got the news while I was sat next to my husband and we were just broken together. He's a rock, though.'

Dawn: 'I got the news on my son's seventeenth birthday. I desperately didn't want to ruin it for him but when I got home, he just knew.'

Aundrea: 'When I told the boys I sat them down and said that I had a tiny bit of cancer in me. I explained that it was nowhere near as big as James's (Aundrea's son who battled cancer successfully as a young child) and that he was only a baby and he beat it. I told them that I was much bigger and stronger so I would fight as hard as I could. My dad told my mum, as I couldn't face telling her as I knew she would go to pieces.'

What are the scariest thoughts you have?
Negative thoughts induced by fear are undoubtedly natural for those with a terminal diagnosis, but it's what you do with those thoughts that really matters.

Heidi: 'From the moment I was diagnosed I've hated the thought of saying goodbye to the boys. I can see it in my head. It'll be in a hospice, the boys will walk in and I won't know if it's the last time I'll ever see them. I'll try and have this heartfelt conversation with them and one of them will have a tantrum and then them leaving and not knowing if that's it. It plays out in my mind every day, usually at night. I try and distract myself to get it out of my head and then remind myself there's a long way to go yet.'

Mary: 'Sometimes I wake up in the middle of the night and start thinking about my husband moving on; even though I accept that and I don't want him to be lonely, it can start feeling like he is cheating on me because the thoughts seem so real! I have a daughter in the States, so I go on Facebook and just start having a conversation with her, then the thoughts drift away.'

Dawn: 'Not seeing the boys grow, not seeing the grandkids grow. Not being able to communicate at the end. I know the pain will be managed but I want to be "with it" at the end. I don't think I know how to get rid of these thoughts, it's always there, but you have to get on with your life and try not to let what you are feeling impact the people around you. I think that's why I'm always upbeat, as I don't want my life to have a negative impact on people's lives, I don't want them to be sad or feel sorry for me. I'm always thinking about the memories that I'm leaving behind, and I don't want them to be sad; I want fun memories that will maybe help my family if they ever have to face something like this again. I pray they don't, but it could happen to anyone.'

Aundrea: 'Scariest thoughts . . . me dying and how my boys will cope without me. Them growing up and I'm not there to look out for them. Knowing my parents would never get over it. I worry that my mum will have a breakdown.'

4

Adjustment and Acceptance

Adjustment to a terminal prognosis

There seem to be two categories that an individual with a term may at first fall into: someone who accepts the prognosis and the term they have been told to expect and another who simply doesn't or cannot. Which camp are you in and are there any benefits in that for you?

Why adjust?

There are two schools of thought here. It really just depends on a number of variables, such as the stage of the illness at diagnosis, your attitude towards your illness, your strength and determination, your experiences in life, influences and support around you and, most importantly, the motivations you have for going on.

Those who feel partially or fully responsible for their illness (for example, lung cancer in frequent smokers) may be more inclined to accept their term than someone who feels that they have no reason to have been struck with any ill health.

If you feel like you probably deserve the illness through choices you have made throughout your life, then this may lead you to a different type of acceptance, 'because I deserve it'. I'm not sure anyone particularly deserves an illness of such devastating capabilities, but the specific mindset may be that 'I have treated my body badly, therefore given the risks, it doesn't come as a great surprise that I'm now ill.'

An older person who has lived a full and satisfying life may also be more accepting of their prognosis because they may think, 'If I was ever going to get something terminal, it's better that it waited until I'd seen a respectable amount of life.' Again this depends on the individual and their attitude towards their reality and their expectations of life.

What do I get from adjustment?

Time to prepare. Those who refuse to accept run the risk of running out of precious time – time that could have been spent preparing their families, themselves, their finances, their belongings, maximising the memories they're leaving behind that become tools for a more manageable experience of loss. For one person, time spent refusing to acknowledge the prognosis is time wasted; for another it is time spent being positive, attempting to extend life, daring to defy the odds and dreaming of a miracle. There is no right or wrong, only the instinct that comes naturally to you. I believe the way you are coping with your prognosis was preconditioned by your experiences in life long before you knew of any ill health, but there are no rules against changing your mind if something you've spoken of or read about makes sense to you. Ultimately, it's your time to do what you want with, ensuring that what you are doing is for the right reasons.

Personalising the details

You can exercise 'choice' in many ways and decide the arrangements for your final moments and beyond by arranging the funeral and celebration of life afterwards. Family members take comfort in your being in control because it eliminates the stress of getting it wrong for them.

You can be more purposeful in the memories you leave behind, making events for family and friends, given the likelihood that you will be in better health closer to the beginning of your term. You have more time to plan and more time to enjoy those significant moments knowing the value of them to everyone around you.

I also believe the period of acceptance, whether it comes to you straight away or not, grants you the ability to focus on your quality of life. You may have two years doing all of the above, feeling a large element of control in the process and doing things on your terms. Alternatively, you may have four years of fighting, prolonging a life with a purpose to fight, defy, push and refuse only to submit in the end.

The Negatives of Acceptance

The Unknown

How will you know what you could have achieved if you had battled the news for longer? In contrast to the above, you could be given a prognosis of two years and with a fighting spirit, live for ten. I think it's one thing accepting and adjusting to the presence of the illness and that it may one day catch up with you, but another thing to accept the length of term. To accept the dates is to assume that doctors get the timing right every time, and I don't think that is the case.

Demotivation

Having the mindset that 'I'm going to die' without allocating any kind of timescale is the most harmful form of acceptance. The worst-case scenario may feel realistic to some, but it's possible that it could simply diminish your fight and will to live, and any time available may be cut short as a result.

There is a great deal of interest around just what decides how long we can go on for after we have been given a time to live. Is it our mental strength, the existence of strong motivating factors such as reaching anniversaries, seeing a grandchild born or being at a wedding? Is it that our religious or spiritual beliefs make a difference or can we gain time by telling ourselves we must stay alive because there are things we fear will happen to others around us if we don't?

It's hard to prove or disprove these theories either way, but what really matters is that we have a reason, a motivation, a goal or a person that gives us the energy, the strength and the belief that we cannot just create or extend time, but that we can enjoy it and achieve many things with the time that we are alive.

5

Staring Life in the Face

In the final stages of our lives there are many things we can be doing to ensure that we leave as much of us behind as we possibly can. Some of us are waiting to die but some are too busy living. Whatever it is for you, there is still choice. There are usually other people for us to think about, so how can we help them and continue being ourselves in the process?

Making those final arrangements

Music, hymns, readings ... Families can really benefit when you choose it all for them, because then they get the satisfaction of knowing it's exactly what you would have wanted and it avoids your family having to make potentially contentious decisions at a time when they are likely to be in shock or disbelief. That said, relatives may want to put a personal touch to the service too, so it's important that families know that while you've provided the backbone of the ceremony there is always space for them to add to it.

Mary Turner told me: 'I'm going to be cremated some distance away from the committal, so I've arranged for my husband and daughters to go for a walk on our favourite beach and then I'll come back the next day in a jar. My friend has a boat and my family will go out to sea and scatter my ashes for me. Incidentally, my friend bought a bigger boat a few weeks ago. I called him up and said, "I'm arriving in a jar, not a coffin. You needn't have bothered!"'

Heidi Loughlin reluctantly stated: 'When, if I feel really ill, I might start thinking about it, but until then I just can't see myself not being here. Everything I've ever done has been done with humour so there would need to be some in there on the day.'

Dawn said: 'I can only go on what I learnt from when Jamie's dad died, Jamie felt so left out of the arrangement for his dad, and he wanted to arrange everything but the family took over, I saw how important it was to Jamie to do this himself, so I have left little notes and ideas for him and Conor to make my final arrangements. I would hope that it would be funny and not too down, I would like different people to speak for me, I don't want everything spoken by the priest who doesn't know me. I would like you Jeff, as my friend, to speak about my cancer journey and how I have dealt with it. So that was me asking you to speak at my funeral.' (As a good friend of mine, I told Dawn that it would be my privilege.)

After the funeral

In our multicultural society there are many mourning traditions, such as a Jewish shiva, a Muslim family gathering post-funeral, or Hindu tradition where a number of days after the funeral mourners bring food to a relative's house and have a ceremony to liberate the deceased's soul to heaven.

More generally, outside religious traditions, people might like to hold a wake, which can happen at a home, a hall or maybe a pub. Family members can gather and drink to the memory of the deceased, celebrate their life by exchanging memories and maybe even having a good dance to their favourite songs. You might like to decide the venue and type of music, and put a few quid behind the bar, or like Mary, you might like to actually have the wake before you say goodbye.

Mary: 'We've had the wake already! Didn't make sense not being there, I didn't want to miss out. Everybody had lots of fun and I said a few unofficial goodbyes. If I'm here in another year I'll have another one.'

Dawn: 'After the funeral I would like for everyone to have a party, maybe a bit of karaoke, have a few southern comforts on my behalf, lots of lovely food, and remember me for being a bit of a party animal. The idea of a living wake is appealing but not just yet, but it is something to think about. I'm not too sure I could handle my family responses to it, and I'm not too sure I could hold up and keep the smile on my face.'

How and when do you want to be remembered?

When you can tell your family how to feel either generally or for specific occasions, you can actually provide their coping mechanisms with a set of rules and boundaries that make their relationship with grief far more straightforward and permissible. Imagine the difference if, on your birthday, your family know to get together at a particular restaurant where they are to enjoy a nice meal and raise a glass in your memory, because that's what you requested they do once a year. Jade instructed me to never let the boys forget her. We've comfortably ensured that could never be the case, but if she had been a little more specific in her requests I suspect she might have told me to go to Smiths in Ongar with the boys, because it was her favourite restaurant.

Heidi: 'I want the children to know if they want to cry it's OK for them to feel sad, but on those special occasions I want my husband to sit down and remind the children how everything I ever did was for them. I want my husband to have a few drinks and I want my mates to get involved in that, have a bit of a party. I don't want to be responsible for making people feel sad, so I'd like them to have a good story-swapping time and maybe go to the beach, because we go there a lot to eat our sandwiches.'

Now this is an example, of course, but without some kind of direction from you, that anniversary could go by without a get-together and everybody just staying at home feeling very sad because they didn't have a clear picture of what is acceptable on the day.

Lots of families are obviously very capable of arranging their own celebrations and appreciate the benefit of talking together about the person they all miss, but if you feel like you are going to leave a big gap in the family structure, a little encouragement for their own benefit might go a long way.

Dawn: 'I would like my family to continue to celebrate my birthday; maybe come and visit me at the grave, as I'm being buried, then to go out and have a meal and a few drinks.

I come from a very large, close-knit family, we have always spent lots of time together and hopefully that will never change. One of my fondest memories will always be dinner at Mum's, all the brother and sisters' children, and now grandchildren, sitting around Mum's big table with more tables added to it so we can all sit together. I ask that every time there is a family gathering, please set a place for me. I will be there.

My children and friends' family know that I wouldn't want them to be sad. Always remember me with a smile and a giggle, it's ok to grieve and it's ok not to. I want them to live their lives to the fullest, so when their times come they can look back and say "that was one hell of a ride."'

Other than your goals, what is there still left to do in your life?

Bucket list aside, I want to alert you to the benefits of organisation, because I don't want there to come a time when you are not as strong as you have been and you suddenly remember there's something you haven't taken care of. In the early stages of diagnosis, you may face some kind of feeling of indifference, some shock, maybe even a period of denial, which might take you some time to confront and overcome. The frustrating thing is that it's in this period that physically you are in the best condition to look at making the choices detailed in this chapter.

Heidi: 'I use visualisation to imagine myself hitting the milestones, like being there when they start school. A lot of people in cancer-land don't allow themselves to see any further than six months ahead and while I can hugely relate to that, you've got to get on with life in the best way possible. When I take Noah to his first day at primary school next year I know I'll be a mess because at one point it was suggested I might not get that far. You've just got to aim big and what will be will be.'

What happens if you don't get all of the life admin tied up? Your family have to do it. There is usually one among the group who naturally elects themselves to take care of the finances, bills and other responsibilities, and there are professionals that can be hired if there isn't such a person. Don't feel like if you don't get to that stage everyone is going to suffer, because let's face it, the inconvenience of closing an account pales into insignificance, compared to the feelings they are about to encounter when you pass on.

The main benefit of being organised is to gain the feeling of control. In illness, which can be an out- of-control situation, you may take great strength from making decisions while and where you can. It's also a way to maintain a healthy mind when your physical health is in question and, as many people believe, a healthy mind can make a positive difference. If your mental health has been affected then you might like to share control of your personal details and arrangements with a trusted member of your family so you have the peace of mind that the vital information has been passed on while you are in good health.

Mary: 'I'm lucky that I'm older. I've done a lot of research and there's so much to learn about dying. Did you know they close your bank account down on confirmation of your death? I want to be organised so I know it will make things easier for my husband Phil. He'll have less to do, so he and the girls can go away for a few weeks after the event and just concentrate on themselves instead of paperwork.'

How do you want to be supported after your life-limiting prognosis?

Heidi: 'I don't want to be mollycoddled. I just want to be treated normal unless the treatment has made me feel like crap, in which case I want to be given a sick bowl and made a cup of tea. It's people that I don't see very often that are different around me. It's annoying being around people that are uncomfortable around me. They just ask me the same old questions and it gets really boring. I just want to have a laugh.'

Aundrea Bannatyne: 'I surround myself with positive people. I avoid negativity at all costs to protect my mindset.'

Where do you want to go after you die?

This one is completely down to your own interpretation and will depend upon your religious, spiritual or individual views. Whatever brings you comfort is all that matters.

Mary: 'I'd like to see my mum and dad and I have a feeling I will be born again.'

Heidi: 'I like to think there is "somewhere" that we go. I think there has got to be more, otherwise what's the point? I like the idea that I'll be reunited with my daughter again.'

What do you want to come back as?

Imagining a life after death can bring comfort to those enduring their last days; it can also provide the family with a few priceless laughs in a pretty humourless time. When you are no longer here in body, your family can look out for you and gain comfort from questioning if that butterfly or robin perhaps is you. You don't, obviously, have to believe in reincarnation, but I definitely feel like I've been here before – maybe you do too?

Mary: 'I want to come back as a builder or an architect. I'd like to still be a Mary too.'

Heidi: 'I used to like the idea but now I don't because it might mean that I won't meet my daughter again, unless you think that all souls congregate together through the generations.'

This is a challenging time, so how do you feel about it? Do you take with you any regrets?

It's hard to accept the reality of the fact you may not be here forever, and it's even harder to accept when you feel there is so much you haven't done. There are two types of regret: for the things you've done and the things you won't get round to doing. By splitting our regrets in half we can see that the things we haven't achieved are out of our control, which makes them less of a focus.

We can, however, do something about any regrets for the past. If you really want to set yourself free, you can divide that list into two separate columns – people to forgive and people to apologise to – and it goes without saying that if you can take that list and cross each name – or as many as you comfortably can – off after a phone call, letter or text, your feeling of peace is going to multiply.

Your actions would create a very powerful and positive ripple when you do this, but if there are one or two you can't forgive, the exercise of having achieved at least some of the names on the list will still have moved you forwards in your pursuit of an emotional unburdening.

What is the biggest mistake you've made since your diagnosis?
When faced with the most traumatic news – that life will end prematurely – everything we do afterwards can be under extreme stress and sadness, so it's likely we would look back at those early stages after the news feeling like we could have handled one or two things differently.

Heidi: 'I've done some media because of the rareness of the type of cancer I have, and I read some nasty comments about me online, and the biggest mistake is letting those people get under my skin. Because what they said reaffirmed the doubt I have in myself.'

Mary: 'I was looking at some sandals shortly after I was told I had eighteen months and I told myself, what's the point of buying anything now? After thinking about it later on that day I was like, "Hold on! I'm still here!" You can't deny yourself the right to carry on living right up until the end. I went back and bought the sandals and I wear them all the time.'

With life-limiting illnesses, how will you know when it's the right time to go? Is it a date? A number? A feeling? An event?
My grandad Charlie Faldo died in February 2016 and he waited until my brother Lee, his grandson, came back from being on a submarine for three months. When Lee had visited the hospice, he let himself go. There is arguably an element of control we hang on to in deciding which exact day, hour or minute that is.

Those battling a life-limiting illness can gain great comfort in reaching a certain point or milestone and then granting themselves permission to set boundaries around how and when this is to be. Many people I've spoken to prefer to go peacefully in their sleep.

Mary: 'For me it's a quality of life. When I'm stuck in bed doped up on morphine, that's my time.'

JB: 'What if others ask you to hang in there?'

Mary: 'I've asked them not to.'

Heidi: 'I don't think at the age of thirty-four that any time in the next twenty years is acceptable for me. If I had to, I'd say when my first grandchild is born. I've been given a guideline that statistically shows that I've got two and a half years left.'

Deciding for yourself what that right time looks like is the very epitome of taking control in an ultimately uncontrollable scenario. It's a personal decision that you may need to ask your family to respect, because although you may be ready, they might have other ideas.

What can't you do that you wish you could have?

A cruel question to ask someone in their final phase of life? Not if you consider the closeness your family can generate by going there or doing it on your behalf – this one's for you, Mum! Let your family know something you always wished you could have done and they'll do it for you to great satisfaction for all involved. If you do not have close relatives or friends, you should focus on what you did achieve in your life, the places you went and the experiences you collected along the way.

Mary: 'I was really keen to go to the Maldives but we didn't quite make it. I feel really lucky that that is the only thing I don't feel like I got round to doing with my life.'

Heidi: 'I really want to go to America for a six-week trip that we had planned before I got ill, but no fucker will insure me to go there now. I really hate that I can't go there now. I also really wanted a tattoo of my daughter's butterfly but I can't have one because of the risk of infection. I also wanted to tattoo my eyebrows on because drawing them on every day is doing my head in!'

What to do for others: making it less excruciating for those you're leaving

Here are some examples of how our inspirational contributors have ensured their memory will live on in a number of ways.

In memories

Many of us make a bucket list that creates purposeful memories that provide places, objects and moments of comfort for those we leave behind. For example, a family picnic at your favourite beach, park or lake will make that particular spot priceless to those you share the moment with, or a trip to a clay pottery that put your hands next to your children's to create a physical memory that will allow them to feel like they can almost put their hand in yours for the rest of their lives.

Heidi: 'Because of my blog "Storm In A Tit Cup" I've had lots of people giving me great ideas, like a book called "Tell me all about Mum". It's got sections like "What was your favourite music when you were a teenager?" so they will be able to remember the little facts about me that might usually be forgotten. I'm also giving them memory boxes that all of my friends are writing letters to contribute to so they can keep my memories alive.'

In still and moving images

In the age of social media we're not lacking in pictures or videos, but beyond putting photos in frames and gifting them, you could arrange a photo shoot with the family in a location you love, to create a double whammy of positive memory material.

Heidi: 'I'm making a photo album and I filmed a documentary called *Extraordinary Pregnancies*, so that's great for them to look back on, but I also film a lot of myself on the camcorder, just normal stuff, keeping a video diary, talking to the camera so they can see my mannerisms and hear my voice, because that's the kind of thing a photo doesn't get.'

In keepsakes

We need to eliminate the possibilities of misinterpretation, the very catalyst of the family feud, the time-honoured art of falling out over the wishes and belongings of the dearly departed. If you deem it appropriate you could just give keepsakes to people before you die. I think it might make the item even more valued, although I understand the apprehension some might have that once all your bits are given out it may feel like you're bringing the date forward.

If you were ever going to take a minuscule positive out of knowing roughly how much time you have left, this would be the gift of time, some being better than none, as many bereaved people will acknowledge.

Heidi: 'We do a lot of scavenging on our local beach, so it's the pieces of glass that have been rounded and worn down over time to look like precious stones that'll probably really mean something to my kids, because we were doing something we all love together when we found them. I will see that they are given to them when they are ready, because it wouldn't make any sense to them at the ages they're at now.'

I do hope Mary Turner ensures that the family continue to play the board game I noticed on her coffee table the day we spoke. The game was appropriately entitled 'Stay Alive'. She assured me it wasn't a tongue-in-cheek attempt at making light of the subject with good humour, but I don't believe her.

In words

Possibly the most powerful way to stay present in the hearts and minds of those you love is to leave something that echoes how you feel long after your death. A precious letter that timelessly encapsulates your feelings towards another can be nothing short of medicinal in its qualities and it doesn't lose its potency when its words are consumed again and again.

Writing letters to loved ones may feel too emotional to bear, so choose the right time, but if you can, just imagine the power of a letter that can be read a thousand times. You could even scent it with your favourite perfume or aftershave to really carry that memory through the senses of those you are leaving.

Heidi: 'I've been writing "Letters to open when . . ." For example, when you start school, when you turn eighteen, when you have your first child. I fill them out and date them so the kids can read them when I'm gone. I got them on eBay.'

Audio

If you don't like the idea of filming yourself and writing, and potentially don't have the energy, grab a smartphone – if you don't have one you can almost guarantee a family member will – and use the microphone app to create a few messages for loved ones. Dictaphones are readily available from electrical retailers or online and are obviously made for that kind of thing. The comfort that hearing your voice will bring to those you love, for years to come, shouldn't be underestimated.

With permission

In grief, people tie themselves in knots questioning their behaviour: 'Is it OK to sell the house? Is it OK to move the children out of the school they are in? What would my dearly departed have wanted?' These are just a couple of examples of the occasions when people will wish that they could just call you for your direction and clarification on something.

You can set people free from their feelings of self-doubt, guilt and blame by simply encouraging them to always do what they think is best when you are gone. Equally, if you have some firm but fair stipulations for matters in your absence, be very clear about your communication of the details so there is no cause for misinterpretation and family division. But remember they must be realistic requests or your words may act as counter-productive shackles that don't allow a family or loved one to move forwards with their lives independently of their grief.

Heidi: 'Life is short. If you want to travel the world for ten years, do it! Do whatever you want, whatever makes you happy. I wouldn't have said this before but actually this has taught me that telling your kids what they must and mustn't do is absolute bullshit. I wouldn't want them to ride motorbikes or smoke, but that's normal mum stuff.'

Mary: 'I want my husband to be happy and I don't want him to be on his own. I just hope that I don't come back in spirit in a way that means I can see it all!'

Typical of a strong character like Mary to give her husband permission through humour. It's not her decision to make, but her accepting words will indeed allow her husband to make choices for himself in the future, free from the guilt induced by the constant feeling of wrongdoing by Mary's standards.

Heidi: 'I'm honestly too alive to even think about giving him permission to move on, but maybe I will later. I really don't want somebody else to raise my children and I'd also prefer that my husband continued to bring our children up in the same area because of all the people we have here.'

Where do the children in the family think you're going?
Heidi: 'My two-year-old is too young to understand, but over the years we'll probably drip-feed something about heaven into his mind. My three-year-old understands a little more because we lost his baby sister at only eight days old, a year ago. We're very clear on the words that we use. We won't ever say "going to sleep" because it might give them a complex on going to bed. "Death and dying" sounds so harsh, but it's very definite and they need that.'

If there are young children, grandchildren, nieces and nephews, godchildren and neighbouring children who see you regularly, creating a story that is helpful to their comprehension of the facts is a delicate yet important factor to consider. What is right for the age and level of understanding your child has is up to you to decide. Children are very perceptive and are completely in tune with their parents' emotional state, so it would be a shame for parents to try to deny the need to broach the questions and fears of the young.

Naturally the children will grow up and their understanding of death will mature, but don't ever worry about a child feeling they have been lied to in years to come because a story was given for their own good or because maybe that was the belief of the individual passing that things would be that way in the afterlife.

The general idea is that if it comforts you it comforts them, but please take note of two key considerations. Firstly, the story you tell should be maintained before, during and after death, with the consistency required to make it a comforting belief for the child.

The story may be religious, spiritual or complete fantasy. If the details are consistent throughout, they'll accept it.

Secondly, children are not great at verbalising the confusion and sadness they experience in loss, so we should give them regular opportunities to air any concerns and ask any questions they may have and would like the family to talk to them about. 'Would you like to talk about what is happening to Mummy?' is a straightforward way of giving them the option. It is also important to be aware that children's minds are most active when the daily distractions subside at bedtime.

If you find it too difficult to communicate the facts to yourself, let alone the children, buy some children's books that explain the imminent future to them via words and pictures. Let's protect the children involved from those thoughts in their heads that turn into assumptions and permeate as great fears that create stress and anxiety. This is all avoidable if they are presented with the right detail at the right times.

What's your gift to those you leave behind?

We all want to have fulfilled a purpose in our lives and to find some meaning to our existence other than the fact that we have lived. If we can feel that we were an influence on others it can help us to feel a level of acceptance that helps us to stay focused in our final stages.

Heidi: 'I'd like to raise awareness of inflammatory cancer. Nobody seems to know that there is a type of breast cancer that doesn't involve lumps. I want to have taught my children that anything can be overcome with the power of the mind, what true strength looks like, and I want to be an inspiration for them.'

Three biggest tips for those you're leaving behind?

Remaining family members love receiving instructions from their loved one as it makes life after the loss make sense, like there's a purpose. This could come in a challenge that you have set them that they are going to carry out in your honour. What do you want those three instructions to be?

Mary:
1. Talk, unburden yourself, show others that it's healthy to talk about life and death and everything in between.
2. Express your feelings! Share how people make you feel and what they mean to you.
3. Let people in, let them ask how you are, let them care for you. They will need to fulfil that purpose.

Heidi:
1. Don't sweat the small stuff.
2. Relationships with everyone are the most important thing.
3. Always have an adventure.

What will your last words be?
If you are a good communicator it's likely that you won't have any because you'll have been saying them all of your life anyway. If, however, you struggle to verbalise affection, refer back to the ways you can communicate it in written words or audio. In your last moments words carry more value than ever, they become almost magical, so ask yourself what magical spell you'd like to cast on those who are with you in that moment.

Mary: 'No need for last words, I'll have said them all already a hundred times.'

Heidi: 'Words of love and always be kind. It wouldn't be pull my finger, that's for sure. I'd tell my husband to eat some fruit and stop biting his nails.'

How will any inheritance work for you?
Mary told me about how she had met all of the children and godchildren in the family to gift them some money ahead of her death, while she was healthy enough to enjoy seeing the kids receive their present. Of course she knew they didn't understand what the money was for, but what was most important was that she made an often sticky matter of consequence into an enjoyable experience, not just for the beneficiaries but for her too.

It's by no means conventional to do this ahead of time, but who's ever read that bereavement rule book? I haven't, and this certainly isn't one either! Remember, if it works for you, do it in your own style. It reassures everyone around you when you take control of your life – at any stage, and especially now.

Heidi: 'I don't really have fuck all that's worth anything! We don't have bugger all to lose, we've hit rock bottom now, so let's just get on with it and have a bit of a laugh. My husband will get anything of value so I can ensure it goes to my boys.'

People could fight over the most innocuous objects in your absence, so if you'd prefer, you could save them the undignified conversations and decide who gets what. I know it's a really tough conversation for you to approach with others, because some may not like to hear you talk about a time when you won't be here, but it's really your job to dictate what is to be spoken of. If you pander to the sensitivity of others, as understandable as that would be, then you will not achieve as much in the time you have left as you could, and your loved ones will not be as organised and prepared as they could be.

6

The Mindset for Miracles or a Failure to Face Facts?

In speaking to numerous people with a life-limiting term I've learned that while there are common themes, there are also some real inherent differences between the philosophical way they look at what they've got and what they've had in life.

You may come across a person who has lived a full and satisfying existence and whose children are grown adults; another who is leaving far too soon, with or without young children, and who is struggling to find acceptance; and yet another who is not content with the life they have lived, irrespective of age. The way that this news is interpreted is purely down to the individual perspective of the person in question.

It seems as though many fight the prognosis in disbelief or shock. Sometimes their reaction is termed as denial, but from another angle you could just as well call it positivity and courage.

Does that mean that those with less acceptance are in turn more likely to have a greater motivation to fight against the prognosis and therefore have a longer term than expected? It depends on whether the main aim is to have as long as possible, or alternatively to focus on a quality of life. It is in essence a decision of quality over quantity.

Some perspective in conversation with Heidi Loughlin

JB: 'Say someone had a prognosis of five years and someone else had one of ten. The person with five years goes out and seizes every opportunity that comes their way, making the most of every day, while the one with ten years potters about expecting their next day to be their last, but if it isn't it might be the one after. Which person would you rather be?'

　HL: 'Absolutely the five years!'

　JB: 'Then let's take the emphasis off time for a moment and the "stopwatch" that someone has on their wrist somewhere and put the emphasis back on what you control, getting as much as possible out of each day you have.'

In this chapter we will look into the mindset of those who are resisting the apparent shortage of time to see if the absence of the expectation of an imminent end really does buy you more.

Should you accept your prognosis?

Aundrea Bannatyne: 'Doctors just go on statistics, but it makes no sense given the fact that pancreatic cancer is most common in seventy-year-old men that have drunk and smoked all their lives, so how on earth does that represent me, a relatively healthy 42-year-old woman?'

　Aundrea has a point. If we all took the doctor at their word each and every time, it would surely limit our chances of prolonging what time we had left.

　AB: 'I have zero acceptance for what the doctors have told me. I'm really angry about it. They tried to tell me it was a kidney infection, then kidney stones, then a urine infection before they actually took the pain I was in seriously. If I had any advice for others in a similar situation it would be not to listen to it. We are all unique individuals and not a statistic, so fight and prove them wrong!'

This is very typical of Aundrea's defiant attitude towards her prognosis. She truly believes she will get better. Her youngest son battled with a brain tumour at two years old and overcame it. This has given her all of the belief she needs in her ability to come back against all odds.

AB: 'My son had five operations and they didn't give him any hope of pulling through but he's ten years old now, so if he can do it, so can I. I have to set an example to my children.'

Some might feel that Aundrea could potentially be in a form of denial and that her inability to accept a supposed medical certainty will give her less time to get her head around the preparations she will need to undertake, just in case the doctors are right – but who are we to judge people taking control of their lives?

Aundrea is so certain she can beat her cancer that she has taken drastic steps to give herself the best possible chance of survival. If she was a family member of yours, wouldn't you want her to do exactly the same?

AB: 'I have discovered a pioneering cancer treatment in Germany called "immunotherapy". Its side effects are like chemotherapy, but not so harsh. Some people on the programme have beaten their illness and are completely in remission. If it shrinks my tumour by two centimetres, I can have an operation to remove it completely. I get the results in two days' time.'

On that occasion Aundrea's cancer hadn't reduced but it also hadn't grown in any way, so there were pluses to take from the results and grounds for her to continue in her resilient approach to the treatment.

There is obviously an expense to this treatment, but Aundrea has proven an inspiration to others, who have rallied around her to raise £130,000 to go towards the costs.

AB: 'I'm so grateful that friends, family and strangers are so willing to fundraise on my behalf. My friends are literally keeping me alive.'

After all of the treatment and general devastation you may have experienced, it's understandable that positivity and fundraising may feel a little beyond your capabilities, but I want to ask you this: what took the wind out of your sails more – the news you were ill or the fact that you had been given a life term? If you can question the validity of the prognosis like Aundrea, does that leave any more room for hope?

Hope will look like different things to different people. For some it might be more time, for others it might be less pain, more support, not to be alone, to raise awareness. I think people are entitled to dream at any point in their life, especially after prognosis, and it is in the absence of fight and ambition that hope may be lost and time might be at its shortest.

Dawn Sharpe is a veteran of terminal prognosis. She learned of her stage four cancer in 2004, yet has defied the predictions of the professionals by outliving her two-year prognosis given in 2009 by a staggering five additional years. She has two children, Jaimie, 29 and Conor, 21. She obviously knows something about surviving when others see little hope.

Positive affirmations are a powerful tool for anyone, but how's this for a statement the moment she was given two years to live: 'I'm Dawn Sharpe. I don't die.' She's proven for a good while now that she meant what she said.

I wanted to investigate what has helped Dawn get so far. Is it just about positivity? Surely there is more to it than that? Luck? A great consultant? A body that responds really well to the treatment offered?

'My GP calls me her miracle, they use me as an example. They say that I shouldn't be here, so I know I've exceeded everyone's expectations, which means a lot to me. When she told me two years, I told her: "No! I'm a single parent, my youngest has just lost his dad and I need to turn a fourteen-year-old into a man, and you will get me there. I don't care about my quality of life, I care about his. You watch what I do to this cancer."

I was told I was incurable and inoperable. I had all the words thrown at me. I don't think they should have used the word terminal because it made me feel like I was at the end there and then and I quite clearly wasn't.

'I use turmeric, which helps with inflammation. I'm not saying that's why I'm still here but I take three turmeric tablets a day, and who's to say it isn't really helping?

Another patient told me one day: "It isn't about you any more." Every year I'm still here I push the barrier back. I'm one year closer to them finding that cure. Who knows, maybe they'll find it in my lifetime.'

Obviously in a great position to comment, Dawn gave me a few examples of people who haven't faced up to the battle in a way she would recommend.

'I met a woman with stage two cancer. I didn't tell her I was terminal. I didn't want to get people down. She cried through her chemo every time so I took it upon myself to rally around her and told her that if she cries through her treatment she's making the treatment less effective.

'I told her how I imagine the chemo attacking the cancer like space invaders, but all she kept saying was, "I can't believe I've got cancer!" She was so down and in the end I felt like I had to get away from her because she was going to kill me. I heard not long after that she had actually died. She was only stage two at the time, she shouldn't have died.

'I really believe in a healthy mindset. You know who's going to be alright. There was a girl with breast cancer, devastated she hadn't yet had babies, but she was so positive and that was her motivation. We used to sing together. I used to sing James Ingram's "Keep the Music Playing", but she always wanted to sing "Somewhere Over the Rainbow" and she would get everyone crying but it worked for her, and she got healthy again and went on to have three children.

'Then there's this one bloke whose wife had stage one breast cancer which is luckily very early, but he was going on about how he had to give up work to support her. I think he should have carried on as normal and not let the kids see them like that. He said, all pleased with himself, "We've got a car now off the bene-fits." Mate, please don't make your cancer about money and about what you can get! Then there were other negative people and I just knew I had to steer clear.'

Hearing Dawn's examples reminded me of something I'd seen on Twitter earlier that day. Some people have their illness all over their profiles on their social media accounts. I think it's a bad thing. You might like to raise awareness of a rare disorder, but it makes a very powerful connection between you and it, as though it is who you have become now, and everything you were before no longer exists. As the saying goes, 'Where attention goes, energy flows.'

Dawn has never been one to publish what's bad, only what's good. Her Facebook profile is a feed full of mischievous jokes.

'I looked for positive influences, people in the same situation with the same mindset, so I went around all the support groups because I wanted to get some strength. There were only outlets for young women or older women at the end of life anyway, and in the end I actually found that it made me worse. I couldn't cope with the depression, so I just went to the pub with my mates instead.

'I stopped the Macmillan nurse coming round because when she was there she would always bring it back to me, the prospect of dying, talking about funeral arrangements, and when she wasn't there I always felt better.'

Dawn is clearly a survival expert, or at least someone with the strength to decide what is good or bad for her and then to implement or remove it. Listening to her, it started to make sense that having a clear and powerful motivation is vital to prolonging life.

'In a terminal diagnosis it isn't about you; it becomes about the people around you. I don't want people to turn around after I'm gone and say it's a good job she went because she wasn't half struggling. I hysterically laugh and mess around all the time.

'The thing I still need to do is make sure Conor is a man. He was fourteen when I was diagnosed and he's twenty-one now. I've tried to force him to tell me he's going to be OK and he's gone backwards as a result. I'm trying to turn him into a man as quickly as possible. I've done it wrong and I'm paying for that now.'

By doing it wrong, Dawn means she has created a young man who has cleverly worked out that by being less than he could be, he is contributing to his mother's survival. We focus on Conor's perspective in Chapter 25.

'He won't talk to me about my health any more. He won't say if he feels ill or anything to do with illness. He doesn't tell me anything about his life in case it upsets me. He's so dependent on me and it's like he thinks that it's his immaturity that's keeping me going. "The less I can actually cope for myself, the less likely it is that Mum will leave me." He's not preparing himself, so I haven't done my job with Conor yet.

'I also need to outlive my mum! She already lost my brother and I don't think she could go on if she lost me too. I want to do this the right way round – the children bury the parents, not the other way round. I can't have me being the reason for my mum's death. I can't put her through losing a child again.'

I think motivation is key, and Dawn has two huge self-motivating reasons for staying alive. She really has put others before herself, namely her younger son and mother, and I have no doubt that these factors form a large percentage of the reason why she is still here.

The danger of setting expectations you have no power over, such as outliving your healthy parent, is that Mum could go on for another twenty years. If it's in any way possible that you'll fail in that attempt, are you making for an awful and desperate final few months when the reality of your motivations not coming to fruition sets in?

Is there such a thing as an unhealthy motivation? Is gaining years on your life ever a bad thing? Does it matter what your motivation is as long as you're still living? Or does a potentially unhealthy motivation with risk attached actually make for a harder run-in with the fact that forcing something may have lasting repercussions after your death?

How much more of a 'man' does Conor need to be before Dawn decides it's enough? Would it be her death that actually instigates the need for him to grow up? I feel happy to be acquainted with this inspirational woman, but I have a tinge of sadness for Dawn in that she isn't powering through because she wants or chooses to; she's potentially soldiering on because she's told herself she has to.

I think whether the motivation makes sense to you or is irrelevant, that's how Dawn has chosen to live her life. The fact that it is motivated by two substantial fears is fascinating, seeing as the fear that most people have – the fear of death – is actually the furthest from her mind. Perhaps this is how you turn two years into seven . . . and counting.

7

The Final Stages of Life

In pre-bereavement, you can do a varying job of making those last moments as comfortable for your loved one as possible. In doing so, you can also do a varying job of leaving yourself with little regret and the peaceful confirmation that you did a good job of caring in those final stages.

The final stage is inevitably scary and daunting for all involved, but just how can you make this part go 'well' and what are the ways that you might actually make things harder for yourself and your family?

I consulted with Beverley Warner, a grief counsellor from St Clare's Hospice in Harlow, to hear about her experiences of how families tend to cope, and whether people in their last moments are able to exert a small amount of control as to when they take their last breath.

Some people spend months in hospices, hospitals and homes before they die; some spend weeks; others days. It's important to recognise that we're are not dead until we die. An obvious enough concept, but we need to acknowledge that we should make the very most of every minute we still have collecting memories and giving love. This is what life is about.

What could we do better as families?

The disturbing transference of unrealistic expectations from one family member to another can be damaging for the person on the receiving end. For example, 'Come on, pull yourself together' and 'What are you crying for?' prevent the dying person from displaying emotions that threaten the speaker's own mortality.

Here the accuser is displaying their own denial. They can't deal with the loss so they need everyone else to stop dealing with it too, or they will feel exposed and left behind.

There are so many fears that can be generated from the final stages of the life of someone we love and we should forgive ourselves for feeling out of control. However, the way we express those fears is all-important, and by projecting them on to others we reveal our inability to accept the situation at hand.

Questions may arise such as, 'Will it be me next; will I die of cancer too?' That's when we need to find a different, more honest way of communicating the fears, rather than taking our anxieties out on others. If being straight and honest is difficult, has it always been difficult for you individually or as a family? Do you find it hard to allow others to express themselves how they wish?

Self-sabotage

We also put incredibly limiting rules on ourselves and make negative predictions about our supposed ability to cope. When you hear yourself say 'I'll never get over this' or 'I'll never be able to have a life again', these statements are far more than a little bit of negativity; they are the parameters and boundaries of your experience of grief that you are imposing on yourself. Use your language wisely and be kind to yourself, because you decide with these statements more of what's to come than you will think possible.

How does denial reveal itself in the hospice environment compared to hospital or home?

Because of the nature – the finality – of a hospice environment, you will find yourself facing the inevitable ending that you may, in a hospital or home environment, have been able to put to one side. There is a difference between being positive and 'holding on to positivity'. To be positive in the final stages is to create a togetherness, bring comfort, share happy memories and to foster a restful, calming environment.

The significance of communication: plan, talk, prepare

Don't forget to ask them what they want . . .

It's important to understand – and where possible, implement – the final wishes of your dying loved one. Your job is to create peace for your dying relative and you should ask them how they would like everything to be when they depart. We encourage birthing plans at the beginning of life, choosing how we want our children to come into the world, and it should be no different when we come to leave it. If you can't ask your relative because of ill health, come to an agreeable conclusion with your family.

You can make their environment as comfortable as possible. What music might they like playing? Perhaps they would like to have their nails painted each week if they have always prided themselves on having nice nails. What photos might they like to wake up and look at? Who might they like to visit? Might they be cheered by flowers or pictures drawn by the grandchildren? If you can make their bedside as comforting as possible, this will make them feel content and cared for.

Have you said everything that needs to be said?

It's important to clear up any unfinished business while we can and to say any words that should be spoken before it's too late. Hearing is the last sense that leaves us and so, even in the last moments of life, they can hear you telling them that you love them or that you forgive them or thank them for sharing your life and enriching it with all the things they did for you. Before the last stages, you can ask your loved one how they want you to remember them. What would they like you to do at the anniversaries? What would they like you to think about when you are really missing them?

Even at this stage, the rules and boundaries of your bereavement are being decided for you. Listening to your loved one's wishes, their desires as to how they are remembered, what they want to tell you before they die, can take a huge weight from your shoulders. It's incredible how a little permission from someone you're about to lose can go a long way, and it also saves disagreements within the family, such as what's to be done with certain keepsakes or what kind of funeral they want.

I wasn't there when they died

Those you may rely upon in a hospital or hospice will always make every effort to monitor a change in a patient's breathing and relay that instantly to their family, so, if they choose, they can be near. Ultimately, though, responsibility must rest with you, the family, so that someone is always there and can make the necessary contact with the family members who wish to be present when the time comes.

This is, of course, presuming that the patient wants to have people by their side at the time of passing. We must remember that it's all about the wishes of the person in the bed. From their point of view, they may feel that you being present at that precise moment might be too hard for you to take. Ideally, all of this should be clarified as early as possible in the stages of prognosis or through the illness, or even in conversations before anyone is ill.

Supporting their spirituality

Your relative may have a specific belief about what's going to happen to them after death. If you don't know what it is, find out. They may want a visit from a religious or spiritual leader and the hospice can help you arrange that. Most have a chaplain who visits regularly. If they would find comfort from a picture or photo of their place of worship or a spiritual leader who has inspired them, place these by their bedside, even if you are not of the same belief or faith yourself.

For many, you will be their most pleasurable and happiest achievement, and so a photo that contains as many of your family as possible may be the best image for them to hold in their mind's eye as they open the door to what comes next.

Inside the mind of a dying relative

Your loved one may spend a lot of time looking back over their life, thinking, and if they can, talking to you about what they felt went well and the things that didn't, and you will need to be sensitive to their needs.

If you sense they are consumed by regrets, you can help bring their minds back to the things that went well by talking about them, helping them to forgive themselves for the things they may regret. It's common for someone who is dying to think a lot about their childhood, so you can encourage those memories.

They also may like to talk about a future they won't be a part of, to comfort themselves that life will go on and that everything will be OK, eventually. It will help them a great deal if you take part in these conversations.

Can they speed up or delay their final moment?

My brother Lee is a submariner and he made my grandad promise him that he would 'wait for him' to return from a few months' service. My grandad stayed true to his word and died very shortly after Lee walked through the doors of his room at the hospice.

From a medical point of view it's impossible to know if my grandad was able to defy his symptoms and stay alive, but if my brother's request allowed him to exert some control over his life, then that is hugely poignant.

Regrettably many people's final stages are far from controlled or peaceful, but they – and you – will be helped and guided through a difficult ending by the hospice or hospital staff.

Parting gifts, or not

Words spoken by those departing the world can be like a bouquet of flowers or an invisible shield that will be by your side through the grief. However, some words, instructions or demands can feel like a heavy burden, a pair of handcuffs or an electronic tag that you may feel limited by.

I've heard from a client how her father told her to stand by her husband – he couldn't have known of the difficulties she was having. She took that as a rule she dared not break and displease her beloved father, so she stayed with her husband for many more years as a result – years that were filled with verbal abuse and great unhappiness.

We can't necessarily control the words we speak as we die and we all hope that parting words will be full of love and comfort, but if they aren't quite what you were hoping for, just remember that while these wishes are important, they have to be right for you first.

Jade left me only one instruction, which was that I should always keep the children in private school. This was something she had worked so hard to provide the money for, so naturally it was something I agreed to respect. That is, until it became clear later that Freddy and private school were not a great match. He was diagnosed with ADHD at the age of 11, but for years before that, especially at one particular school, there was a never-ending feeling of him being nudged out, and as the increasing threat of exclusion loomed, I took the step to remove him from a place where he would always need to conform to standards that he couldn't achieve at that time.

Because this was going against Jade's dying wish, I had to think long and hard. The fact that Freddy can now be himself in a more patient and understanding environment, where it's in the school's interests to provide him with the level of learning support that he requires, means that I was able to forgive my decision, because I felt that it was a decision made on account of new information, and that she would have concluded this too.

Even though we are describing the trials and tribulations of these last moments, it's most important to recognise that they offer potential nonetheless. Make the most of them in all the different ways detailed in this chapter. Leave as little as you can to regret and find comfort in the words and support that you have been able to afford others in those final stages.

8

Common Emotions Felt Throughout Grief

There are so many stages and phases on your journey through loss. Below are some examples of the predominant emotions you may experience, what they represent and what you can do to reduce them.

Anger

Someone or something has taken away a loved one who was not just important to you, but also played a major part in your sense of purpose, position and security in the world. Without them you can feel disoriented, as if the rug has literally been pulled out from underneath you. Their death can leave you feeling that you have no sense of who you are, where you are and where you are heading.

You may feel furious about the way that that person was taken from you. However, a lot of the anger you may be feeling is not down to the finer details of their death – you didn't get a proper chance to say goodbye; you didn't have a chance to fulfil all the experiences you were meant to have with them – but might be because it has reminded you that you haven't really lived your own life to its fullest potential.

You won't get anywhere unless you express your frustration. Only then can it reduce. Does the reason for your anger have anything to do with someone else who you might be able to talk to? Is there any assumption at play or is your rage based strictly on fact? Have you considered how realistic your expectations were? Is it down to something that *you* controlled, so is this something you need to take responsibility for and own?

Denial

Loss can be such a shock to the system that our defence mechanisms take over and protect us.

Denial is a desperate attempt to alter the course of reality by simply not recognising its existence, but sadly it doesn't work and just delays the inevitable. When the barriers of denial finally erode and the truth sets in, it will have an almighty impact and send you straight back to square one on the road to acceptance.

Guilt

We have the tendency to self-sabotage in moments of disappointment, pain and failure, and some of us have the ability to take responsibility where it doesn't apply. This can also apply to the experience of loss. I have met clients who have taken responsibility for the failure of a loved one's body; I have heard people repetitively berate themselves for 'not being there' or for 'not doing enough'. These sorts of thoughts can induce the kind of guilt that will stop you from living, from feeling any sense of entitlement in life. When anything bad happens, it may mean that you attribute your lack of luck to the fact that you didn't stop the loss of your loved one.

Carrying this level of guilt can be a ticking time bomb in some who may subconsciously be searching for a reason to not live, to not try, to not enjoy themselves and to inflict pain internally, and when they suffer, they extend their suffering far beyond the 'normal', especially when their loss coincides with the complexities of a negative and limiting experience of the past.

Loneliness

It's inevitable that when someone who has been so intrinsically linked to our life has died, we are going to be confronted by the blank void where that person once stood. The sense of loneliness, even in the presence of others around you, can be crippling and when, day after day, hour after hour, your loved one still isn't there and you can't, as you may have done for years, call to tell them your good news, wish them happy birthday, invite them to your wedding, the loneliness can be overwhelming.

Loneliness after a bereavement can persist until you learn to replace the habits that involved that person with new habits that involve others. Slowly and respectfully the memories will be in places we choose for them to be, and not in the difficult moments when we go to reach for them and they are no longer there. Loneliness is the body's reminder to the mind to think about what you had. It's a tough thing to break but we can learn how to see that as a positive and be grateful for the message. Continuing to feel lonely is a personal choice, because while we won't have the company of our loved one, we can immerse ourselves in the company we keep with relatives and friends and always make new friends too.

Resentment

Following the death of a loved one you may find yourself in a state of mind that makes you particularly aware of what you no longer have and others do have, and this may in turn produce feelings of resentment. This is the mind's way of coming to terms with the unfairness of the situation and sometimes we express that negativity outwardly at others. Why should they be so happy? Why should they have their happy life and I don't?

People remind us of what we don't have by walking down the street hand in hand or by cuddling their child in a way that you once held yours. We can make things the fault of others, but the simple truth is that we need to find some acceptance for what has happened within ourselves. A loss can create bitterness, but the path forward requires you to look at yourself and ask if it is right for the negativity of your loss to be expressed through the hatred of others who are no more responsible for this unwanted reality than you are.

Resentment can be reduced and removed by finding and trusting the right people to talk to. So often we bottle everything up, and if resentment is your tool of expression you're putting as much effort into talking about your loss indirectly as you would if you were expressing yourself productively and honestly. These are two very different routes to managing your grief: the latter involves acceptance and finding yourself, the former a cycle of negativity that will not just come from you, but also be reflected back to you as long as you remain this way, making it very difficult for your friends and family to help and care for you.

Shock

The initial reaction to a loss is disbelief. Everything we ever believed in has been found to be untrue. You are overtaken by the realisation that life should not be taken for granted; the pain at the knowledge that you may not have done or said all you wanted to your loved one; and the undeniable but baffling reality that they are no longer here. The combination of all these things is nothing short of incomprehensible, so to protect ourselves, we simply don't believe it. We go into a state of shock.

The shock passes when the truth and reality settles in and it can be an almighty fall when it does, but that reaction can be delayed. It took my children ten months of a mixture of shock, disbelief and denial, until it finally struck them that their mum was not coming back.

Shock is not something we can snap our fingers and come out of – it requires time, patience and understanding that the processes of grief are complex – but we can help ourselves by not adding further complications in fighting against the stages as they manifest themselves.

Yearning

We want something we can't have, the very epitome of grief. To want to feel their skin on yours, hear their voice once more, smell their scent, are all very natural reactions to loss. There is a point where yearning for them will be balanced by acceptance, but while the scales are tipping, you need to be careful not to hold on to that yearning so that it becomes a tool you use to hurt yourself with.

Yearning, needing, wanting your loved one is normal. They have left a space in your life that you may not feel you can fill. You can imagine those natural reactions to loss as stops on the train line of grief you're now riding on. After yearning, needing and hoping, further down the line comes wanting, regretting what you lost, and missing, and after you've travelled a little longer follows accepting, remembering and feeling grateful for what you had.

Some of those stations will continue to echo; you'll visit them more than once on your journey through grief. Before you begrudge that train too much for taking you to some difficult places, try to see it as love. It's love that will take you on that journey and it will go as fast or as slow as your relationship with that person, your relationship with grief and your relationship with yourself dictate.

Emptiness

Emptiness is the void left in the space your loved one once inhabited. There will always be a place for them in your heart and in your thoughts, but physically, there is a deep chasm and you don't know how this can ever be filled.

Your life's purpose may now be less clear and if the person lost was a huge part of your daily life your 'reason for being' may actually feel entirely non-existent. In order to survive you will eventually need to find a new meaning to life alongside existing for the person that you have lost.

Irrespective of our loss we are always changing, and things around us are constantly on the move too. If this process seems to stall when we are grieving, we may feel that we are stuck or weighed down. However, we are still moving in a direction; it's just far less noticeable, because we are constantly looking backwards at what once was.

We may not like to think of ourselves as being OK one day because it feels somehow disrespectful to our loved one. The truth is, we need to give ourselves permission to grieve naturally, to feel the emptiness, to go through it bravely accepting its validity but knowing that it is not forever, unless we make it so by refusing to let it.

The cavity is not a space next to you that you must keep open and available. It must close steadily and you mustn't be abrasive to friends, family and new friends yet to be made when they start to inhabit space and time that once belonged to you and your deceased loved one.

Disbelief

For some reason we go through life completely oblivious to the fact that these relationships we have with friends and family are not guaranteed to last forever. It isn't until we experience loss for the first time that we are exposed to the process of grief, and when loss happens for a second time we realise that the first experience didn't even prepare us.

I don't think we should go through life feeling like at any time someone we really care about will die, but I do think we should have a healthy attitude towards the importance of making the most of every moment we have, knowing that we can expect the unexpected.

Disbelief is natural when it simply wasn't someone's time, when it wasn't in the script or written in the stars. Disbelief belongs to the beginning of grief's journey but again should become just a 'belief' when you've had time to process the nature of the loss.

Numbness

Shock is synonymous with grief. Even in cases when the loss was expected it still doesn't feel real when the news hits home. We have an involuntary inbuilt mechanism called 'fight or flight' that helps us cope with psychological trauma, and loss is no exception.

Our body goes into a state of threat, secreting cortisol and adrenalin into our system, and our feelings then seem hard to access simply because our body is protecting us from the trauma we face. The numbness inevitably passes because we can't stay in that state and at some point we fall to earth with a thud and all that we couldn't feel is suddenly very much there.

Regret

Often mistaken for grief, regret very often pertains to what we feel we should or would have had if the loss had not happened. Grief is more about the *actual* loss – what you had that is no longer present in your life.

To regret is very natural given the finality of the circumstances, but you need to be careful not to allow your mind to spend too much time on a projection of what you would have had if the loss were not to have happened. It's natural to feel like your life is worse off and the absence of your loved one will shift the way you experience things, but in your journey through grief it will help you a lot to focus on what you did have in far greater depth than what was taken from you.

In the early stages you may find this impossible to comprehend. How can you not have regrets? However, nearing the end of grief's journey, we learn to acknowledge that it was a devastating event but also that our life would have been infinitely more complex and strained if we were stuck on the question 'why?'.

Blame

A not-so distant relative of regret, blame is another tool we use against ourselves in grief. We have a propensity to need to find a logical reason for everything. Sometimes in death there is no acceptable conclusion, certainly not one we control, so then we might find one that fits no matter how tenuous the link.

We may not go as far as blaming ourselves for the death but we can start to do so for a part we played in the build-up – words we did or didn't say, feelings we didn't acknowledge or time we didn't spend. We have to ask ourselves how much of this is justifiable and how much is a form of self-sabotage.

Of all of the claims of responsibility you may be making, how many of them are things you control and how many are perhaps things the person you've lost was responsible for? We don't just use blame against ourselves; often we point the finger at others, generating and maintaining a justification for all of the hurt and pain caused by the loss, masking it with anger and frustration directed at the behaviour of those you see as responsible.

Acceptance

This is the ability to rationalise recent experiences of loss and agree that the reality is permanent. You may not want to face facts, but you will need to live in your new reality so that your life does not become one of avoidance. Adjustment is the twin of acceptance. Some prefer one to the other, but for me we can start to adjust to our new reality before we even contemplate accepting that it is the case. Which one best fits for you? Do you accept certain elements of what has happened to someone you know or would you say you have come to adjust to it very gradually without feeling like an acceptance in any form has taken place?

Moving on

The feeling of 'moving on' can be both positive and negative. You may be happy that the pain has started to subside but feel guilty that you are 'forgetting' or not 'being sad enough'. It would appear that in grief we almost can't win.

Moving on simply represents a form of progression. It's widely accepted as being preferable to its distant cousin, 'getting over it'. As many come to realise, you don't get over a death as if it's a fence between you and the rest of your life. Rather than move away from grief, you can move on, forwards, with it a part of you but not overwhelming you.

To learn to move forwards, with your loss over your shoulders, on your back or in your pocket, is to start to 'manage your grief', manage being a significant term here. Once you see that you have a great deal of control over the terms of your bereavement, you will be able to move forwards.

9

Anticipatory Grief

We typically assume that you can only grieve when someone dies, but there are many forms of grief that we can experience – separation from a long-term partner; leaving a job or career that you have put many years into; and sometimes even when your children leave home. Grief isn't exclusive to a death; it's a natural reaction to losing something that we love, need or want. When something that we are used to seeing, feeling, knowing on a daily basis suddenly ceases to exist in the way we have always known it to be, this can induce feelings of grief in itself.

If someone close to you has dementia or Alzheimer's, you may experience loss as the degenerative disease sets in and your relationship will, inevitably, change. You may find it hard to recognise the person they once were, and you may grieve for how things were before, even though physically, your loved one is still here. You can also feel like this if your loved one has terminal cancer – maybe a brain tumour that is degenerative and causes them to lose the power of speech or movement; or if they are in a coma after an accident; or if they have had a stroke.

This type of grief is known as 'anticipatory grief' or 'living bereavement' and in many cases it feels as powerful as the grief felt after a death. Acknowledging feelings of anticipatory grief does not mean that you are giving up on the person or that you love them any less, but that you are adjusting to the change in circumstances both on the outside and on the inside.

Understanding what people you know are going through

My interest in 'grief before a loss' is heightened by the fact that my girlfriend's grandfather has had dementia since 2012, so I want to know what it's like for her and her family, his daughter especially, to feel like you're losing someone so special to you, one visit at a time.

I wanted to investigate the effects of feeling as if you had lost someone mentally before they had left you physically. Maybe it's a feeling you just can't imagine unless you've been through it personally.

I met Nikki Truman, whose father Ernie Moss is a 67-year-old ex-professional footballer and Chesterfield's all-time leading goal scorer. Ernie has dementia and, according to his family, has been 'disappearing' mentally for the past few years. Dementia in ex-football players is a hot topic. Jeff Astle and World Cup-winning Nobby Stiles are just two of many high-profile names to have died of dementia, and there is much concern about the long-term impact of heading the ball on an almost daily basis, even if balls are much lighter in the modern game. Once a fit and active man who was full of banter and never short of an opinion or two, Ernie is now unable to speak or follow instructions, he needs twenty-four-hour care and he won't leave the house unless it's to go to the football ground to watch his beloved Chesterfield FC. His daughter Nikki even married her partner at the club as it was the only way she could get her dad to attend. Slowly, his ability to do even the simplest of tasks – make a sandwich, or shave – have ebbed away.

For Nikki and her mother, it is nothing short of torture that physically Ernie is the same but mentally and emotionally, he is unreachable. Where once her relationship was full of conversation and life, Nikki's mum now inhabits a house of silence, caring for her husband who functions as if he were a child. When people tell her 'at least he's still here' she wants to shout back at them that he's not, that he's a shell of the man he used to be and his soul, his very essence, has long since departed and his mind has been stripped of all his cherished memories. Keeping him alive by feeding him, clothing him, caring for his bodily functions, is necessary but can feel futile and empty. What will happen when he doesn't want to go to football?

Nikki is convinced that if Ernie was aware of what he has become, he would be devastated. He would have swallowed a pill at the first opportunity so as not to have suffered the indignity that his life has become. Despite her own terror, Nikki is glad that he has no idea of what is going on or what is to come. Death will, she thinks, be a small relief to her family, because of the loss they have already encountered. Keeping his body alive, without him being inside it any more, is a devastating situation to be in and a constant emotional and physical drain on the family, not to mention Ernie himself.

Is it the same for everyone?

My girlfriend's grandfather, Alfred, has dementia. Like Ernie, he too had been full of life before the onset of premature dementia, caused by a stroke. Alf's short-term memory is affected more than the long-term and it is heartbreaking to know that he can't remember visitors who have been with him a few hours previously. His family can't reconcile the fact he may be feeling desperately lonely inside, despite friends and family being with him a lot of the time.

Alf has begun to talk about things that are not real; for example, there being 'tigers on the roof', and the family have found this distressing, initially trying to explain things differently to him, until they learned from the professionals that they should 'go with the flow' so as to not cause Alf any further stress. They continue to keep memories alive for him by telling him stories of their past and comfort themselves by his ability to listen, even if he can't remember what they have just told him.

Alf can recognise his close family and friends and is able to feed himself but he is unable to care for himself in any way and cannot walk. He now lives in a care home and his family are terrified that he is on borrowed time. They are dreading the day he can no longer recognise his children and grandchildren and Debbie, Alf's daughter, can't get it out of her mind that several years before his stroke, Alf said that if he ever got dementia, he would take a pill so he could die with dignity.

Debbie has a strong sense of regret for what her father is going through and that the stroke he suffered didn't actually take his life instead of leaving him to this cruel existence, which is completely alien to his previously active and fulfilled life. She admits to feeling relief at the thought of him dying so he can be at peace and out of his misery.

It takes a lot of courage to say something like this about your father. Life is precious, but maybe it is only precious when we have the mental ability to enjoy certain aspects of it. Alf, in the short intervals when he is lucid, will say that he has little or no enjoyment in his life. Whenever I have seen him, I have detected an embarrassment on his part to be the focus of everyone's attention due to his incapacities and when someone you love doesn't want to be around, it is difficult to imagine that death would be a less desirable outcome than months or years of a reduced and diminished life.

In some respects a family may feel like they are keeping a body alive. You can't let it go even though you know it isn't your loved one inside it any more. It must make it so much harder when your loved one just looks like the same person they always were.

Feeling that your loved one would be better off dead defies every human instinct we might ever have had. To survive and to protect the life of those we love is at the centre of our existence. But maybe, to see a beloved close one deteriorating miserably in front of your eyes with no hope of a cure or improvement, you just want that day to come.

10

I Didn't Get to Say Goodbye

There is no rule or advice that could ever prepare you for the sheer desperation and crippling helplessness that receiving the worst possible news will cause you. You must simply accept that you are going to need a prolonged period of time off from normal duties in order to come to terms with the incomprehensible fact that your life has changed suddenly, unexpectedly, and that you are powerless to intervene.

I have experienced many losses at the hands of cancer but there has, mostly, at least been time to attempt to prepare for death. The one exception was in 2009 when I was in Australia with the children, shortly after Jade had died. As I answered the phone and heard the tone of Mum's voice, I knew instantly that something terrible had happened.

And it had. My grandad had taken his own life. A terminal prognosis of a throat cancer, which that he had watched rip through his own father when he was a child, was not the way my grandad was prepared to go and so when the cancer had developed to a point far enough, he took matters into his own hands and shot himself in the head.

As my mother's shocking words hit home, I fell to my knees. My grandad's death, and the nature of it, were far from expected. Out there in Australia, so far from home, looking after my children who had just lost their mother, I had no choice but to try to rationalise my grandad's choice to end his own life.

Our experience with grief often begins with a sharp jolt caused by devastating news. My biological father drowned on the *Marchioness–Bowbelle* disaster on the Thames in 1989. I didn't know him but I have never stopped imagining the pain and anguish my family went through waiting to know whether or not he survived. When, as was the case with my biological father and my grandad, you can't say goodbye, issues such as blame or guilt, compounded by the suddenness and injustice of your loss, sit on top of your grief so there is even more for you to get to grips with.

Amy, 36, lost her husband Keith, under horrendous circumstances. In July 2011, Keith was made redundant and one morning in the school holidays, he spent the morning with their kids before going up to London for a job interview. After that he had a drink with some friends, caught the last train, fell asleep, missed his stop and, while walking home in the early hours, was knocked down by a hit-and-run driver who had mounted the kerb. Keith was never to return home to his family.

Amy's last interaction with Keith had been an argument, something she found very difficult to forgive herself for. But how could she have known that that argument would have been their last, precious conversation? A few weeks before, Keith had gone out and got pretty drunk, and, keen not to see him in that state again, Amy had begged him not to go out drinking with his friends after his job interview. Keith had defended his choice and, as we know, had gone out just as he said he would. He had called Amy at 12.45 a.m. to tell her that he had fallen asleep on the train and left her a voicemail asking if there was any money at home for him to pay for a cab. Amy left a message at 12.50 a.m. to say yes, but didn't hear back. She fell asleep and in the night woke briefly when she thought she heard the porch door close. In a sleepy state, she assumed Keith had come back and she fell asleep again. But when she woke in the morning and saw he wasn't in bed, she went downstairs to see if he had fallen asleep on the sofa. And when he was nowhere to be seen, she had a very bad feeling.

She asked a friend to look after her children and then phoned a couple of the friends Keith had been drinking with and they confirmed he had left town to catch the last train, before they went clubbing. So Amy went to her local station, which happened to be the last stop on the Central line and where she reckoned Keith had called her from about the cab.

Before the station, she was met by a policeman who was blocking the road to traffic. She told him that her husband was missing and that as she knew he'd been on the last train and hadn't had money for a cab, it was likely that he would have walked down this road on his way home. The officer immediately asked Amy for her husband's name and before she had finished she saw the policeman's face drop. He waved her through the road block and another policeman came forward and told her the devastating news.

Amy was on autopilot. From the very moment she discovered Keith hadn't come home she had expected this outcome. Sometimes we think of the worst and believe that it's happened as a way to pre-empt and soften a blow. Fight or flight, a shot of adrenalin and a clarity of mind that doesn't befit the situation, and certainly doesn't last.

No one had had a chance to say goodbye to Keith and Amy was faced with breaking the news to his family and of course her children. There was so much to take in and try to get to grips with – the hit-and-run was a crime scene and there were going to be no answers for some time to come – but fortunately there were family members and friends on hand to help.

Amy will never forget the day she had to tell her children that they would never see their daddy again. Flynn was only three so he really didn't understand Amy's explanation that Daddy had been hit by a car which had hurt his head and caused his body to stop working, and so his soul had gone to heaven. Ava, who was five, had asked lots of questions when Amy Winehouse had died only weeks before her daddy, and Amy felt that this may have helped her comprehend slightly.

Amy had thought about how she was going to explain things to her little children. She told them to close their eyes. 'You know you can't see your body but you know you are here?' she asked. 'Well, that's your soul.' I thought this was beautifully put and it would leave them both believing that there was a part of their father that existed somewhere even if his body no longer worked.

What we tell our children is always dependent upon their age and their ability to understand the facts. If the facts are too complicated it's then that we should find a way of simplifying the details, but however it is put, spiritually, religiously or just as plain facts, it must introduce the children to the inexplicable fact that it is irrevocably final because if we don't, we're leaving them with the agonising hope that the dead person might somehow come back tomorrow, the next day or the day after that. The damage created by an open-ended explanation will absolutely echo with them in later life and delay the grieving process from starting.

Over and above the fact her husband had died, Amy struggled with many aspects of her loss – the fact that Keith had been alone; that he hadn't died instantly (his body moved before he was found) and that because the driver handed himself in forty-eight hours later, he couldn't be tested for drink or drugs. He claimed that he'd had a small beer and a small glass of wine but thought he'd hit a deer. Amy was keen to pursue justice for her husband. After a half-hearted reconstruction, she paid for a private one and the insurance company settled with her out of court because the evidence for

Keith's case was so conclusive. The moment the police saw that Keith had alcohol in his system, they wrote the case off because it was cheaper to do so and meant less work. With Keith no longer able to give his account it was one man's word against another. The fact that a seven-minute phone call was made on the driver's handset at the exact time Keith was hit was overlooked because it was an incoming call. I am furious just writing this. Imagine what Amy had to endure as she fought for answers and closure as to what had happened to Keith on the way from the station to his home.

How to cope with unresolved issues

There were so many things Amy had to deal with. Not just trying to find out what had happened and who had killed her husband and the pursuit of justice, but also complex emotional issues such as how she could ever forgive herself for her last argumentative conversation with Keith. She was also desperately upset that he hadn't heard her voice-mail telling him there was indeed enough money for a cab at the house.

Of course Amy's main priority as a surviving parent was to her children, helping them come to terms with their father's death and the suddenness of it. But that is a tall order and unless you are mentally and emotionally prepared and robust, day-to-day living is difficult enough, let alone having children to care for and explain things to. Amy found that she was comfort eating, a sign that she was punishing herself for Keith's death and the suddenness of it.

Soon she realised that she had a duty to not only maintain herself mentally, but also physically. She didn't want her children having to face another loss, and maintaining her health was crucial to that. I can relate to this. Whereas I may not have thought twice about risking my life before Jade died, I wouldn't throw myself out of an aeroplane or bungee jump off a bridge anytime soon because it feels like a gamble too far. I also try to eat healthily and keep myself fit, all the time knowing I have a responsibility to look after myself for the children's sake as much as my own.

Amy couldn't actually hold the funeral for a whole five weeks after Keith's death. This meant she was in limbo: 'completely helpless and out of control' was how Amy described it. It was during this period that she formed some behavioural tics that she is still affected by: 'Little things, having my pillows in place, towels hanging correctly, all of my tins facing front, really small, meaningless things that do not even register with most people but really started to bother me. I had to have it all a certain way and try and plan things in my head so they happened with ways in which I felt comfortable.'

Through a general lack of control during that period Amy became very aware of the little things that she *could* control and became obsessed with ensuring an outcome 'so she knew what would happen', all signs that this was a way of restoring some balance at a time where she had nothing but uncertainty.

It may have served a purpose at the time, but over the years we often forget to 'reset' this sort of behaviour once we have regained a normal element of control in our lives. This leaves the bad habits in place for so long we almost forget they were something we introduced for a specific purpose and they simply remain in place and we somehow believe they're just 'who we are'.

'The truth will set you free'

Part of the acceptance that enabled her to move her mind away from these tortuous thoughts was by studying the sequence of events that made Keith responsible for being there in the first place. When we lose someone it is highly forgivable for us to find blame in others, and only others. It takes guts to allow ourselves to see responsibility lying with the loved one we are grieving for, but if there is responsibility there then to accept it is a vital catalyst for freeing ourselves from the memories and assumptions made by what happened and how.

There were undeniably so many opportunities for Keith's evening to have played out differently, so instead of continuing to ask 'why, why, why' for the rest of her life and driving herself to distraction, it helped for Amy to admit to herself that she is bringing up two bereaved children as a widow purely because of two grown men's choices that evening. Keith didn't ask to die, nor did the driver set off intending to kill, but a combination of chosen actions led to the consequence, and that is the reality that Amy has been able to accept.

Guilt

Amy remembers that her guilt was sky high. She had literally argued with her husband the last time she had ever spoken to him and she agonised over the fact that she couldn't tell him she loved him and she was so grateful for the nine wonderful years she'd had with him.

She recalled how she would moan about the socks going in the wrong wash, about him not helping enough around the house and spending money unnecessarily, and how she realised all too quickly that none of this really mattered in the grand scheme of things.

Amy believed she had been able to overcome her feelings of guilt by accepting that Keith's death had happened as it had but that she needed to choose to live her life and bring up their children. Through her spiritual beliefs, she made peace with not telling him how appreciated he was and believes that he knew how much she loved and appreciated him and continues to know to this day.

Amy was right to find responsibility in the actions of others. It gave her clarity and peace of mind and protected her mental and emotional wellbeing as she set out on the path of being the sole carer and provider to her and Keith's children.

She also realised that those repetitive thoughts – the regret for those last words and the anger that he went out – were hers to own, that they came from her own mind, so she had to take responsibility for them. At first and for a period of time, those thoughts of guilt and longing for what she could no longer have and what had been taken from her felt involuntary, but there came a point when her mind took back control and she was able to make choices.

The wait: delayed response

There were, understandably, many people around Amy at first, helping her absorb the shock. Her parents were a wonderful source of support, especially with the children. When Amy was overwhelmed by emotions and questions about what had happened to Keith and to her and the children, they were there to listen, sometimes sitting with her in silent disbelief. Along with friends, they allowed her to shout, to cry, to express her darkest thoughts and fears. This sort of support enabled Amy to not judge herself for having those feelings. To react naturally is more constructive in the long term – even if the long term feels a long, long way away.

Amy was well supported, sometimes too much so, and this meant that the reality of her situation didn't have a chance to set in until everyone started to ease off. 'It wasn't until a year later that I could see what my reality actually looked and felt like,' she told me. 'The hardest thing was adjusting to weekends, because that's when it was most obvious that Keith was missing.'

It may be that this feels harsh, but as important as it is to have support, it is also very important to have space. Overcrowding can sometimes stifle the ability to think. Friends and family, those supporting, like to give their interpretations of how you should feel, how you should think, how you should cope, but ultimately, you are the only person who can make those decisions.

When you are ready, you should balance the company you keep with friends and the company you keep with yourself. The right people encourage you to talk and express your feelings without judgment or opinion and are simply happy to listen, but you will find YOUR answers in your quiet moments. The point of equilibrium lies somewhere between the two. Share and search, feel comforted and find your path.

Letting someone else get close again

Amy started a relationship two years after she lost Keith and this lasted eighteen months. They were making a great go of it and he was seemingly OK with his role in the children's lives until one day he seemed to lose his nerve and made for the door proclaiming he 'didn't want to bring up a dead man's kids'.

Understandably, Amy's experience of being let down by this guy in such a harsh way has made her wary of men and getting hurt. The kids had grown to like him and then one day he was gone, which no doubt reminded the children of their father, compounding an understandable fear for all three of them that they had been abandoned again.

The legacy of sudden loss

Dealing with sudden loss can take years to come to terms with, and in the case of Amy's young children, the fallout continues as the children get older and understand more about what happened to their father. Flynn has become hung up on the guy who ended his father's life. He talks about him a lot and for a while spent half the time screaming in anger and hating his life, wishing he too were dead.

From very shortly after Keith's death, Ava has suffered from separation anxiety and finds it difficult to let Amy out of her sight. At bedtime she watches Amy on a baby monitor so while she falls asleep she can see that she is still there, and it has only been the last few months that she has started to go to bed by herself and sleep through the night. She has been too scared to go to sleep in case something was different when she woke the next morning.

Amy's children are not only having to deal with the finality of their loss but also the nature and suddenness of the way Keith died. They have reacted in different ways, Ava internalising her grief, rarely talking about her father but thinking about him, as Amy often discovers when she mentions him to her; Flynn asking questions all the time, wanting details and answers.

I didn't get to say goodbye to my grandad and it's hard when you spend your whole life with someone only for them to leave without getting to have those last words or the final embrace that the magnitude of love shared between you deserves. The funeral is often a way of saying goodbye to the living memory of that person, but if a child wasn't old enough or it wasn't deemed appropriate to have them at the funeral, it might be good for them to feel like they have said goodbye with a gesture like lighting a candle, sending a balloon up to the sky or drawing them a picture so they feel like the person who died will have received their thoughts. The child would like them to at least know that they are thinking about them at that time, then the child is less likely to feel guilty for somehow not being there to let them know they loved them and that they will be missed.

Is grief particularly different when you've said a goodbye to when you didn't get the luxury? Only in that when it's sudden you'll experience a greater degree of shock, which is a stage not always experienced by those who had months to prepare themselves. That said, even when you have said goodbye, maybe on several occasions, it never seems enough anyway. If saying final goodbyes to people was easy you wouldn't be reading a book about grief.

11

Denial in Grief: Pretending it Hasn't Happened

I had a client describe to me how he had managed to keep busy for ten years, running from the feelings he knew he had suppressed by focusing so heavily on his four children while running a busy pub. What happened the day he decided to sell the family business? It hit him hard.

You can run from the facts but you can't deny something that lives within you. Losing a loved one and not dealing with how it makes you feel will lead to greater problems in the long term.

People often misinterpret strength as having the ability to pretend nothing has happened or that it doesn't really hurt. However, strength in bereavement is more about being able to share feelings; when you share the grief it releases something, albeit temporarily, and you have allowed yourself to be present and honest with yourself and others.

Here's an example of denial in the case of Vikki, 38, a dance choreographer and mother of two, Molly, ten and George, seven.

Vikki's situation

Vikki lost her father to cancer in February 2011. He hadn't been a great father – in fact something he had done in the past caused her a lot of hatred towards him – but when Vikki had become a mother, something changed in her father's behaviour and she was more than happy to forgive anything he had done before Molly's birth, and she enjoyed seeing her children having a good relationship with their grandad.

Vikki's denial was that she didn't want to acknowledge that he was dead because she figured that she would have to take time out from being strong and perfect and maybe then she would cry and be weak.

Vikki was in fact living a very time- and energy-consuming reality, one created by avoidance and fear held in place by the belief that to think of her loss would send the world around her tumbling down. She did not realise that the denial was slowly eroding her life anyway.

Vikki couldn't say that her father was dead. She referred to his death as 'the going part' and she found it very hard to complete a sentence on the subject without giving a great deal of thought to every single word that came out of her mouth, as though if she said something out loud, it would make it real. She had her head in her hands, her knees tucked close to her chest and her head on the table. Her body language told me that she was fighting hard against something in addition to the loss.

Denial needs a good back-up story, one that makes the person's version of reality so convincing that they start believing it. Vikki's denial went along these lines: 'I haven't got time to be weak or acknowledge any of that stuff [reducing all the things that loss denoted to 'stuff']; that's like a luxury [a luxury she couldn't or wouldn't afford herself]. People discuss their grief on your bereavement group on Facebook and I think, how can people be so inward-focused and self-indulgent? Those contributions are so vulnerable. I have kids to tend to and the minute I'm weak my little family falls apart [setting self-imposed rules that make it near on impossible for her to break free]. It's been so fascinating seeing people's comments on the Facebook bereavement group [said with a degree of envy] and I don't mean it rudely, but how do they have the time and energy to be so open? I can't be that open, so I just make out I'm funny and make silly comments. I haven't got time to be vulnerable. It's really difficult to see everyone so comfortable talking about it. There's no way I could sit with my mum and brother and have a conversation about my dad – daft to even think so!'

What denial says about grief

Before you judge what Vikki was implying about people's relationship with grief, remember that when people are particularly down on something, it generally comes from a place of longing for something that they don't feel they can have, so they downgrade it, pull it to pieces, devalue its whole existence.

I wanted to examine her fallacy that grief was self-indulgent, so I asked her if it was OK for me to talk about losing my grandad. 'You're asking me if I think you are self-indulgent for wanting to talk about your grandfather's death?' she replied. 'Not at all. If it feels right for you and it will make you feel better, that's fine by me. If you need to talk or scream out about it, that's your right. It just feels that when it comes to me, I don't deserve to feel better.'

Vikki clearly believed that she couldn't express her grief, that to do so would be going against some rule she had imposed on herself. It wasn't that she was denying others' grief, and later on she told me that she helped her children grieve for their grandad, even telling me it was good for them to express their emotions.

So I asked her what she thought she had done wrong and why she felt she didn't deserve to feel better. And she looked at me and said, 'I don't know.' Somewhere in Vikki's life she had learned that she didn't deserve to feel better and I wanted to unpick what it was that someone had done or said to make her feel unworthy of her natural human reaction to loss.

When loss and separation combine

Vikki started to talk about her ex-husband, although it wasn't clear for a while if she was with him or not with him. Shortly after her father died, Tom, her husband and father to her children, decided that Vikki 'wasn't what he wanted in a wife' and told her that her father's death had made 'everything fall into place'. He left the family home five months after her dad died and stayed away from his children for long periods of time. On top of losing their grand-father, to whom they had been very close, Molly and George had to cope with missing their dad and they found that very hard.

Being on the receiving end of separation can have a very similar effect to having had a loss. For Vikki, just as things had come good with her father, he was taken away from her – through nobody's choice – and then her husband – who did have a choice – chose to take himself away; another loss.

It isn't difficult to see why she put all her focus on the loss of Tom – there was a possibility, however slim, that if, as she put it, she 'worked hard enough' she could get him back.

I asked her how she thought she might have grieved for her father if Tom hadn't left. She replied, 'It would have taken it all away.' She meant that if Tom hadn't left she would have grieved a lot more naturally; there would be no denial, no need to avoid and maybe it wouldn't have been as hard to cope.

Somehow I doubted that. Not only was Vikki distracted from grief by her relationship issues and her learned behaviours from the past – 'I don't deserve to feel better' – but she was also playing a role to her mum and her brother, as there were family issues at play with her father's side of the family leading up to, and after, he passed away.

Vikki described some awful behaviour from her aunts and uncles that had made the whole funeral a disgusting and dirty experience, totally destroying it for her mother. Vikki's mum had been slapped in the face by a sister-in law-for not ensuring they were there when Vikki's dad had taken his last breath, something that would have been impossible for her mother to have instigated because she had only just got there herself.

Vikki was trying to keep her mum safe and make sure her brother didn't react physically to the lying and deceit that was taking place. I asked her what role she was playing and she concluded she was the 'manager of everyone's feelings'. 'And what about your own?' I asked her. She didn't need to answer – it was all too glaringly obvious.

Vikki has made a life's habit of putting everyone else's needs in front of hers. She had helped her mum and brother through those difficult months following the unpleasantness with the family, and looked after her children, helping them to grieve and cope with their dad effectively abandoning them, but hadn't thought about her own needs.

What Vikki didn't see was that the more focus she placed inwardly, the more everyone around her would benefit. We should always make sure we look after ourselves as much as those who depend on us – mostly our kids – and more than those who don't really depend on us but who we sometimes convince ourselves do come before us. For, if you're deeply unhappy but are putting on a good front, how able are you to enrich the lives of those around you? I wanted to show Vikki that if she had the right balance between her own needs and the needs of others, she would be capable of enriching their lives no end.

When denial is shown to be a learned behaviour

I had gathered from the way Vikki spoke of her past that something had taught her that she doesn't matter and that even with the trauma of her relationship break-up and the difficulties of wider family issues, all she still wanted to do was to help everyone else with how they were feeling. Why?

Vikki said that she hadn't told her mum that Tom had left until recently, when the matter had been taken out of her hands by a mutual connection who just happened to tell her mum that Vikki and Tom had split up. Until this point, her mum had thought Tom and Vikki were still together, probably made believable by the fact that Tom was allowed to use Vikki's home as if it were still his, which Vikki thought would be best for the kids. For the first year and a half she told them Daddy was on a night shift, so she hadn't told the truth about what was going on.

Vikki and her mum, for all the love that they shared for one another, clearly didn't communicate about things with an emotional value to them both. Even when her mum found out that she and Tom were not together, Vikki forbade her mum to ask her any questions about it. It was like there was a wall of silence between them. I asked if her mother ever spoke about the loss of her husband. 'Oh no!' said Vikki. 'We don't talk about that. Neither of us choose to.' So it went both ways.

Vikki's mum had been with her dad for over forty years when he died. She had thought of leaving on many occasions, but when something changed in him (around the time of Molly's birth) and he became a better person, everybody enjoyed a wonderful three-year spell until he got cancer. The interesting thing here was that Vikki saw it as a successful marriage. Her mum had got what she wanted in the end; he came good for her. When I questioned if three out of forty years was a good return and could be deemed a success, Vikki looked at me as though I'd said something revolutionary. Putting it into numbers seemed to change her mind. 'She gave half her life to receive three years of something most would deem acceptable. It wasn't a success after all, was it?' she reflected sadly.

That her mother had lived unhappily for so many years made Vikki see that her mum had put herself second and that she herself was mirroring that behaviour. She reflected on whether her relationship with Tom felt similar to her parents' relationship and she told me that she had tried everything to get Tom to stay. She was so desperate for their relationship not to fail that she would have put up with anything to have held it together. She could also see that now, letting him come and go as he pleased, even though he treated her badly and put her down in front of their children, kidding herself that this was for the benefit of Molly and Tom, was harmful and setting them a dangerous example. What was Molly learning from her mum about relationships and how we should allow ourselves to be treated? She could now see that hanging on to the idea of Tom and her being together was mirroring her mother's efforts to make things work with her dad, despite his challenging and unkind behaviour. 'In my family,' she explained, 'traditionally couples didn't separate. My nan and grandad, until his recent passing, lived together much of the last twenty years, even though they had actually split in the 1990s. Separate bedrooms was enough distance for them; splitting up just wasn't the done thing.'

The chronological facts

I often show a client their life through timeline therapy to make it visual for them so they can see the course they've been on and where they're heading. Before Vikki's dad's death there was a whole lot of history that had resulted in her feeling that she didn't deserve a certain outcome in life. It was also clear her parents' relationship, particularly her mum's example in remaining in her unhappy marriage, had had a huge influence on Vikki. After her dad's passing came the dismantling of her family, when Tom left and the need to look after others – her children, her mother, her brother – became even more pronounced than usual.

When you draw a circle around the post-death distractions and responsibilities it acts as a barrier to grief, epitomised by one of Vikki's early comments: 'I can't think about Dad. I've got too much going on,' and 'If I start showing any weakness, my family will fall apart.' Five years later and our conversation is the first of its kind for her – hopefully a prelude to change. But how and when?

A useful question to ask ourselves is in five years' time, if we change nothing, where will we be? What did we create? How will we feel?

I continued the time line for Vikki to fifteen years from the present, suggesting this period of time because that was how long she was likely to have with her kids until they were likely to have moved out and started their adult life.

I used a technique that I hoped would offer her a glance into the future in order to see two outcomes. Firstly, the outcome she wouldn't have wanted. I asked her to imagine her children fifteen years from now and to see and hear how they were doing, how they felt about their childhood, to ask how it affected them and what about it they would have changed if they had the choice.

Vikki looked shocked. Thinking these things through was painful for her. The harsh reality, given that she had already offered me some insight into how her kids were coping, was not what she wanted for them. I then asked her what would they be like in fifteen years if she started to focus on herself a bit and believe that she deserved nothing less than happiness. I asked her what they would say about their last fifteen years if she had joined them in grieving for their grandad openly and honestly. And crucially, how would things be different if she let Tom go and had been able to have shared this loss with her mother?

Vikki smiled. She was visibly enjoying the image that was playing out in her mind. I added some weight to the impact by asking what would happen with every year that now went by with no change? It would mean the effects of her behaviour would continue to take hold of the kids and with every year that passed this would be less reversible. A childhood is not something to be taken for granted; each year is precious. Now was the time for her to make some changes.

How to break the mould – where do I start?

It was now over to Vikki. I asked her what her three priorities would be after she walked out of my front door and started the next fifteen years of her life. Without missing a beat, she said that she would talk to her mum about Tom. (I happen to know that she texted her as soon as she got in her car and that as soon as her mum received the message she replied, 'Thank God! At last! I'll bring Prosecco.') Step one, she said, would hopefully give her the strength to carry out step two – letting go of Tom. Step three was to tell the kids how she felt about Grandad, allowing herself to have a good cry in front of them and let them see that their mum was looking after herself now, as well as them.

The purpose of denial

Denial protects us. It's a defence. It keeps us from dealing with our loss and having to deal with the issues we have hidden and potentially lied to ourselves about for so long. Pretending the loss didn't happen can feel like a favourable option.

Vikki didn't just decide to deny her grief because she had a few things going on around the same time. It was so much more to do with how her life had actually already given her the ability to deny other things and that was her preferred and embedded way of coping. She'd watched her mum brush her problems with her dad under the carpet and utilised it to good effect with her own husband and even carried that on when he walked out, only telling her mum (who she is incredibly close to) that they had split five years after the event. She was trained to use denial and she had proven herself a great student.

Something traumatic or something learned will give you the option of using denial as a means to cope. Some take it, some don't. I don't think grief alone is enough to spark denial; there have to be other factors present.

The opposite to denial is simply acceptance. An ability to face the facts and work on the feelings and thoughts that grief provokes the moment they strike. You accept that you're going to feel certain pain and that you're going to go on a journey you don't wish to embark on, but nonetheless you'll go voluntarily because you know that you're no exception, you're only human and you have little choice but to engage with grief, whether it's straight away, in five years' time or beyond.

Playing hide and seek with reality – the truth – is a short-lived game because at some point it will catch up with you and you'll have to answer to how many years were wasted thinking you would get round to dealing with it later. Denial is a damaging defence. It's a complete contradiction in terms. It keeps you safe from one thing and creates so much more of a dilemma than the thing you were avoiding in the first place. Have strength and allow yourself to face anything undesirable in life with the knowledge that it's part of being here in the first place.

You don't control what happens to you, but you do control how you react to it.

I later spoke to Vikki to catch up and see how she had been getting on since our discussion. She told me that she spoke to her mum and now they can't stop talking. She is also making small steps with Tom. He doesn't stay at the house any more and she is quite businesslike with him now. She reflected that her new partner is a great talker, and that she feels she is immature emotionally but making improvements with his help, as he does not let her get away with pretending she is OK. Although this makes her uncomfortable, she knows it is good for her in order to help her come to terms with her loss.

12

Acceptance of a Loss

Why, when the loss of a loved one will cause us so much pain, would we want to accept it? Avoiding grief, not wanting to face the reality of our loss, keeps us bound to a myth that it maybe hasn't happened, which in turn leads us to create so many unhealthy conditions for ourselves and others in order to keep the denial alive.

Plainly put, you can deny the facts but all around you see them. It's a common and understandable defence mechanism to not want to believe the truth when that truth is tragic, but it can alienate you from anyone or anything that threatens the structure of your false reality, leaving you with a lot of pieces to pick up when your structure collapses and the truth prevails.

In many of the case studies in this book, acceptance and adjustment are highlighted as being key ingredients to reaching a constructive level of grief management. And when you do take the incredibly difficult step of accepting the circumstances of your loss, you allow all other aspects of your life to unite. Effectively, you rejoin reality.

It's perfectly normal to have a period of time after your loss when acceptance and adjustment may seem a million miles away. When shock and bewilderment take a hold, you have to allow them to run their course before you can even ask yourself: 'How do I feel about this?'

There will be a transitional period after any shock you experience, dependent upon the nature of your loss, until it will become clear and you are completely aware of what has just happened to you, and it's then that you're in the clutches of grief. At this point there are choices to be made.

As I see it there are ten main factors around acceptance that I believe are the key ingredients in either having it, wanting it but not being able to achieve it, or it being available but the individual not wanting it.

To accept is not to forget. You can't forget and you should not worry so much about doing so. To accept is to begin to adjust, to overcome the barriers, some self-imposed, that will help you stop replaying the incident or the bleak facts of the loss and take you to the stage where you'll be able to remember positively and keep the memories of your loved one alive – a better place for your mind to be.

If you've lost more than one person, consider the questions posed below for them individually. They are in death, as they were in life, completely separate people and should always be recognised as such. If you haven't already read it, I would suggest going to the chapter on multiple loss before you go any further here and return when you're ready.

1. Our relationship with the individual. How close were you?
The closer you were to the individual who died, the harder it might be for you to accept their absence. Some people leave a gaping hole in the middle of our daily routine and for them to not be with us every day is obviously excruciatingly difficult.

If we were to focus for a moment on what you had, instead of what you're missing, would you say you had a number of incredible years with the person you lost? Was it a relationship that gave you many happy, comforting memories? If so, this can very much lend itself to greater acceptance because the person fulfilled a very important purpose in your life. It wouldn't hurt so much if they didn't.

When grieving, we very much focus on what we have lost. If you had a good thing with that person, a relationship to be proud of, you may feel that this warrants a higher score. However, you may also feel that the fact you had such a good thing warrants a lower score because it's harder to let go. Be prepared that this perspective of yours can change with time, so you could revisit this chapter in the months to come to assess what has changed.

There may be something about your relationship with the deceased that you can't let go of, or some unanswered questions, and this will affect how accepting you are. However, if your relationship with them wasn't, on balance, a strong or positive one, your score here may still be high because it's your acceptance of your loss, not your acceptance of the relationship and its complications, that you are scoring here. In other words, and in light of the relationship **you** had with **them**, how much do you accept what **you** have lost?

2. The individual's circumstances before death. What sort of life did they have?

In this component of acceptance, we look at what was going on in the person's life leading up to their death. The measure of this is down to how we perceive how much they valued their life and how fair or unfair we feel their passing was as a result. For example, some feel their life to be directionless and empty, in which case do we feel worse about their death or the potentially hollow and unsatisfactory life they led?

Alternatively, some people fulfil a tremendous amount of purpose to many, living their life to the full and leaving a footprint on many others'. Do you feel they had a good life and believe they were happy and content? Is it better that they lived a shorter yet more fulfilling life than if they had been desperately unhappy and lived until old age?

The circumstances of death are vital to our acceptance, but again your interpretation will be unique, so in light of how you perceive that that person was living their life, how much do you accept, given what **they** had and what they lost?

3. The nature of the loss. How traumatic was it?

What happened and how? This is a vital area to explore. Some find acceptance less of a struggle if their loved one died of old age or if the deceased had battled a disease with every ounce of energy, prolonging their life beyond prognosis, making all around them proud while also giving them time to prepare.

Arguably harder to accept might be death caused by an accident, a death by violent or criminal behaviour, the loss of a child, or by someone taking their own life. When these sorts of deaths occur there are many more complex factors that come into play. In scoring yourself you need to be aware of how you feel about the nature of the loss. How do you feel about the circumstances leading up to the event? Was the loved one in any way responsible? How predictable did you feel the event was? Did you get time to prepare or was the death sudden? What is it about the events themselves, beyond the fact that someone you care about has died, that stops you from feeling acceptance?

Does the nature of the loss make it more or less acceptable to you?

4. The time since the loss. Is time the greatest healer?

The old adage 'time is a healer' gives the impression that things just sort themselves out if you're patient. But for me, we are the healer. Time is perhaps the vehicle that takes us through the stages but only if we do the work, have the right mindset and make good decisions both for ourselves and on behalf of others. Even if the wheels of time will always be turning, the direction they point in is up to us.

Preoccupation with time can result in unnecessary pressure. If we come across someone who says she got over her loss within a year, we can set unfair pressure on ourselves to expect to do the same. The truth is, when it comes to acceptance, time is irrelevant and just one of many elements of grief. You are on a unique path in your bereavement and it is immeasurable against anyone else's experiences, quite simply because they aren't you.

People often use time against themselves. Believing you can outrun your grief – 'I'll deal with it later' – will keep you at square one and ensure that you carry a bag of complicated and unrefined emotions. You will have to force the way you operate and how those around you are allowed to act and talk in order to maintain your procrastination.

If your loss is recent then you might not be at the stage where acceptance is even feasible. Some people do find acceptance straight away or have even been able to make an agreement with themselves before the death itself.

How does the time you've had relate to where you are with acceptance? How much time do you feel you will need before you accept? What is in the way of that? What needs to happen before it is possible? Do you control the time it will take or does someone else?

Exactly what is an adequate amount of time before accepting and adjusting to your loss is up to you. Give yourself a higher score if you feel as though you're at the point of containing the negative thoughts you've had swirling around in your mind since the loss. Mark yourself low if those thoughts are multiplying with very little to supposedly reduce them.

5. Blame and guilt. Whose fault do you think it is?
Blame is one of the key blockages that might prevent you from feeling the relative peace and calm of acceptance. We have a propensity to want to point a finger thinking it will help, but I question that. The people we blame may absolutely deserve it, but by pointing the

finger we immediately put ourselves in the path of bitterness, a path that once we start on it may be never-ending.

The problem is we can't change the outcome of death, so unless we find some forgiveness, apportion responsibility for the loss elsewhere or realise that we are perpetuating a cycle of negativity by blaming, we won't and can't accept or adjust to what has happened.

Even worse than wasting years blaming others for something we can't change, is spending years pointing the finger at ourselves. Self-sabotage is a dangerous thing. You may have had an argument with your loved one, you may have felt there was more you could have done before they died, you might have missed that vital phone call that would have stopped them from walking into the scene of an accident. If you're of a certain disposition, taking responsibility for something that wasn't your fault, you'll always find a way to make the blame fall on your lap. Maybe you were taught to do this during a childhood of being made to feel you were not important or that your feelings didn't matter.

If we blame ourselves for things we may or may not have been responsible for, we stunt our progress through grief. Your justification for feeling blame could be because you have played a part in the events leading up to the loss. You may have been driving the car, you might have given them the drugs, but whatever the circumstances, you may need to take a closer look at whatever it is you are blaming yourself for and allow yourself some forgiveness. Let's imagine your case was being argued in court. You know what the prosecution would say because you have been hearing that over and over, but consider this: what would the defence lawyer say? Why might you NOT be to blame?

You can do this by looking at the bigger picture, accepting that the way to bring meaning back into your life might be by making the necessary changes to your lifestyle or mindset that would have averted the actions that led to your loss and use that knowledge and remorse to stop others from taking the same actions that you regrettably once took.

Give yourself a higher score if you feel less blame. If, however, you're in the process of acknowledging your blame, which is based on something you would and should wish to change, mark yourself lower but know that that your score will increase as you take steps towards turning your regrets into ideas to inspire others and prevent the same thing happening to someone else.

6. Our relationship with ourselves. How kind are you to yourself?
What has our sense of self and our internal dialogue got to do with acceptance? Some people are incredibly hard on themselves, only seeing negatives that they can't let go of. Being kind to yourself in grief is to forgive the indiscretions that you could spend hours thinking about – the things you said that you shouldn't have and the things you didn't say that you should have!

Being kind to yourself through grief is to allow yourself to be at your worst, and to experience the many components of grief such as anger, frustration, confusion and vulnerability.

What do you do that gives you the best possible chance of coping with grief? What do you do that makes your day harder? What thoughts do you have that are helpful, and which ones that are unhelpful? Have you always taken responsibility and blame for everything? Are you always quite self-critical or did this start with your loss?

The ultimate kindness to oneself in grief is to carry on being you, to withstand the potential pull towards denial and delay. Score higher if you are facing everything with the sole intention of working with yourself, for yourself and never against yourself. Score lower if you find yourself putting more on your shoulders than you seem to be taking off. Who taught you to do that to yourself?

7. Our mental strength. How in control of your thoughts are you?
A big element in the management of our grief is in fact the management of our mind. We can't control memories triggered by the most unexpected of words, actions, TV shows, music, people, old neighbours, etc. What we do control, however, is the time and focus we place on those memories.

In our collection of memories, we will, regrettably, have a file full of negative moments that most commonly belong to the time leading up to the actual death or things we didn't see but imagine happened. These are the thoughts that most commonly flash into our heads after loss and we can absolutely influence them by imagining them as appearing on a big cinema screen. As we didn't ask for this film, we can say, 'That's enough. Dim the lights, turn the volume down,' and change the reel ourselves. We can then show the film that has the good memories, crank up the lights and volume, and watch that one instead. Try it! Actually put yourself inside the old-fashioned projector room and see yourself changing the reels next time.

Of all the thoughts you have for the person you have lost, what percentage of them would you say are negative and what percentage are positive? Your score is 6 if it's 60% and 4 if it's 40%, and so on. This is another figure that is absolutely fluid; you can change this result tomorrow now you know you're able to control these thoughts.

8. Our ability to be present in the moment. You can busy yourself to buy time, but will you?
What was going on for you at the time of your loss? Were you distracted by the kids, by work or a house move, or a relationship struggle? We have to be careful not to take the very tempting route of being too busy to understand what has happened to us.

There really is no limit to the amount of time that someone can spend distracting themselves from grieving properly. Stillness is the ability to stop at a time where we prefer to keep moving. Being present in the moment is to be bold enough to stare grief in the face and say, 'I don't know what you're going to put me through, but I'm not going anywhere.' It's about engaging with all your responsibilities outside of grief but being mindful enough to leave yourself sufficient time and space to have moments of your own, instead of supporting everyone else.

How distracted are you? What are those distractions? Can you see how you potentially use them to avoid facing grief yourself? What is the correct balance so that your world doesn't fall apart but you still give yourself the time you need?

Score yourself higher if you are really good at taking the time you need for you, if you recognise that you avoid distraction and you don't run from the feelings of grief that are now a part of your day. Score lower if you recognise the distractor in you and maybe that you keep yourself busy for its own' sake, just so you don't get hit by a wave of grief.

9. The reality of grief. What do we expect?
Realistic expectations are important in all aspects of our life. If we are unrealistic with our expected outcomes then we are simply setting ourselves up for failure. In grief, it's hard to be realistic if it is our first experience of loss. Even if it's your second or third experience, the ones before it barely prepare you because no two losses are ever the same.

To be realistic in grief is to understand there is no 'getting over it'. We learn to manage our loss, not forget it. We wouldn't be taking a realistic approach if we gave ourselves time limits or banned ourselves from crying or refused to talk about the person we have lost, or did things like taking down photos so as not to be reminded of them.

We impose rules on ourselves in all areas of life and don't always realise we're doing it. Have you ever noticed when you say 'I must' or 'I can't'? Usually anything that follows these kinds of directives are a command we give ourselves which after much repetition becomes a belief. We have the freedom to influence how limiting those beliefs are by either continuing to use negative commands or by choosing to rewrite those statements into a more positive example, like 'I can' or 'I will'.

Are you realistic in your expectations of grief? What do you base that on? Other people's opinions? Assumptions? Hope? Do you expect yourself to breeze through it because you're going to use mind over matter, or do you think you'll just save it for later? Are you communicating about grief regularly, and are you refining your expectations based on all of the helpful conversations that you're having?

The reality of grief is that if you're not feeling anything then you're not grieving. You'll score higher on the scale of acceptance if you are not setting yourself unreasonable targets such as 'I can't cry' or 'I mustn't show emotion at the funeral'. However, you will score low if you often tell yourself exactly how it's going to be or 'needs' to be, even though you haven't experienced it before. Assumptions become the reality because you have thought them into existence.

10. Our past. How influential is it?

The experiences we've had will affect our ability to accept. Grief has a habit of awakening, activating and justifying pre-existing issues that we have experienced in the past. The result of this can often be the tendency to use our grief against ourselves as a punishment or something we deserve. Grief is enough to deal with without making it harder for ourselves.

We might have had some awful experiences as a child that gave us low self-esteem, resulting in our being less likely to feel worthy of feeling better or doing OK. We may have communication issues due to something in our past, that stops us from wanting to talk about our loss because we don't want to impose on others. There are many examples of how the past can stunt our ability to manage our grief. Is there something that you can see is very much about your past that is making your acceptance of your loss harder?

What are the big knocks in your life that have hurt you and set you back? What were the effects of these tough breaks? How might these effects be echoing in the loss you've just experienced? How might your cocktail of grief be mixed with other elements that relate to your previous experiences?

Very often what we think is grief is actually a combination of other elements and we are always better off for identifying the factors in play. In thinking about other factors, you will score highly if you are firmly aware of the ways that your past may have crept into the way you are coping with your loss. A lower score is for those who know there is something that pre-existed before their loss but cannot or will not look at it in order to find acceptance. Maybe for you the thought of dealing with the old defence mechanism constructed for other reasons is far scarier than the reality of your loss. If so, make sure you read the chapter 'When Grief Combines with Pre-existing Issues'.

This chapter will no doubt have helped you to identify what you are doing well and the areas that you're finding harder. Now you have broken down your adjustment and acceptance of grief into smaller aspects you'll have a finer understanding of what it is you would benefit from focusing on. If you had lots of new thoughts and ideas during this chapter it would be an idea to get them all down on paper. Each new perspective you have can lead to an action, which will change something and take you closer to where you would like to be on the path to adjustment.

13

Losing Someone Later on in Life and the Burden of Blame

My grandmother Molly Faldo and I sat down to lunch one day to talk about her recent loss of my grandad Charlie Faldo, who had died from cancer just a year ago, in February 2016. She had told me many things that she didn't like about him, which I always found to be her natural response to being asked how she felt about him.

This was her way of being honest, not wanting to dress her life with Charlie up as something it wasn't. But even though he is no longer here, it's also her way of continuing a good few decades of justifiable cause to be a little disgruntled by him. And I say little, when really, I mean a lot!

Nan shared a lot more with me once she had warmed up a little later. Initially she was far more interested in telling me about her parents, so we started with her father – her first loss – who was 79 when, in 1988, he died of a sudden heart attack while shaving.

Molly described the shock she felt in losing someone she thought would go on forever. She recalled what an incredible man he was, a wonderful husband and father, and how she had felt more sorry for her mother than she had for herself. She accepted her loss because her dad had a good life and had died at a good age.

Molly was 50 years old when he died and because of the emptiness she and her mother both felt immediately after the loss, she decided to move in with her mother to her home in East London.

Loss of her mother

Molly's mother was incredibly strong mentally, but not so robust physically. After a bout of flu in 1996, she died at the age of 88. Molly described how she had lost a good friend in her mum. They were affectionate with one another and her ashes have been with Molly ever since.

Molly takes great comfort from the fact that her mother is still there with her. She talks to her all of the time and relishes the idea that when she dies she will be placed somewhere with her mother: 'Wherever I go, she's coming with me.'

Are we forgetting someone?

We had jumped from a loss in 1988 to another in 1996, but there was a loss to us both that Molly had chosen to skip. This, I think, is because there are losses that you can accept and there are losses that take on a whole new set of parameters – and the loss of her son Steve Faldo, at just 29 years old, was one of those.

Just to explain one thing

You might wonder why I haven't referred to Molly's parents as my great-grandparents. They *are* my great-grandparents, but I didn't actually come into the family until I was 13 years old, in 1992, by which time my father Steve, who I had never met, had drowned in the *Marchioness–Bowbelle* disaster on the Thames in 1989.

My mother and Steve had met working on the river in 1978 and after a short fling my mother became pregnant. Steve wasn't in a position to support her so she went ahead with the pregnancy on her own (phew!) and at just 16 years of age brought me into the world.

Ten years later on the day after Steve died I was staying with my auntie, who just happened to work on the river too. She would have known that my dad was missing and she would have known that it was likely I would never get the chance to meet him. I was oblivious to the significance of the events that evening and I feel sad for my auntie that she would have known only too well what it all meant for me. How incredibly strange that I still recall that day I was in her office on 'the Regalia' looking out on to the river, wondering why all the police boats were frantically circling around not far from Swan Pier.

In case you're wondering why I wasn't told about my dad then, my mother had since married my stepfather and he forbade her to let me or anyone else know that he wasn't my real father. So while she remained in that relationship, I was never to be told.

How did I not know he wasn't my real dad? I have no idea how I was able to forget the first five years of my life when he wasn't actually in it! I was fostered in those years, but I don't look back at that time with any negativity. In fact I have many early memories of being safe and happy in my foster home. I did actually think my stepfather was my real father – maybe we only see what we want to see.

Just to completely bring you into the picture, in 1992 my mother, myself and my younger brother Spencer ran away from my stepfather, fleeing to Great Yarmouth to a women's refuge. We were later housed in Tiptree near Colchester and it was then that my mother sat me down and unexpectedly asked if I would like to meet my real nan and grandad – Molly and Charlie.

In that very instant she asked me I had a flashback to a moment when my stepfather had punched his way into the council flat I grew up in, which we had been evicted from for not paying the rent on time. As he sat on the edge of the bath nursing a cut hand I recalled a comment that would reveal the truth of my conception. 'Paul, your hand's bleeding,' I said. I realised in that moment. Why would I call him by his name, and not 'Dad'?

My immediate response to my mum was, why was I not meeting my real dad, and it was then she told me that I wouldn't get to meet him because he had died in the accident, and she went on to tell me about it. In terms of my feelings I remember finding acceptance very quickly and being excited about meeting a family I never knew existed. The next evening there they all were in the living room, and they've been in my life ever since.

The contention

Back to the story in hand. My grandmother recalled how Steve, my real dad, was talking about the loss of his grandfather to Molly and said to her that 'life was going to be really different now Grandad wasn't going to be around'. Little did they know that in a matter of months his life would be lost trying to save others, when the boat he was the skipper of was completely submerged in just thirty seconds as the dredger hit it and it rolled beneath the vessel as if it was a toy boat.

Two crewmen stationed on the bow of the dredger failed to see the *Marchioness* ahead, and the skipper of the *Bowbelle*, Douglas Henderson, was not at the helm. He was later criticised for having drunk six pints of beer on the afternoon of the accident.

According to the dry narrative report of the Chief Inspector of Marine Accidents, the *Marchioness* was hit by the dredger *Bowbelle* at 1.46 a.m. With 127 passengers and four crew, the party boat had just cleared Southwark Bridge.

The *Bowbelle* was behind the *Marchioness*, both boats adjusting their course to stay in the centre of the river to go under Cannon

Street Railway Bridge. Somehow they converged, although crew members on the party boat had already seen the dredger coming up behind them and assumed it was going to overtake.

The dredger had passed a similar party boat, the *Hurlingham*, a few hundred yards upstream. At eight-and-a-half knots, the dredger was moving twice as fast as either of the pleasure cruisers.

As the collision became inevitable, at least one deckhand on the *Marchioness* shouted a warning to Steve and he applied full throttle to try to escape the bigger boat. To no avail.

The *Bowbelle* weighed 1,880 tonnes and was more than 260 feet in length. The *Marchioness* was just 85 feet long, and weighed only 46 tonnes. The dredger's iron hull swept the party boat's wooden superstructure aside, crushing the *Marchioness* with such force that her upper deck separated from the hull.

The aftermath was protracted and messy. A public inquiry was refused by the then Transport Minister Cecil Parkinson, and again in 1993 by his successor Stephen Norris. A report by the Marine Accident Investigation Branch was criticised by relatives and survivors as a whitewash.

Though the *Bowbelle*'s skipper was twice tried in court for failing to keep a proper lookout, the juries could not reach a verdict either time, and Henderson was acquitted.

Criticisms of the coroner's office, the crews of the *Marchioness* and the *Bowbelle*, the Port of London Authority and even the lack of preparedness of the Thames River Police were swamped in a complex legal row that continued until a coroner's inquest finally ruled in 1995 that the victims had been 'unlawfully killed'.

Not until February 2000 was a formal investigation launched by John Prescott, then Transport Minister. Lord Justice Clarke then reported that a formal investigation should have been held earlier.

Criticism, blame and regret to one side, for my nan, the damage was done and the protracted to-and-fro turned a devastating loss into a bitter battle to defend her son's name and to prove his innocence in the face of extreme hostility from some who were accusing her son of murder.

Molly was incensed. She wasn't just dealing with the loss of her son, she was dealing with hatred and accusation. Loss can be very unfair but this was something else. She was angry. She would look at people on a bus or train and tell herself that her son should be there instead of them. She was trapped in a world of hatred for what her son was being subjected to and she was expressing it in worrying ways, allowing her grief and anger to seep out in the direction of others. She realised she needed to stop.

Nan openly admits that she doesn't accept the loss of her son and that she has never got used to it. She can't forget it, she has just learned to cope with it. Her most frequent thought is: 'Why didn't you swim, Steve?'

Going back to Charlie . . .

'Sir Prancelot' (this made me roar – I've never heard anyone call him that but it was very apt) had been gone almost a year and Nan began with the leveller that 'He wasn't a good husband', followed by fonder memories. 'He was always a character; he made me laugh as much as he made me angry.'

Molly was softening and she added how grateful she was that he had given her three fantastic children. The grandchildren and now all of the great-grandchildren were all down to him.

They split up twenty years ago and although there was a ten-year period when they lived apart, Charlie wasn't doing particularly well on his own, so she took pity on him and allowed him to live with her, staying in separate bedrooms for the remainder of that time.

Charlie was never one for apologies but it meant a great deal to her that he thanked her for putting up with him while he was in the hospice, which she said made her 'feel a bit pleased'. I thought this might be something of an understatement.

What did Molly lose?

She loved my grandad like a brother in the end, and together they had produced a great family. While she doesn't miss the memory of his gambling, drinking and general selfishness, she does miss the talking, the laughter and the companionship. When you have spent so long with someone for better or for worse, it's hard not to feel a great hole in your life where that person once was.

How she is coping with the loneliness?

Molly tells me that her biggest rule is to not get stuck indoors. And that where she used to say no, she now says yes. She gets out as much as possible, volunteering in a St Claire's hospice charity shop, and she meets up with friends, stays incredibly close to her daughters and grandchildren and has allowed the holes left by her losses to be filled by the rest of the family, who are always there to help and listen.

Regret?

My nan is no stranger to bereavement, so I wondered how she felt about the way she had grieved for her four losses. She regrets not talking to a counsellor about her son, especially as she felt she couldn't talk about him to her other children, because they had their own feelings of grief to contend with. They have long since been able to discuss Steve together, so I let this one slide. There were, however, a few things that I could not because they are very much affecting her on a daily basis.

Dividing the feeling of loss

I didn't need to be especially perceptive to see that while talking about the loss of her mother, father and Charlie, Molly could never resist bringing it back to her son Steve. Acceptance and non-acceptance obviously play a big role here. In less obvious cases it's particularly helpful that we know exactly who our grief is for and to understand when grief and other emotions like regret, resentment and blame combine to create something very different.

A small chink in the armour – the coaching begins

Hearing my nan describe how she is living for today and making the most of other people's lives and that it was her wonderful parents who gave her the ability to look forwards and not live in the past, I had no option but to help her see the contradiction she had just made. She was very much living in the past, not in the act of remembering – that as we know is vital – but in the act of choosing what to remember and being responsible for how those memories affect her. I wonder if anyone who holds on to blame after a loss does something similar?

I asked Molly to think about how many of her thoughts about Steve on any given day were positive and how many were negative. She replied 60% positive and 40% not. The smaller yet still quite significant quantity of negatives that still endured were 'what if's' and of course not actually real-life memories of her son.

I asked if those thoughts were a choice. Did she have control over having them? Molly agreed it was a choice. She could stop thinking about the 'injustice' of her loss but she doesn't want to. Why not? 'Because it would feel like I was pushing Steve to one side,' she told me.

I asked Nan to clarify what her 60% represented. She said it was all of her wonderful memories of the twenty-nine years she had of her son. I asked what the 40% was. This was the accident, the blame, the injustice, the hatred. So the 40% isn't Steve at all, I pointed out: 'It's the pain of the circumstances and the effect it had on your life and others' actions, but it isn't actually Steve.' She agreed.

I asked (without pushing her too far; I doubted she had ever had a conversation like this before) whether she was happy to hold on to 40% of what she despises when she could let that go and enjoy 100% positive thoughts about her son, whom she loves and misses incredibly.

How interesting and sad in equal measure that my nan had found that for the twenty years since she admitted she had got to the 60/40 mark (it was initially 100% negative) she had chosen to put the brakes on acceptance and hold on to that 40% simply because she felt she would be letting go of Steve if she did.

This is a conversation I have yet to continue with my nan. I hope to be able to help her relieve the feeling of resentment and injustice she feels over Steve's death, because as we agreed, it doesn't change the past but it very much affects her present and future. Imagine how all of the subtle changes would add up when she extracts the negativity from her thoughts!

The truth about blame

Holding on to blame is a form of self-sabotage. It's a state of mind that was useful to my nan in the moments after the disaster, but once the powers-that-be had all had their say it was the battle mode without the battle. Nobody is fighting any more but her, and she is standing there occasionally with her teeth gritted and her fists clenched with no opposition. Everyone else has moved on.

There is a significant difference between letting go of the memories of a loved one and letting go of the contention around their death. A mother's role is to fiercely protect her offspring, but it would not be the wish of her son for her to carry on fighting long after the bout ended.

Letting go of the controversy is not to give in on her son. It's to understand what is best for her personally and for her family members around her, who just want her to be at her happiest.

I will tell her: 'Nan, remember that Steve is more to you than the *Marchioness*. To some, he was the skipper of a boat in a tragic accident. To you, that was one day of twenty-nine years' worth of memories.'

If you want to be free of your blame

If blame is a big, enduring part of your loss, no matter how long ago this blame became a part of your thought process, I have put together some questions that will help you to break it down.

1. Measurement
How much of your grief is positive memory and how much is negative regret?

How much of the negative percentage can be changed? Is there something that might change your feeling of injustice? Is the apportioning of blame, fair or not, concluded as far as others are concerned?

2. Timescale

How long have you been at that percentage? Get some paper and chart chronologically how your percentage has changed from the day you lost your loved one to the present day. What sent it in a certain direction? What happened at those points on the scale? Is it consistent in its progress or did the transition from total negativity to joint feeling stop somewhere? For what reason might this have happened?

Now you know where you have been it's very important to know where you're going, so plan the next five years and then dare to plan the next ten. Where do you want your balance to be in the future? What's going to get it there? What do you need to do to let go of the negativity? What actions on your part would represent the progress you wish to make, and is there something you need from someone else that gives you permission to progress? if so, what, and when will you go and get it?

3. Imagination

In order to achieve this, try out what I had my nan do. I divided a bit of tissue up and wrote '60% Steve's positive memories' on the bigger section and '40% injustice' on the other.

Physically take the injustice away for a moment and focus only on the remaining part containing good memories. How does that feel? What are the benefits of seeing this and only this? What do you feel you're missing?

Bring the smaller bit of tissue – the injustice/blame – back and place it in front of the larger one representing the good memories. How do you feel about the fact that the negative clouds and overshadows your precious invaluable memories? Now remove the negativity again and throw it on the floor and ask yourself what are you afraid of and what do you lose by doing so?

Lastly take the positive memories away and put them out of sight. What do you have? How did you end up with that? How does it make you feel to be completely alone in that conflict? Is it even possible that you could ever forget all of those memories? Does it make you feel like the positive is indestructible but yet the negative is literally only held in place by your own will and nothing else? What wins in a fight – the positive memories or the negatives attached to blame?

4. Perspective

You can never go far wrong by placing yourself in the mind of your deceased loved one. In my grandmother's case it would be to imagine what Steve might say about the fact she is still gripping on to the cause and effect of the accident and allowing that to influence her life, marring her ability to remember positively without limitation.

Would he say: 'Don't let go, Mum, it's still not fair.' Or would he tell her to free herself of the burden?

How do you feel about that? What message would you get back? Not many would see the point in continuing the fight when the outcome cannot be changed.

5. Courage

The glue that holds it all together. We won't stumble across the answers; it takes conscious effort and the courage to go against the notions that we repeat so often in our minds that they have become beliefs invisible to the eye but not to the ear.

One final exercise. Imagine yourself on your rocking chair just before your time is up. Imagine you became aware of your propensity to hold on to negativity in the form of blame, regret or something else. Now imagine how you feel about your time since the loss of your loved one.

Was any of that time wasted? Could you have put any of it to better use? How do you feel about the fact you carried around something negative all that time? Does it serve you any purpose now?

Lastly, move position in the room, change chairs and then switch your thoughts to being in that rocking chair just before your end of life and imagine how proud and grateful you are that you made the very most of your time since you lost your loved one.

What did you do with your blame? How did you spend your time? What did you do to your thoughts? How did you speak about the past around others? What agreements did you have to make between yourself and others in order to achieve that feeling of pride?

It's hard to witness first-hand how thirty-odd years of blame can become such a permanent fixture of someone's outlook on life. My nan had an opportunity to put her blame to rest after we had exposed it as being a matter of choice, but she has carried them for such a distance over the last three decades that it was apparent she would rather the devil she knew than the one she did not.

If you're inspired to take the opportunity to recognise how your blame works and slowly but surely disconnect it from your person, you may initially feel like you are letting someone or something off the hook, but you will soon realise that you have let go of a weight that will absolutely alter the course of your life if you don't do so. The longer you carry the feeling of blame and resentment towards others, the harder it is for you to put it down, it will just become a part of who you are.

14

The Grief Guilt Trip

We often fail to give ourselves permission to continue living our pre-loss lives in the face of a bereavement. How can we be happy when our loved one is no longer here? What gives us the right to enjoy life when they have been cruelly denied the right to enjoy theirs? If we enjoy ourselves or even so much as smile or feel momentarily happy about something, is this in some way disrespectful to our deceased loved one? But how much of this is what we truly feel deep inside us, and how much is to do with our being afraid of being judged as disrespectful by others, for seemingly not caring enough, for not grieving the way others want or expect you to grieve?

I'm a great believer in the idea that a loss should inspire us to want more, be more, have more. For in the face of loss, we have seen first-hand that life is precious and to be made the most of, seeing as there is absolutely no guarantee as to how long any of us have. For us to impose limitations, born from our desire to load guilt upon our shoulders and to avoid judgment by others, is to start to descend into non-existence. Why do we do that? What purpose does it serve?

Maybe there's a part of us that feels like a justifiable limitation is in some way useful, a reason to not try? We must never feel guilty for being human; sadness doesn't equal respect. The greatest positive that can be generated from a loss is to inspire.

I could have done more

You're right. With hindsight we would all have done things so differently. Talked more, laughed more, experienced more. Some of the greatest lessons come from the biggest tragedies. If you have experienced loss, does it not make you appreciate life and those you share it with?

We tend to punish ourselves generally in life, bereaved or not. If we could see the potential value in learning the lesson of how precious life is, and use that to improve our relationships with friends and family moving forwards, we wouldn't spend so much time punishing ourselves for not having gained that insight before we first tasted the pain of loss. We typically dislike taking positives from negatives and whether you're ready or not is up to you, but the positives are there when you're ready to take them.

I never met my biological father. Undoubtedly this was a negative in my life and no doubt if I had met him, my perceptions of fatherhood might have been different growing up. But letting the fact I never met him negatively influence how I father my kids is not something I have been prepared to allow to happen. Our pasts, difficult as they may sometimes have proven, shape us into the people we are today or will one day be, and that can undeniably be positive. We don't always control what happens to us, but we do control how we react later in life.

Ask yourself what you can do to change what you have lost. Very little, sadly. Then ask yourself what you can do to change your outlook on what you do have. It's limitless in its possibilities, isn't it? We have a tendency to focus on the past so much we can literally be camped in it. In bereavement we have to start in the present because it's very hard to see the future at first. The future can suddenly seem foggy, unclear, bleak and dark and so because we inevitably are remembering our loved ones retrospectively, it's understandable that we tend to look backwards when faced with loss. But focusing on the past ensures you remain firmly on the spot. Learning to be present in the moment is like being on an escalator in that you may not feel you can see ahead, but day by day, you are undeniably moving forwards.

Living in the past is not the same as *remembering* a loved one. Living in the past represents a lack of acceptance, denial of the truth and facts and a failure to acknowledge your feelings and the emotional experience you're having. You can remember a loved one with great positivity and eventually with great joy, but that isn't the same as being rooted to the past, unable to move forwards with your grief or your life.

The apportioning of guilt

Jimmy told me about the overwhelming guilt he experienced after the loss of his mother. On the anniversary of her death he decided he would have a tattoo done to 'take his mind off it' but then directly afterwards he felt selfish and disrespectful that he hadn't spent the day with his family. When he then told me that the family had got together to have a meal that evening and he had been there with them, I could see that in his own eyes, Jimmy could do no right. I asked him what he thought he should have done that day:

'I should have been with Dad, but then I didn't want to go to the crematorium. Maybe I could have gone to lunch with him but then I would have been on a downer.'

When explaining why he didn't like to be around his dad for the whole day Jimmy said, 'I can't take away Dad's pain, so I don't want to face it.'

Talk about bestowing yourself with some pretty large and unrealistic amounts of pressure and expectation! Is it really Jimmy's role to take away his dad's pain? There are no magic words or healing embraces that can truly take away anyone's pain, so to look for such miracles is to expect too much of yourself.

To help him choose what's right for him and realistic above all else I asked Jimmy what he wanted from days such as the anniversary of his mum's death.

'To remember Mum.'

Good start.

'Did you remember Mum?'

'Yes. Before getting the tattoo I imagined what she would say about me getting another one. "Oh James!" she would have said, and that made me hear her voice and feel she was there for a moment.'

'How about during the tattoo?'

'No, the pain took my mind off it; it gave me a focus.'

'Straight after?'

'Yes. I thought about her on and off for the rest of the day.'

'So did you achieve your objective?'

'Yeah, but. Well. No.'

'But you said your objective was to remember Mum and you did that.'

Jimmy looked confused and dissatisfied so I gave him a chance to be more specific with his objective; maybe then it would explain why he felt so much guilt for his supposed audacity to do something for himself on such a day.

'What specifically was your guilt about?' I asked him.

'Not being there for other family members on her anniversary,' he replied

Jimmy then told me about the family meal.

'The whole gang are there for Mum,' he said. 'But there was no mention of Mum, no sharing of memories. We raised a glass but it was silent. But we had all gone out of our way to be there and we knew what we were there for.'

'Did you achieve your objective that evening?' I asked.

He described how his mum had become the '... elephant in the room. We all knew she was there but nobody said anything in case we upset one another.'

Jimmy then thought about how his mum might have felt that all of her family who she had loved so much and had left behind were all together and hadn't mentioned her. He was upset by this, and very much guiltier about it than he had been about the tattoo session. Going forward he vowed to remember her as positively as possible, to celebrate her life and discuss his wonderful memories of her.

This sounded like a plan. Literally a plan. And with that plan Jimmy felt he would know what to do with himself on special occasions. But while he himself wouldn't be able to accept silence again he was worried that other family members may not agree and would find talking or explicitly acknowledging why they were together to be incredibly painful.

We do have a habit of thinking that talking about the facts and reality of loss is in some way insensitive or damaging. But suppression is just about the most damaging factor in grief. If you want to truly help, short- and long-term, my advice is to be bold and brave. It just takes one person to say what everyone is thinking and suddenly everyone has permission to share and to feel and to adjust and be real.

The way Jimmy decided he would bring his mum up on the next occasion was to ask everyone, 'What's your favourite memory of Mum?' He would share his first so everyone could see how good it felt for him to talk about her with everyone there. Jimmy had been taking responsibility for things he couldn't control and it was good to see him start to take charge of the things he could.

We too might be concerned about upsetting someone we love, but so much of this is based on assumption. Jimmy didn't actually know that nobody else wanted to talk, he just felt it was best to be safe. But what if everyone was thinking the same as him and they were all longing to talk about his mum, to share their precious memories and bring her alive in a moment of shared love?

Collectively, we can only grieve like everyone else is grieving. We become a product of our environment just as we did growing up generally, and if you are wittingly or unwittingly engaging in a 'culture of suppression', then unless you break the cycle, you will be party to it.

Jimmy didn't need to wait until the next anniversary. He called his siblings the next morning and told them that they needed to talk about their mum, that he wanted to ask how they were coping and if there was anything he could do to support them.

And you know what? They all opened up. They all admitted they wanted to talk about her and they all agreed to meet to talk honestly about what they found hard. Jimmy had instigated the way they would move forward and I can bet you that you'll never catch that family being silent about their mum on her anniversary again.

There are countless reasons we could feel guilty and some are maybe more valid than others. But when you level accusations at yourself: I wasn't there when they closed their eyes; I didn't do enough for them when they were here; I didn't forgive them before it was too late; I didn't tell them I loved them when they walked out of the door, then this is more about self-sabotage, and you need to let go of these feelings and instead focus on the responsibility of others.

If your guilt does lie in actual circumstances that led to a death then you will need a level of self-forgiveness that will come from a greater understanding of the free will exhibited in the actions and behaviour of the individual you feel responsible for.

They will have no doubt made choices along the way, decisive actions that would have led to those circumstances surrounding their death. You'll need to look at what or who influenced their choices, at the state of mind they were in at the time, and to identify the risk they knew they were taking leading up to the event, and in so doing, you may find some answers that will help reduce your feelings of guilt.

Carrying the burden of guilt for too long can be very damaging and you need to be given the tools to challenge it and to find perspective. This may be too big for you to take on alone or for your friends and family to be able to dig deep enough to really help, so always keep in mind that professional guidance is available to you.

It may have been your fault in some way, but what will this change? Holding on to blame won't change the outcome of your loved one's death and will cause you untold difficulties. Once you have learned to unburden yourself of the guilt, you can then think of ways in which you can make their death really mean something – maybe creating a legacy for them so they didn't die in vain. For example, could your experience help save the lives of others who would otherwise follow the same tragic route?

Whatever you feel you were responsible for, let's take your focus towards taking action to save the life of another. How about volunteering at a homeless shelter and giving the people your time and effort? Or becoming a donor, giving blood, raising money for a charity that saves lives like the air ambulance? Whatever fits for you, really, but the bottom line is the only way to get yourself out of a hole is to look up and head back in the direction you came from. These ideas represent a few ways that you might do that.

15

The Delayed Start

Grief may not obviously kick in after a bereavement and you may at some point wonder if you might have got away with it. It is common in the early stages following a death to feel confused about what you are feeling and for other factors to be at play that may mask your grief. The grieving process has many identifiable stages and only truly begins when you give it permission to.

Many clients have told me that the best way to describe grief is like a build-up of pressure, a black mist that engulfs you. We can try to convince ourselves it isn't there, but even though you can't see it, you know it exists. When you release some of the pressure by crying or talking it's a relief, but when you aren't talking the invisible black pressure holds you in its grip.

You may find that you lost a loved one some time back and have only just begun grieving, having suppressed your emotions in order to press on with life. But that's like not sorting out the garage that is packed with junk; you can pretend it doesn't exist because you aren't opening the door. For a few years you'll probably get away with it, but eventually when you are moving house you'll have to deal with the junk and it'll make you wonder why you didn't just get on with it in the first place.

People see grief as the enemy, an unwanted burden, so they try to close the door on it. Sadly, it's not until we learn to manage our relationship with it that we start to truly heal. Battling against grief's existence is a futile exercise that does little more than put much of your life on hold. Imagine grief as a person who knocks on your door. He doesn't want to knock on your door, but that's his one and only job. If you don't open the door, he will come back and knock again every day until you finally let him in and form a working relationship with him. When you begin to do that, you gradually stop begrudging his intrusions because you expect him, he is familiar to you and in some way you realise he helps you to remember some special memories of some special people. Eventually, he becomes an employee with you becoming the boss, managing his shift until you one day send him off to semi-retirement. And he doesn't always make you sad, he simply reminds you the person isn't here any more and you can be grateful for his appearance because it reminds you to remember what you had.

Stephanie, aged 40, has had a bumpy ride in life, and we have spent many hours unravelling a complicated sequence of events, of which grief was a central underlying factor. For years, Stephanie has hidden the extent of her true identity and purpose by disconnecting herself from everyone except her work colleagues and a handful of friends in her new life on the coast.

Stephanie bravely shared with my online bereavement group how she had suppressed, denied and delayed her journey through grief, and with her kind permission I am able to share this journey with you.

Hello everyone. I am about to take one of the biggest steps of my entire life by writing this.

I have been quietly and occasionally taking a very quick peek into the various discussions in this group, but usually the sheer panic and wave of horribleness that engulfs me each and every time I start to read a post is overwhelming, and, in the same way that I have tried to deal with my grief for so long, after about twenty seconds, I have simply closed the page.

You see, the thing is, grief and I do not have a very good relationship. It's kind of like one of those bad dreams we all have, you know the ones . . . when something is chasing us, and we keep running . . . and it keeps chasing, and no matter how fast or far we run – it keeps trying to catch us.

On 19 March 2004 I was out for the night having fun with my friends when all of a sudden I just felt like going home. I didn't want to go home to my own flat, instead I felt an overwhelming urge to go back to my mom and dad's. So, at about 2 a.m. a rather tipsy me arrived back at my family home.

I still had my own key and after letting myself in I was surprised to find my dad still awake in the kitchen. It's a moment in my life that I will never forget. He smiled and said, 'Hello, sweetheart, I've been waiting for you.' I asked him how did he know that I was coming? He just smiled, shrugged, and said, 'I just did.'

My dad and I had one of those special relationships. He would often say that I would pluck his thoughts out of his head and then say them out loud. I would always think of him just before he called and he could second-guess my every reaction. We were partners in crime, two of a kind.

He knew exactly what to say to make me smile; we had the same sense of humour and laughing was just a normal part of every day.

He was super protective of me and it was an ongoing agreement from way back between him and my friends that they needed to look after me when I was out of his sight with requests like: *Make sure Steph looks when she crosses the road, please; don't let Steph get too close to the sea; keep an eye on her speed, she drives too fast; can you make sure you see her into the door safe; don't let her walk home in the dark; do you have my number, call me if you need to.* Having an over-protective parent was at times frustrating, especially for a freedom lover such as myself, and I'm sure you can imagine my teenage tantrums, which, as I got older, turned into eye rolls and smiles.

I would do anything to have that back.

So, that night, after saying goodnight to Dad and telling him that yes I did know that he loved me, and that I loved him too – I went to bed. The next morning – 20 March, a date that is never far from my mind, was bright, sunny and beautiful. Dad was a car salesman and had people coming to view a car. Afterwards we planned to spend the day together, nothing special planned, just catching up.

I was relaxing in my childhood bedroom and joking with Dad, and as he went downstairs, he laughed at the joke I had just finished telling.

This was the last time we spoke.

Ten minutes later I heard a loud crash and loud, laboured breathing. The house suddenly went completely silent. I ran down the stairs and shouted to Dad and the next few hours are a vivid blur of me shouting through the toilet door to Dad, me on the phone to the emergency services, me in the front garden scream- ing, my friends rushing to help me, me calling and shouting for the ambulance to hurry up, the next-door neighbour trying to open the toilet door, me frantically calling my mom and my sisters and not being able to get through. Me smashing my phone up.

My grandparents arrived at the same time as the ambulance and the paramedics told them that I needed to be sedated. But I didn't allow anyone to touch me and got in the car with my friend as we followed the ambulance to the hospital. Arriving, I fainted, and when I woke up I was told that my beloved, precious dad had died.

And in a heartbeat, my whole world changed. Everything was still and silent. Grey. Black. Empty.

Desolate. Wretched.

My mom initially fell apart, as did my sisters. I am the eldest daughter so I felt that I needed to take care of everyone and I felt the responsibility fall on me, and as everyone was caught up in their own grief, I was left to just cope. No one knew what it was like to have been in the house on my own with my dad trapped inside the toilet, and no one mentioned it. I wished that they had. I wish that someone, anyone, had asked me how I felt.

As the world moved on around me and people cried and gathered together, my world, well, it was silent. As I tried to look after everyone and be brave my insides were in turmoil. If my eyes dared to even think about crying I would quickly swipe the tears away with the back of my hand and press on. But. A slow burning fierce anger was building, like a small puff of smoke growing into a massive fire.

I just wanted to escape into starvation but instead, after being a vegetarian for seventeen years, I thought sod it and ate meat – out of anger. I had terrible road rage and I walked out of my job. I just couldn't wait to wake up and be happy one day, that this was all just a bad dream.

It was only six months ago that I accepted that moment is actually never going to happen.

The funeral was three weeks after my dad's death. Over 200 people came to say goodbye to my wonderful, beautiful father. In a true reflection of him, there was a lot of laughter as one by one his friends told funny stories about him. I had written something, which my uncle read out on my behalf. I can remember everyone laughing as I recalled him calling me a flaming idiot as yet again I ran out of petrol at the top of a hill.

And then after the funeral life is supposed to go on. Just like that. You are expected to just carry on as though nothing has happened. Looking back – this was when I desperately needed help, and maybe if I had been offered or sought help then maybe I would have dealt with things more easily.

After six months or so of going around in an angry/shocked/emotional/empty shell I decided that I could no longer live in the same town and moved 100 miles away to London. I managed to get a position in a very sales-focused company in Central London and buried myself entirely in my job.

Over the next few years I became very successful in my career as I worked incredibly hard – and partied even harder. Long working days would be followed by even longer nights and I became a social butterfly. None of my new friends had any instructions to look after me or keep me safe. I became the life and soul of the party, I was always the one who stayed out the longest, and always the one who looked after and cared for everyone else . . . other than myself.

I would flit between starving myself and over-eating as a comfort. I would promise myself that I was going to have a healthy fresh start. A calmer lifestyle, and enjoy the things I used to enjoy before Dad died, but I just couldn't seem to get my head around any of it. I became more and more deeply buried in work, and any family commitments took second place.

I was becoming more and more tired and I had put on a lot of weight. I put every effort into being constantly busy or preoccupied and if I wasn't, then I would read or stare vacantly at junk television. Everyone was important to me except for myself.

Years passed and Dad became one of those unspoken subjects. Family members and friends would tiptoe around the subject as I would shut the conversation down – I just couldn't talk about him.

I have always loved to drive. Dad taught me and it was another one of our things, and I had – and still have – a car who I have named Bean, which he bought for me. It's a little red Vauxhall Corsa that he found in an auction and it was my pride and joy. As Bean has gotten older I haven't been able to let him go. So now instead of having a car as I always have had, I now have an unused car that sits in a car park, never moving but never being replaced.

In time, I developed my own specific version of OCD. If I drank tea made with water from anyone else's kettle, it would mean bad luck; if I didn't kiss a photo of firstly my nephew and then my grandparents on my screensaver before bed, a family member would die; if I didn't count things five times it would be the same result. If there was a black bit on my food and I accidentally ate it, the world would fall apart and it would be my fault. I was consumed with guilt over everything and anything and regardless of the situation, I would blame myself.

I love people to the extreme; I care about everyone and don't want anyone to ever feel pain, so much so that I have accepted people treating me very badly. As long as they were OK, so was I. I have allowed behaviour towards me that I never would have in the past. It was OK to treat me badly – because I didn't matter.

And all the while I was wearing my smile, still the joker of the pack, the one who made everyone laugh. I was becoming more and more successful at work, and despite my terrible inner pain, I was travelling the world and having fun. No one knew what was going on inside.

And then . . . exactly this time two years ago I did something that changed my life forever – I reached out for help. I knew that

I wanted to try to do something about my situation, but I also knew that I was terrified – terrified of letting my very controlled and protected little bubble that I had made for myself burst.

It had taken me a while, because the side effect of being so successful at blocking my grief was that I had created various other issues, but I got myself there eventually.

In June 2016, I sat in a coffee shop and, with Jeff's help, I voluntarily admitted to myself what everyone else already knew: my dad is never going to come back. No matter how much I smile, no matter how hard I work, no matter how guilty I feel, no matter how much I avoid it, my dad is dead and is never coming back. No matter how angry I am that the ambulance took forever to arrive, or that I couldn't get him out of the toilet in time, my dad has gone.

It was without doubt a very difficult day and I am not sure how to explain it exactly – but the next day I kind of felt a little bit more alive. A little bit lighter and a little bit more . . . here.

I had passed from denial into the early state of acceptance – which I guess is a bit of a weird place to be considering I have been unable to accept my dad's death for twelve years. I can be having the best of days when suddenly a wave of sadness will come from behind and crash over me. It appears to have no warning, or sense of timing, it just comes.

On Dad's birthday in December, I sent a message to this group for the first time and then afterwards I sat in a room with my friend, and I cried and I cried. He sat with me until 5.30 a.m. and just let me cry, and let me laugh, then let me cry again. I felt as though every bone in my body was wailing, that my heart was crumbling into a thousand pieces that I would never be able to put back together ever again. I wanted to scream out in agony and at times I thought that I might stop breathing. I thought that perhaps I would never stop, that I would spend the rest of my life in tears.

That the awful pain would never subside. But it did.

Now, each time I cry, although it's bad at the time, I always feel so much better the next day. I feel so much more like the real me. I feel better. I feel less anxious, and I feel much stronger after crying – every single time.

It sounds very odd but I have a found a strong connection with the colour orange. It started with me feeling happy when I poured orange pop into my glass and it's grown from there. Bonkers, I know . . . but it helps me.

Now, when I see orange, or I think about orange – I feel a connection to my dad. I walk to a special part of the beach where I often watch the sun set, and I feel that I am with my dad.

On some days I will buy easy peeler oranges and place them all around my desk at work; I buy tomato soup, which feels as if I am eating a huge orange cuddle. I smile so much more than I ever did – but now they are real smiles. I have lost three stone without dieting, and although I have some major things that I need to sort out in my personal life – I am getting there, slowly but surely.

I now feel that my happiness does matter, I am important and my dad would be heartbroken himself if I didn't look after myself.

I have also changed my name by deed poll to Stephanie Orange-Hicks. Only a few people know this at the moment, but one day soon I will tell the world.

The strangest thing is that, by accepting that Dad has died, I have him back in my life. I have started to enjoy memories of him. I can listen to his favourite songs without going into a blind panic; I can look at photographs and smile and I am starting to plan for my future.

I have a long way to go yet, but I am finally starting to move forwards. After ignoring my grief for so long it is amazing how much better I feel after finally talking about it. Accepting that Dad has gone doesn't mean that I have forgotten him; it means that I can now actually remember him. There are days when sadness will hit me square in the face and my heart hurts so much that it could bring me to my knees, but there are also the days when the funniest memories will pop into my mind and a bubble of laughter will burst out of me. I have rejoined Facebook and reconnected with some of my oldest and dearest friends. My sisters created a photo film of me and Dad for my birthday and posted it on social media. Instead of running away, I now wanted the world to see it. I was proud, proud of Dad, and proud of me. I have joined a steel-pan band, which I love! I have made friendships and I have helped others who are struggling. Telling people that I needed help has opened up my world. Talking to someone, reaching out and asking for help is brave, and it's terrifying. It is also the most important thing I could have done. Now each time I remember Dad my world becomes slightly brighter. Almost as though I've got my fingers on a dimmer switch and I am slowly making the light brighter.

There will always be a Dad-shaped hole in my life but I am starting to look forwards with excitement, rather than with guilt. I am grateful for being brave enough to face this, I am grateful for having my dad, but also, I am grateful to be alive.

Stephanie demonstrates the before and after of years of suppressing to finally expressing her grief perfectly. What made the difference? Taking that bold step to talk. In Stephanie's case she came to me and after we spent many occasions talking about things other than grief, it become apparent that all roads led to her father, and I remember vividly the session that Stephanie finally stopped running from the undesirable truth about her dad. It isn't as simple as that makes it sound – there will have been times after this realisation that Steph would try to revert back to the shadows of avoidance – but for entrusting someone else to 'see her' even if she didn't like to see herself meant that she was able to stay present, to slowly increase her capacity to live with the truth and to begin to see that sticking with reality not only made many improvements to the way she felt emotionally about her loss but added focus and strength to all areas of her existence.

Not everyone will be in a position to pay for counselling and other talking therapists, so here are my strategies for overcoming a delayed start to the grieving process.

1. **Expose your feelings to someone.** Don't keep your grief a secret. Start by telling one person how you feel and then try telling another. You don't actually need to say anything, you can just cry. It's highly likely they, and quite a few others around you, will have been waiting for you to get to this point for a very long time. We only see what we want to see. We can deceive ourselves no end, but others, the people who know us well, are much harder to fool.

2. **Let support into your life**. Friends play many roles – they are there when we want to go out and have fun, they celebrate our successes and share many memories with us, but the most important part of that job is when things get tough. What is the point of having friends and relatives who care deeply about us if we don't give them the chance to be there for us when we really need them? Is it realistic to imagine we will go through our lives without once needing and enlisting the support of others? It's OK to be vulnerable at times; I've learnt this many times myself. When you do reach out, that's when things can start to fall into place.

3. **Find a mentor.** Someone who has been through the pain of loss but seems to be doing OK. Ask lots of questions that relate to what you find difficult about grief. What can you learn from them that you can apply to your life? There is no right or wrong way to grieve, and you may find some of the answers you receive unsuitable or unattractive, but you need to see that grief is far less scary than the effects of suppressing it.

4. **Start by writing it down.** Keep a private journal of your fears and insecurities surrounding your loss and the journey you have to navigate afterwards. The worst you can do is deny there is a problem, but then if that's how you felt you wouldn't be reading this book. Writing your feelings down is a tentative first step towards an adjustment to the reality of grief and away from the danger of avoidance. You can use different headings, like 'Times I thought about the loss but bottled it up' or 'Times I went to say their name and kept it inside'. It would be fascinating for you to look back and reflect on how many times a day you were doing these things and it's this kind of knowledge gained through self-analytical data that gives you a different perspective on what's actually working for you and what isn't.

5. **Carry on.** Just keep your loss to yourself, shy away from conversations that you know will be difficult, avoid people and places that you know take you back to that person, go missing on certain days of the year and wish that certain months of the calendar no longer existed. Force people around you to believe that your stress is because of 'other things' and that the physical symptoms you experience are down to 'something else'. Lie to yourself in order to preserve the brick wall you've built around your emotions, lie to others in order to make the falseness of your 'I'm OK' seem more

plausible. Well, it's not a very good option, but it doesn't stop some from choosing it.

Summary

Steph's honesty and courage will undoubtedly see her through the rest of her journey with grief. She is communicating, exerting control in areas she had relinquished all of her power over previously, and making decisions that will set her free instead of holding her back. It's incredibly satisfying to see the reinvention of one of the best people I've had the pleasure of meeting, let alone assisting on their way professionally. Steph has continuously astonished me with her solid progress and serves as a continuous reminder that anyone can recover from a long period of grief denial.

16

Dictating Yourself to Grief

To dictate yourself to grief is to walk towards it. What a crazy concept! How, when you are in the throes of bereavement, is it even remotely possible for you to have any control over the effects of your loss? Why would you go anywhere near the experience that you didn't ask for, didn't want and will always begrudge? Sadly, it isn't until you enter into a relationship with grief that you actually learn to live with it.

There are many stages to grief management and in time and with practice you'll see too how the waves of grief can be brought under control in order to reach this stage. However, you must first summon the courage to take a step into the unknown and trust that you can overcome the pain and fear, replacing it with an open acceptance to what each day may bring.

My way of helping my children dictate themselves to their grief is to have a Mother's Day every month on the 15th. There's no actual significance to this date. I just picked a day and it's stuck now, and in this way we choose to make our own special occasions to celebrate Jade's life, inviting grief to join us as we go. If something else is going on on the 15th we are versatile enough with it to grant ourselves the flexibility to bring it forwards or put it back.

It usually entails any activity they enjoy – bowling, go karting, trampolining. They never resist any of these fun activities and it's particularly healthy to attach the memory of Mum to things that they really enjoy, in contrast to the traditional habit of only remembering or feeling for the loss when you visit the grave or crematorium. Because I'm constantly maintaining a balance between homework, clubs and my work it has never been difficult to keep this tradition up. It's simple – we go out and have fun, are especially mindful to talk about Mum, and the boys feel good for sharing and remembering. They get to decide what we do too, taking it in turns to choose, and we usually say you can't pick the same activity twice in a row or we would just end up on a trampoline every time, and although Jade did like trampolining it's good for all of us to get some variety! I like our monthly efforts because it's front foot instead of back, it's progressive instead of destructive and feels empowering and loving.

You dictate yourself to grief daily by remembering on purpose instead of remembering because something made you. These might feel similar but they come from completely different places and have completely separate effects; one is *towards* the positive, the other is *away* from the negative. Imagine being on the beach, standing with your back to the waves. You try to walk inland away from the water but the waves grow bigger and eventually soak you. You feel shocked and upset because you didn't see it coming and you didn't want to get wet.

Say you then allow yourself to stand facing the waves. They may well still soak you but the difference is you had the benefit of seeing them come and you were better prepared by being in your swimwear, so the damage was minimal. One day, you feel like you can go right up to the shoreline and walk a little way into the sea and you find that the water isn't so cold, it isn't so uninviting as you thought. The next time you take your surf board and you greet the waves and while you still get wet and splashed, you come out when it gets too much.

Turning to face the water, choosing when to step into the water, the pain turns into acceptance and through acceptance you start to enjoy the act of remembering and there's no shock left. You have begun to manage your grief.

> Did that make your personal experience of grief visual for you? Maybe you used your own metaphor? Do you feel like you have started to face the waves? Are you dictating yourself to grief by looking at memories, visiting places, and so on?

One particular client's wonderfully visual representation of his own transition from feeling very much like a victim of grief to actually learning to work with grief and the realisation that he could even learn to control it struck me so powerfully that I would like to share it with you.

Kevin came to see me after he had lost his mother to a stroke at the age of 73. He described how since her death he felt as if he had been wearing a lead overcoat that he couldn't take off. To Kevin, grief was the unwanted visitor that came knocking at the door at the most inconvenient of times and he described how these unwelcome guests would visit unannounced, and how they would stay for different periods of time, completely against his will. We explored what might happen if he *invited* them over on a regular basis and after some thought, he replied that it would probably mean they would come less and maybe stay for a shorter time.

This was, for Kevin, the moment when he entered into a 'relationship' with grief, instead of hating it and trying to run from it. He went away and asked grief to visit and he began to actively think about his mother by looking at photos, listening to certain songs and talking about his memories of her voluntarily, not just when they popped into his mind. And little by little, when the unwanted guests visited, he found he was ready for them and more easily able to accept their presence. In fact, when they came it wasn't so awkward and now, they didn't stay so long.

When we spoke again a few months later, Kevin told me that he was now inviting these guests round, sometimes at work and sometimes at home. They now mostly popped in and he found the more he invited them, the more fleeting their visit would be. He no longer begrudged or feared their arrival and now that he was in control of the relationship, sometimes he actually began to like their company. He found too that if they had popped into the office for a quick chat it was unlikely they would come back to the house later on.

When we enter into a relationship with grief, we can start to see the benefits of confronting something we initially run from. Dictating yourself to grief is to proactively encourage its presence, knowing that a 'go to' attitude rather than an 'away from' mindset makes a huge difference.

So you can control grief?

Dictating yourself to the emotions generated by your loss is to have as much control as possible over the guaranteed irregularity of the visits of your impending grief. It's all about pre-empting those visits so they are seen as invited and not unexpected.

Taking yourself to the pain reduces the hurt. Would you rather stand facing a punch in the face that you know is heading your way so you can move away from it, or continue to stand with your back to it so you are powerless to stop your body being knocked to the floor?

If I force myself to think about my loss, does that
mean it won't be able to take me by surprise?

There will always be triggers you can't control. You might be in the
supermarket and your father's favourite song might come on; you
could be putting your bags in the car as an old friend walks past and
asks you how you're feeling since your loss. You could get home
from work and the kids' behaviour might try your patience so much
that you break down because it would all be so much easier if your
partner was still here.

Understanding that there will be triggers that you don't expect
and accepting that it would be impossible to control every environment and situation you walk into and that an effort to do so would
result in an unnatural need to control people, events, outcomes and
conversations, is one way of helping you in your management of
grief.

It all boils down to control. You have a couple of options here.
You can either control the times you invite grief to your doorstep
or you can do what many people do who spend the rest of their
life controlling their family and many other factors of their existence in order to avoid grief and any memories relating to their
loss. They are trying to conceal or outrun the natural process of
grief. Believe it or not, the first takes a year or two to master; the
other creates a lifetime of unrealistic requests and pressures on
yourself, and others, to conform to what you need and want them
to be.

Kevin and I spoke for an update a year after what he described as
his 'light bulb moment'. He told me that grief no longer consumes
him and the main realisation for him was that it was OK for him to
feel like this. His visualisation granted him some acceptance. Grief
was no longer a big, scary, invisible thing, and he felt it was now

'conquerable'. Kevin made the agreement with himself that he could live with grief. He mentioned 'embracing' grief more than a few times, a verb that you wouldn't usually hear in the same sentence as grief, but now he saw his grief through a different prism, Kevin was able to accept and control the pain.

Kevin now referred to grief as an individual. 'Grief is an irritating person,' he told me, 'someone I've got history with, someone who is an irrefutable part of my life, not by choice, but someone who is a part of me regardless. As soon as I stopped fighting him, it got easier, and the more I engaged with him, the less I noticed that he was there.'

To put a face or a personality, or to even name grief, is to personalise and reduce its size and most importantly take away some of the mystery that often makes us feel like it's a giant compared to little old us. If you see it as a huge, unquantifiable entity it will no doubt intimidate you, scaring you into submission or denial. If you visualise it as an unwanted guest – say, your in-laws or a debt collector! – who you can invite in and ask to leave, you realise that you are fighting a very different battle.

The only thing that's worse than experiencing grief is the fear of what grief is going to do to you. Those who allow grief to do what it will, knowing that it's a natural process we all need to face, seem to come out the other side able to take the same direction that they were originally taking; those who hide from grief, denying its existence and consuming themselves with the fear of the unknown, very often take a different path, something more like a ring road, much steeper and far more uneven underfoot.

I read somewhere that grief is just love. It's all the love you want to give but cannot. All of that unspent love gathers in the corners of your eyes, the lump in your throat and in the hollow part of your chest. Grief is just love with no place to go. Not so scary – emotional, but certainly not an unscalable mountain. Don't be defeated before you've even taken a step. The unknown is never what we assume it's going to be.

Dictating yourself in numbers

Let's imagine those moments when grief consumes you are 100%. Of those occasions when grief tapped you on the shoulder X% are triggers you don't control.
Whereas X% of those occasions are times you invited grief yourself. Have a think about your percentages.

Kevin learned that the more he 'embraced' grief and invited it to join him, the more that percentage went up, and so the figure related to the unexpected occasions fell lower.

What would you rather the majority percentage be for you?

If you want to start taking control you can try the following:

1. Have an evening or afternoon of going through photos or watching any home movies you may have. If you can, do this with someone else so that you can share your thoughts and feelings and make sure there isn't anything going on for a few hours afterwards so you don't feel the need to hold anything back or rush.

2. Keep a photo of your loved one next to you at work. Having a constant visual reminder wards off the inherent desire to forget or

ignore, because we can often try to save ourselves from having to feel at inconvenient times.

3. Give yourself a moment to listen to music that reminds you of your loved one. What does the music do for you? Does it remind you of your loss or does it remind you of certain memories? Either way it's a good thing. You might also read a book you both loved or go for a walk you both enjoyed.

4. Arrange a drink with someone who is feeling the loss of someone else so you can have a conversation about your feelings with a person who understands without judgment. It's like finding a grief buddy, someone you have a mutually beneficial relationship with, because not only does it allow you to talk but as the meetings add up you can objectively chart your progress through grief.

5. Plan for the special occasions, don't let them just happen. The unwanted visitors will definitely be visiting you. Do you want them to stay all day or would you like them to come to the balloon release with you and just stay for a short time afterwards?

In order to help you really grasp the practical approach to managing your grief instead of it managing you, here's a step-by-step example for you to try when you feel ready to move forwards.

1. Decide exactly what time and where you're going to experiment with your grief, for example, 10 a.m. at home, when the kids have gone to school.

2. Decide how you're going to take yourself to thinking about your loss and how it makes you feel, for example, I'm going to look at videos and photos.

3. Decide how long you're going to share your memories before you need to get on with your day. For example, I'm going to give myself two hours to talk, cry, hug and be still with my feelings before I think about doing anything else.

4. Reflect afterwards on how it felt to encourage the very feelings that you usually try to run from.

How long was it then before you next got caught by a wave unexpectedly?

If you repeat the process the next day while reducing the amount of time you allocate for active grieving, does it get easier? When it becomes a routine and you have found many different ways to take yourself to an emotional state, do you ever find that the waves find you unexpectedly any more?

Other ways we can dictate to grief

Another way of 'going to' your grief is by keeping a journal. Communicating grief is not limited to talking; you can also write about it. I've even heard of people writing blog-length statuses on their Facebook as a way of letting everyone know where they are with their grief. While being highly effective for some this could be far too public a share for others.

Keeping a journal is more private and will help you track the patterns in your grief, giving priceless detail that will enable you to identify what works for you and what doesn't, as well as the questions that you can't answer one day, but will find the solution to the next. Reflection is important and it requires you to give yourself the time and space to check in with yourself, and recording these reflections is also a therapeutic way of self-healing and will help us to avoid any suppression.

To dictate yourself to grief is to take control of your life in the event of someone you love losing theirs. It's brave and challenging to face the emotions you're experiencing, but face them you must, letting the effects of grief wash over you with a degree of stillness and understanding that it's OK not to feel good, it's OK not to be having good thoughts and it's OK to need support. Please also know that it's OK if you're not ready to dictate yet; you'll get to that when you're ready. Some people never do, but I hope that reading this book will give you the tools to dictate when and as you're ready to use them.

17

Multiple Loss

Losing a loved one is difficult enough, but what happens when loss becomes a repeated experience? Losing more than one person close to you in a relatively short period of time can result in a complete disconnection from the ability to grieve constructively and cause a whole raft of difficulties to occur. But do the rules and complexities of grief change when you lose more than one person?

Loss usually involves either someone we love dying, or someone we love losing someone they love. If we lose someone we love, then we need to address the void it leaves within us, but if someone we love loses someone, then we need to embrace the void this leaves in them. In terms of how we cope and respond, we must be careful in the case of multiple losses not to rate all losses as being of the same value or we really will feel more helpless than we need.

Emma, a working mother of four, came to see me following her father's death from a complicated lung disease. Two and a half years later she was back, upset and worried by her inability to care about others she loved who had lost those close to them, namely her husband's grandmother Beryl, who had died from old age at 92, and her brother's son Michael, who had died from Hodgkin's Lymphoma, aged only 26. Effectively, she had shut these deaths off and wasn't dealing with them – or more importantly, her husband and brother's suffering – at all well.

Emma told me that she was overcome by guilt because all she could think about was her dad. She cried as she told me how selfish she felt and then the worst feeling of all, that somehow Beryl and Michael's deaths had stolen her dad's thunder and she resented them for dying because she didn't want anyone to forget about him. She said she'd just started to really get somewhere with the loss of her father and when Beryl and Michael died, it made her feel like she 'just couldn't deal with it', which in turn made her question if she'd ever actually managed the loss of her father particularly well in the first place.

One thing was certain – as she tore herself up over her inability to comfort her husband or brother or to deal with one of her children who was acting up badly – Emma was pushing her family away in order to protect and justify her decision to shut off from recognising the deaths of Beryl and Michael. 'If I let their deaths in,' she sobbed, 'that would be it.' I asked her what she meant by 'it', to which she replied, 'Falling apart and not coping, feeling sorry for myself, not wanting to be around anybody that I love or care about, like I basically just want to disappear from my life.'

Words of desperation. But to me, clear words of someone who is grieving, having lost one person and then two more. 'Falling apart' was telling – Emma was expressing her fear that she wouldn't be able to put herself back together again if she allowed herself to grieve for her family's losses. I wanted her to hear again, as we had gone through when her father died, that grieving is not the same as 'falling apart', that it is a temporary and momentary sensation and that while the feelings can be overwhelming and last for anything from minutes to days, it is rarely a constant feeling. I wanted her to see that it was OK to grieve for her recent losses and that this wouldn't get in the way of her dad's loss and that in grieving, she was unlikely to 'fall apart' – she hadn't when her father had died, hard as that was – and that what she was experiencing in her fears about letting in the grief for Beryl and Michael was perfectly OK.

Emma was awash with remorse for not recognising the most recent losses to her immediate and extended family. She knew that her relatives were mourning without her by their side, that the kids were waiting for her to come back and emotionally take charge, her husband was waiting patiently for her to help him mourn, everyone waiting for her to remember what had helped her manage the loss of her father so well.

In our first session I asked her to place her hand on the table and told her that it represented her father. I then, with her permission, placed my hands on top, the left representing Beryl and the right representing Michael. I did this to allow Emma to explore the layers of loss that she was subject to and to see how she felt about her father being at the bottom of that pile. I then asked her to take her hand – her dad – away from the table, leaving only Beryl and Michael, and she told me she felt an immediate sense of relief, like a weight had been lifted from her shoulders. I gave Emma permission to shut off from the loss of her father temporarily and at this point, and for the first time, she began to experience the effects of her most recent losses.

I separated my hands and asked her: 'If you think of your dad's loss as a hundred per cent, what would the values be for Beryl and Michael?' Emma was clear in her mind that Beryl's death was more her husband's loss than her own and gave it a value of 25%. While she was upset by it, this was not about her necessarily grieving for Beryl, but more about being able to give her husband support and recognition that he might be grieving for his much-loved and missed grandmother. This, she felt, was something she would be able to do.

As you would expect, it was the death of her nephew, at the heart-breakingly young age of 26, that was causing her the most distress, and we spent some time investigating the feelings that she had been denying for the six weeks since his passing. She put the value of his death at 75%. What was eating her up over and above his death was the fact that she hadn't spoken to her brother about Michael since he'd died.

Things were frosty and resentments were being harboured, and while there hadn't been an explicit falling-out between them, Emma was angry that since her father's death she had been left with the responsibility of looking after their mother.

I passed Emma my mobile and asked her to pretend to be on the phone to her brother. Before she began speaking to him, I could almost see realisation flooding in. 'I feel so selfish,' she said. 'He and my sister-in-law came round shortly after Michael died and told us they were OK, that as Michael had been ill since he was born they hadn't thought they'd have him for a year, let alone twenty-six, so I could see they had the mindset to cope and I shut it out.' Yet Emma knew that this shouldn't be assumed; she would rather have offered her support and love to a greater extent than she had.

This was a big thing for Emma to own up to and expose about herself and once it was out in the open it gave me an opportunity to help her summarise her actions and understanding of where she had removed to since the loss of her three loved ones. Closing her eyes, putting her head down and supposedly sheltering herself from the reality of these losses only served to stop her from seeing the facts and reality of the situation, feeling the way she should naturally feel and recognising the feelings of others who she should be playing a part in supporting.

I gently suggested to Emma that when she was able to lift her head and align herself in grief, accepting that Beryl and Michael's deaths, after the death of her dad, wasn't the reality she wanted but was the one that existed, only then could she start to make herself and others around her feel better.

Emma described her situation and the three people who'd died as a 'complicated mess'. I wanted to show her this wasn't necessarily the case. On the table next to us was a bowl of fruit, so I took an apple, a satsuma and a banana, put them together and then separated them out so we could focus on them as the individuals they were in life.

The satsuma represented Emma's dad. It had been two years and nine months since he had died. Emma went over the three techniques that had really worked for her in making such a good go of coping with the loss of her father. As she turned the satsuma around in her hands, she spoke of how she:

1. Talked about her dad, not shutting him out or putting him away.
2. Remembered constructively, sharing positive memories of her dad.
3. Shared any negative feelings she was having about her dad's death.

In mourning for her dad, Emma had allowed herself to recognise and experience everything that was terrible about the reality of loss but now, in the face of these new losses, she had shut away all the good work she'd done in coping so well. In order to help her to take back responsibility, reduce her guilt and allow her to let in the loss of Beryl and Michael without denying the grief she was still feeling for her dad, I asked her what she needed to bring her dad's memory alive again.

Emma brightened as she remembered some of the techniques that had made her life a little easier when we'd worked together after her dad had died. She said she was going to talk about him, remember him positively in her own mind and share any negative feelings she was having with her family, all three times daily.

I picked up the banana and asked her how she was going to help her husband with the loss of his grandmother. She said: 'First I'm going to apologise for not supporting him in the same way that he has supported me, then I am going to mention Beryl, remember her positively and allow Brian to share his negative feelings with me, three times every day.'

She looked at the apple. 'And,' she went on, 'I'm going to call my brother this afternoon and apologise, giving him an honest explanation for my lack of contact. I'm going to ask him how he is feeling and we can have a good cry.'

I could see how relieved Emma felt. She sounded like a woman with a purpose and I was confident that she was ready to start communicating with her husband, her children, her brother and ultimately herself.

What Emma's story shows us

1. Multiple loss will feel like a congealed mess, and it will be hard to separate each person's death as the individuals they are and will always be. When it comes to your efforts to remember them, you have to focus on them individually. Every loss, in a beautiful nutshell, has to be about seeing and remembering each individual as they were when they were here. Give yourself a visual aid – pictures of each one of them, placed in close proximity to each other – that will trigger thoughts of them individually.

2. Decide on what your recipe is for good grief management. After she lost her father, Emma's was good communication, talking about her losses and expressing negative feelings so everyone around her knew how she was feeling and could support her, as well as purposefully creating the opportunities to enjoy positive memories.

3. Think of a set of scales and how the unannounced negative feelings that grief can bring will weigh down one side of the scale. If you also remember positively, talking about your loss and sharing the negatives, the scales will tip back to the point of balance.

Emma found it easier to manage her grief by putting a number – three each day, in her case – on the amount of time or thoughts she had about the person she was mourning. In mourning Beryl or Michael, she might not have put the same number or weight to her thoughts about them. In dealing with multiple losses the amount of time you spend thinking about each person doesn't need to be the same, as the losses may affect you in different ways.

4. Face your guilt, if you feel it. There are so many reasons why an individual may experience this. It might mean there's something you haven't done or have avoided. Emma had to confront her guilt about not being there for her husband or brother and felt instantly better when she faced it and resolved to do something about it.

5. Don't push people away. Emma put barriers up so she could shut out Beryl and Michael's deaths and that was damaging for her as much as for her husband, children and brother. Emma took down her barriers when she saw how pointless they were.

6. Watch your language. Don't tell yourself you are going to 'fall apart' or that you won't be able to cope. These repetitive yet subconsciously spoken lies we tell ourselves may seem forgivable after what we are going through, but if you make the mountain in front of you higher than it really is, you won't attempt to climb it. Be as specific as you can.

7. Don't suppress your feelings. If you are hiding how you feel, telling everyone you are 'fine' when you aren't, then you aren't

confronting the reality of your situation. Adjustment is the bus that brings you into the town of reality and it's not until you arrive in that town that you can go to work on your grief.

Experiencing multiple loss is debilitating and confusing and makes it incredibly hard to grieve when you don't know which of your losses the pain relates to on any given occasion. The key to surviving the additional layers is to consciously separate them, remembering them as the individuals that they were and not grouping them together as one.

Dealing with one death is quite enough, yet dealing with three is something else. If grief were a path ahead of us, multiple loss produces multiple paths – routes that vary depending upon the relationship we had with that individual, with some possibly being longer than the others.

We are forgiven for imagining that we are progressing down each path equally, but if you focus on one person far more than the others, then you may find yourself feeling like you're literally in three different places at once.

You'll never feel the same about each loss, but if you attempt to keep a manageable balance between the regularity and type of thoughts you have for each, the efforts you make to remember positively, and the time spent simply talking about those individuals, you will be at a similar stage on all of your paths.

18

Becoming an Adult Orphan

Losing both our parents is a significant psychological step in bereavement, and regardless of our age is always incredibly hard for us to accept. We spend most of our life with older people a generation above us, relatives who have the answers, have 'been there and done it' and we can rely on their experience and guidance. But when we become the oldest with barely anyone left above us, grief takes on a whole new form.

While we mourn the loss of someone who meant a lot to us, the death of our parents or older relatives shifts the focus to our own mortality like never before. 'How long do I have left?' we might ask ourselves. 'There's so much I haven't done in life' – questions you may never have asked while your parents were alive because you still felt like someone's child. Arguably, when our parents die, so does a part – if not all – of our own inner child, and with it comes an awareness of time that we had never experienced before.

In order to make sense of the layers of hurt you need to be able to differentiate the contributing factors to what you're going through. If you allow yourself to focus solely on your loss first then you can start to feel your way through the changes that being without both parents will bring to your life over the coming months.

Sometimes, however, what we perceive to be bereavement can actually be a mixture of grief and other issues that existed before our loss. Losing both parents can take you on a very interesting emotional journey and have a significant impact on your ability to cope and your behaviours long after the event. I am going to share with you just such a situation that arose for Michelle.

The facts and surface level complaints

I met with Michelle, a 44-year-old mother of two, who lives with her daughter, aged 14. Michelle lost her father in 2010 after a very short three-week battle with lung cancer, having already lost her mother to heart disease, twenty years earlier. The death of her mother came the day after her grandmother's funeral, when Michelle was just 17, and three months pregnant with her son.

I asked Michelle what the biggest struggle was in losing both her parents before 40. She spoke of the loneliness – how she can't pick up the phone to tell them her good news and how she felt isolated, wherever she was, even in a room full of people. Poignantly, Michelle was waiting for a phone call from a prospective employer while I was sitting in her living room, and at the end of our chat, the phone rang and she heard that she had got the job. She was saddened again by the realisation that as soon as she put the phone down she wanted to call her dad to tell him the good news. I congratulated her, but could see how much she was missing him in that moment.

On losing both her parents she had been left with a stepfamily, relatives who her father had acquired by marrying into another family, and even though she got on very well with her two stepsisters, she always felt on the outside.

Michelle spoke about how memories could sometimes be vague and with both parents gone, there was a big chunk of her childhood that could no longer be accessed as a result. Crucially, she felt particularly saddened by the fact that her son and daughter hadn't spent much time with her parents, as they'd died when they were both young.

'Adult Orphan' – is this an unhelpful stigma?

Michelle hadn't necessarily thought of herself as an adult orphan but on reflection, considering both losses, she felt that was pretty much the way it was. 'People have a lot of sympathy for a child who becomes an orphan,' she said, 'but as an adult there is an expectation that you should be able to deal with it. It's just lonely, very lonely at times.'

I wondered if there was an age when it is no longer appropriate to consider yourself an adult orphan, and Michelle felt that if she'd been in her fifties or sixties it probably would have been less relevant because she'd have been closer to the stages of life that she'd have expected to be losing parents in their old age.

Not all accept the label 'adult orphan'. Fiona, another bereaved client who was even younger, still in her early thirties when she lost both parents, had refused to accept it on the grounds that it might be worn as a badge, a reason to expect less of her life and to justify any limiting beliefs experienced as a result of her losses.

Not wearing a badge is a healthy sign for me. Labels are society's way of grouping us all together, giving us boundaries or categories to exist within. Usually this is what helps other people but not necessarily the one wearing the label. What if that label is wrong?

Dipping below the surface

Michelle was resentful of her parents for dying due to their ill health, most likely caused by their social habits and poor diets. She couldn't help feeling that they could have been there with her still if they had looked after themselves a little better. She understood that they both lived at a time when people were not quite so conscious of the effects, but the fact remained that her mum had said she had given up smoking, but hadn't.

Michelle's father had refused her access to his bedside as his condition deteriorated because he didn't want her to see him in such ill health. Such harsh action can be very damaging for a child, whatever their age, but she can see how for him, he would have preferred her to remember him the way he was beforehand. Michelle knew his decision was made to protect her but wishes she could have seen him as she would have liked to have been in his company for as long as possible and been allowed to say a proper goodbye.

I was interested if her losses felt different in any way and she told me that though her mother was younger, because she had lived with a bad heart, Michelle had been more prepared for her death. She'd also been pregnant at the time, which was a huge distraction for her, although looking back she realised the post-natal depression she suffered had lots to do with the fact that she hadn't grieved at all. The process was completely different for her dad in that she had more time, more memories and they were both adult, which makes her feel guilty.

I asked Michelle to compare herself as a person at the times of the first loss with herself at the time of the second. 'I was messed up when I lost Mum,' she said. 'I was a teenager, my parents had split up, I probably drank too much and I'd fallen pregnant, which was planned.' This was Michelle's chance to be the parent she hadn't experienced. 'I had very much been parenting my parents before that, being the parent to my mother. I think my mum was more dependent on me leading up to when she died, but with Dad, the relationship was a lot healthier. I'd had the opportunity for him to change as a person, and for me to change as a person, to grow older and more mature, so it was a much better relationship.'

Michelle's mum's dependency affected her grieving in that she didn't just lose her mum but she also lost a sense of purpose. She was her carer, and she was very much looking forward to sharing her pregnancy with her. She recalled how she could already see a positive change in her mother, but it was too late. The timing of the loss just heightened the anger; Michelle described how she was given a glimmer and then it was taken away.

Michelle had experienced her dad as a grandfather, but her mum died before she had the opportunity to be a grandma. She didn't get that chance to explore her life choices and potentially to change them, which added to Michelle's sense of injustice.

Michelle's recollections of motherhood after her loss were that it was beautiful but lonely; she had nobody to confide in or to share the firsts with. Every moment she enjoyed also gave her a tinge of sadness that her mum was not there to share it with her and that constant sense that her mum might have become the mother Michelle had longed for all of her young life.

She explained how her dad became more reliable. He kept promises and was a great grandparent; he became settled. Her mum dying was actually a catalyst to him wanting to settle down, because he wanted a mother for Michelle. He recognised he hadn't been much of a father up until that point, so in the absence of his wife, something told him he needed to take action and he found another partner. While it wasn't very romantic for the new lady in his life, he explained that his main concern was that he wanted a mother for his children.

When Michelle's dad remarried it made their relationship stronger, in that he was more dependable. He had a sense of purpose and responsibility to act his age, which hadn't been the case before.

I wondered where her brother featured in these events. Michelle didn't have the best of relationships with him, in spite of their shared loss. Whenever they met up, the memories that they shared were predominantly of the negative variety, and when this combined with other issues, they both agreed that their relationship wasn't a help to either of them.

Reality, or what could have been

I wanted to push Michelle a bit and asked her a tricky question: did she miss her parents as individuals or was it more about what she should have had? Michelle had talked far more about her longing for what could have been than what she actually had, and I wanted to know what that meant to her.

Michelle's honesty was refreshing and she agreed that the parents she could have had today – her perception of what might have been – was more significant than what she had actually lost in reality. She explained that her relationship with her mum would have had a chance to develop and strengthen as she and Michelle got older, just as her closeness to her dad had. 'I saw a transformation from him not exactly being the best dad in the world, to being an involved and loving grandfather. He always said that he wanted to make up for what he lacked as a father by being a good grandfather, and he did that. I would love to have seen what my mother wold have become today. Would she have settled down? Would she have eventually met the right person, who, kind of, made her happy? Was she happy at the end? It makes me sad to think she never found happiness after they divorced in 1981, even though Mum and Dad were back together in1989, the year leading up to her death.'

Michelle had been conflicted by her father's dying words for her to 'stick with her husband 'because he's a keeper' even though he didn't know about the difficulties they were having. If he'd been aware of the reality, he would have instructed her something quite different. It took Michelle years to find the courage to 'disobey' her father and call the marriage off. I've written more about this in chapter 33, 'The Significance of Last Words in Grief'. Words spoken by the soon-to-be-departed can set people free just as much as they can lock people in. It all depends on the relationship, the circumstances and the will of the individual receiving those orders and wishes.

The impact on others

Michelle spoke a lot about the impact of her losses on her children, so to help her along her thought process I asked her to describe which was heavier. I held out two hands and asked if my left hand – her loss of two parents – or my right hand – the kids' loss of their grandparents – was more significant? Interestingly enough, it was again not about Michelle and who she had actually lost but more about what her children missed out on, especially in relation to her mum. While her daughter had had eight years of her grandfather and her son got nineteen years of him, both asked a lot about their nan, and though Michelle told them what she was like and that her daughter was very much like her, she wishes her mum could have been there to be a grandmother to her children.

Making it about the kids and what they missed out on may well have been a subconscious attempt to deflect from having to deal with her own grief. It might have acted as a barrier that protected her from dealing with her own feelings, and Michelle agreed this could be the case. This was indeed the perspective Michelle required to bring her own grieving requirements to the fore, instead of hiding them behind her regrets for her children.

Language patterns

Michelle had a tendency to use the word 'need' a lot in describing how aggrieved she felt by the absence of her mother, although, in her description of her relationship with her mum it sounded like she had stopped needing her at an early age – a slight contradiction maybe? Was that word accurate in relation to her mum or was it creating a greater sense of loss than was actually representative of the facts?

She accepted she was contradicting herself by using that word. She had in fact stopped 'needing' her mum at around 12 years old on account of her mother's dysfunctional relationships, drinking and poor health, which meant that Michelle had become very independent from a young age, something she begrudged. Thinking about her use of the word 'need', she movingly surmised that she meant that she needed 'a' mum to keep her safe, not the version of a mum that she had. Needing and wanting are two different things and come from an entirely different place. Need in this context is hopeless given that it's not possible for Michelle to have her mum back, but want, desiring to be mothered, is natural and understandable.

'I'm protecting her because I couldn't protect me'

When we focused on Michelle's relationship with her daughter, she began to see how some of her parenting traits were very much the result of her own experiences, including losing both of her parents. Given her experience, it was understandable that Michelle wanted to be a better parent to her kids than her parents had been to her, something I completely empathise with, given that I had a non-existent biological father and a temperamental stepfather. I absolutely wanted to go one better than both of them in how I raise my children – my being ever present and very patient is a product of those experiences.

For the first time in the twenty-six years since she lost her mum, Michelle started to link her childhood experiences with how she was parenting her daughter (Michelle's son is 25 and lives in Ireland). Her daughter was unhappy that Michelle didn't give her the independence she felt a 14-year-old should have and this, Michelle could now see, was to do with her desire to stop her daughter from suffering in the same way that she did in her young adult life.

Grief has many layers

In a session that started out about losing both parents, we had found ourselves discussing the effects of Michelle's childhood on her parenting style. In attempting to help her children avoid the same heartache she had experienced, she was unwittingly creating problems of a different nature.

If you have experienced the loss of one or both parents, or indeed of anyone for that matter, do you feel like you are grieving for both what you had and what you didn't get to have? If you didn't have something, can you grieve for it, or can grief only be attributed to something or someone that you have experienced? If we feel grief for something that hasn't yet happened, is that not, more specifically, regret?

Regret is a natural component to grief. We can be forgiven for romanticising about what we could have had, if our loved one had lived for another year or another ten, or right up until we took our own final breath, but it should be understood that grief is initially involuntary, and while regret is very much linked to grief, it requires an adjustment to the facts in order to be overcome.

We can use regret, as I believe was the case with Michelle, to work against us. It is of course far from a conscious decision but it is a means of adding an extra layer to grief. To regret something is to assume that it was ours to lose. I can't regret not meeting my father because I had nothing to do with the choices of others. I can feel that it was a shame that things worked out as they did, but regret is more associated with the outcomes of actions that we personally took.

A few weeks after we met, Michelle was kind enough to send me a summary of how she felt our conversation went.

'Through exploring what bereavement was to me, I found that I grieved more for the concept of the type of parents/grandparents my parents could have become rather than the parents I lost. As a child I parented my parents and they didn't always keep me safe. I thought I had dealt with this, however when we explored the grief I still feel, I was grieving the parents they should have been and in turn I was over-protecting my daughter so that she wouldn't experience the traumas that I had experienced as a child.

This was not a good thing for my children as I was trying to protect them from things they probably wouldn't have gone through anyway. It was like I was trying to undo the harm caused to me. Since our session I have sat with my daughter and gone through the way I was over-protecting her and she admitted at times it felt quite suffocating to her.

As a result, I feel our relationship is now healthier. As a parent I have reassessed what it was about my parents that I miss most and accepted that I cannot change what happened to me, and for my children's sake I cannot try to fix it through my parenting of them. The session was very useful for me and has given me the opportunity to build healthier relationships with them and my wider family, so thank you for that.'

In the session Michelle told me she had some counselling years ago and how 'writing a letter' to her deceased mother had released some of the anger and how having had a face-to-face discussion with her dad had been the positive turning point that had helped her take her relationship with him to new levels.

Writing a letter is a great way of forgiving a person or a set of circumstances; expressing your feelings regardless of whether the letter will ever be read by the addressee, and confronting any issues with someone while you still have the chance is a brave move that can often pay off. The act of sending that letter – actually putting it in the post addressed to anywhere anonymously – will really heighten the release.

To recap, here are the questions that you could ask yourself in order to assess your feelings, if both of your parents have died.

1. Were you the same person from one loss to the other?
2. Were you better equipped second time around?
3. Are you grieving for them individually or together?
4. What roles did your parents play in your life?
5. What role did you play in their lives?
6. If you spent more time grieving what you actually had, what might happen to the amount of regret you feel?
7. Of everything you feel, what's the percentage split for you?
8. Are you regretting/grieving what other family members could have had?

9. Are you affected by any last words interpreted as wishes or orders?
10. Were you more distracted at the time of one of your bereavements?

19

Losing an Unborn Child

Before speaking to Zoe Clark-Coates, founder of www.sayinggood-bye.org, I naively assumed that there was a difference between the grief of a mother who loses her child after a year or so of them being born and the grief of a mother who has lost a child before their birth.

I was sorely mistaken. Why did I think that the grief would be any less if a child hadn't lived for any amount of time? Was it because I assumed the parents and child wouldn't have had a chance to connect physically and emotionally? Did I think that their life had less value just because they hadn't been born? Is the value of a child measured by the days that he or she has lived?

How ridiculous to have been so wrong, but I don't feel like I am alone in my misunderstanding. There is a lot of misconception around miscarriage and stillbirth.

It is a silent grief

Miscarriage and stillbirth are the type of losses nobody wants to talk about, maybe in case it happens to them. People shut them away, because if grief as a whole is a taboo subject, then the loss of a child is the deepest, darkest corner that people most want to avoid.

Because of the way people feel about their children it's the worst-case scenario. It is shut away. Nobody wants to imagine what that loss feels like, and the responsibility for not talking about it is then passed to the parents. We assume they wouldn't want to discuss it, but we are wrong in that assumption. Zoe's website received 650,000 hits last year.

Here's the proof, in Zoe's words. She asked me to consider why there was this generally accepted rule that you shouldn't share the joy of being pregnant until you are at the 12-week stage. Is it because 80% of the 250,000 miscarriages each year in the UK happen before 12 weeks?

If it is, what does that say about our attitude towards the grieving process following a miscarriage? That if we don't tell anyone we are pregnant and then a miscarriage occurs, then at least we won't have to talk about it with our family and friends and share our disappointment or be embarrassed? Why not talk? Why shouldn't you be recognised?

Whatever a miscarriage makes you feel – anger, grief, guilt or a profound sense of sadness – why would anyone think that these emotions are better dealt with internally? If there's anything we have learned through the chapters of this book, it's that grief is most certainly better out than in.

If you are pregnant, tell who you want when you want, and if it doesn't go as planned then the more good friends and family members you have to support you, the better, and yes, you deserve to be supported through miscarriage and stillbirth as much as any other loss.

It should be talked about, it needs to be talked about, and if it's uncomfortable, well, that is society's issue, not yours. Lots of people go through this, and they need to be heard and for their loss to be recognised.

Is one person's grief worse than another?

Absolutely not. There is no competition in loss. All grief matters, and as the Saying Goodbye charity states – every single baby matters. But because of society's generalisation of the pain of loss before, during or after childbirth, those who have experienced the loss of a child feel they need to fight for their baby to be recognised.

Because the loss of a child is considered by the medical profession to be a medical problem, a malfunction of the mother's body in the creation of a child rather than an actual loss of life, you might almost feel guilty for grieving, something that is unique to baby loss. If you lose a partner or a child who has been alive for a few years, people expect you to grieve and give you permission to do so.

When it comes to miscarriage or stillbirth, you don't always get that permission. It can get stolen from you, and you can almost be treated like you're overreacting if you do grieve, so it might be your experience that you either process the loss really quietly or you don't actually process it at all.

So many couples who have experienced baby loss claim to have never been given permission to grieve and have never had their loss validated or recognised. If you don't process it, it just grows and causes mental and physical problems later down the line.

Losing a baby can increase the desire and indeed the pressure to try for another child, and the pain of grief and sometimes guilt can create infertility because of the stress it puts the couple under.

The Saying Goodbye website states that 250,000 babies are lost through miscarriage each year, which equates to 700 every day, approximately 17% of which happen in hospital, the rest in a home environment. Sometimes it's treated dismissively by the medical profession, as though you've got the flu or a stomach bug. The doctors treat the symptoms of the miscarriage, but they don't take into account the severity of the grief.

If you miscarry before 24 weeks the baby is not considered a baby; it's considered a foetus. If your baby isn't born with any sign of life, shockingly, you don't get a death certificate, birth certificate or stillbirth certificate and it's as if your baby didn't exist, but that is never how it feels. If your baby is born breathing or with a heartbeat before 24 weeks, you get birth and death certificates but if they are born after 24 weeks with no signs of life you just get a stillbirth certificate.

The Saying Goodbye charity is running a huge campaign for anyone who loses a child before 24 weeks to be offered a new Loss Certificate and the opportunity to have their loss registered on a new baby loss database. This has proved a popular campaign. Everyone wants their child's story to be heard and recognised.

Medical termination

Some couples have to take the excruciatingly painful decision to abort their child before the 24-week cut-off point, often due to serious medical complications. It's not so well known, but a mother can have an abortion right up until she is in labour or before 40 weeks, a provision for people with severely disabled babies, and sometimes the NHS very much encourage (and allegedly pressurise) people to take that route.

This can often leave couples with the grief of losing a child and the guilt of having made a decision to end their baby's life, and again, you can guarantee that this is a grief they won't find many willing to talk about.

The facts (in the UK)
Early Miscarriage: 12–14 weeks.
Late Miscarriage: 14–24 weeks.
Stillborn: Over 24 weeks.
Miscarriage: You bleed heavily, and the baby comes out – 'Miscarried'.
Incomplete (Missed) Miscarriage: You don't know you've miscarried. You're told at your routine scan, and you learn the baby is dead and is still within you. You then go into full labour and delivery.
Stillbirth – When a baby dies in utero after 24 weeks and is then born without signs of life.

Saying Goodbye offers great advice about what not to say to someone who has lost a child at any term.

Zoe Clark-Coates has this advice for us all:

'The human spirit always wants us to say something positive, but speaking to a bereaved couple who have lost a child, a situation we might not know much about, we can sometimes panic and say the most horrendously insensitive comments, such as:

"Well, it's not as bad as losing an 18-month-old." Each loss is individual; how can we possibly presume one is worse than another?

"Oh, at least you can try again." Like an unborn life has no value. If someone lost a husband you wouldn't say, "Oh, it's OK, you can go and find a new one."

"Well, at least you've got two children already." It's not about being a parent, it's about losing a child.

"You'll get your baby one day." Oh, and you know that for sure, do you?

"At least your child is in a better place." You might think heaven is a better place than your life, but I disagree.

"At least you're still fertile; my friend can't have children at all." But what's the point of being pregnant if it doesn't result in a child in your arms? Where is the consolation in coming close?

Sometimes it is best to say nothing, merely offer empathy and compassion, and accept you cannot just make it better. If you're going to say anything, try: "I can't even imagine how painful this must be for you" and sit there with a box of tissues.

Don't say, "Let me know if there is anything we can do." Offer practical help. People who have lost a child can be lost in a fog of grief and can find it hard to consider what they do or don't need, so just take the initiative. Perhaps drop them off dinner each night for a week.

Sometimes people send friends or family articles about how to avoid baby loss from magazines. Obviously, people are trying to be helpful by doing this, but it can be so painful for the bereaved parent, as it can suggest to them that they could have avoided the loss, and guilt is the last thing they need.

The best thing to do is listen, show love and kindness and simply say: "I can't even begin to imagine the pain, but I am here to listen and help in any way I can."'

Zoe's personal story

Having seen a close friend go through the horrendous experience of miscarriage and stillbirth I had put off having children, as I actually didn't know how I would personally cope with such a loss. However, having been married for over twelve years to my soulmate (we married young), and after setting up a successful business, suddenly my biological clock started ticking . . . Yes, I too thought this was an urban myth, that one day you could be satisfied with no children, then the next you have a burning desire to reproduce, but it happened to me; I can confirm it is real.

After a while I knew I was pregnant, but sadly it ended in a miscarriage, and my way of coping was to almost pretend it hadn't happened. I didn't want to be one of those statistics, which state up to one in four pregnancies end in miscarriage, and surely if I didn't acknowledge it, it didn't really happen.

Within a couple of months, we were blessed to get pregnant again, and this time it felt more real. We decided to keep it a secret from the family, and tell them at Christmas, as we knew they would be surprised. There seems to be a presumption in Britain that if you are going to have children it will happen in the first three years of a relationship, and if there aren't signs of tiny pattering feet by then, maybe it's just not going to happen!

We went for our first scan, and we had a heart-stopping moment when the sonographer said, 'Are you sure you have your dates right? I can't see anything.' Following our assurance that the dates were indeed correct, she suddenly announced, 'Oh, there it is,' and on the screen we witnessed the miracle of life, our tiny little baby wriggling around, with its little heartbeat fluttering away. We were, of course, over the moon. She did mention that she could see a pool of blood in the womb, and warned me I should expect a little blood loss at some point, but not to worry about it at all. That evening I did get a little spotting, and if I'm honest I did panic. I think any woman will tell you if you see any signs of blood while pregnant, this fear just swells from nowhere, but by the following day the spotting had stopped, so peace returned.

A few days later I caught the flu and was bedridden for the rest of the week. Then, as quickly as it had stopped, the bleeding started again, but this time it felt different. We found a clinic who agreed to scan me. After an age, we were called in to the scanning room, and the doctor immediately activated the all-telling machine, and there on the screen we saw our baby for the second time – kicking away, showing no signs of distress or concern . . . what a relief!

We were due to go to a party on the Saturday evening, so figuring resting might stop any further bleeding I stayed in bed, constantly doing that maternal stroke of the stomach, which somehow feels like you're comforting and caring for your child within. But when I got up that evening I felt a sudden rush of blood, and I knew, my baby had just died. I lay on the floor begging God to save her, crying out to the only One who truly controls life and death, but I knew it was in vain; I knew she was destined to be born into heaven, not on to Earth. Mother's instinct? Who knows, but I knew her little heart was no longer beating within her or me.

We rushed to A & E where I was sadly met with little concern; I was even asked if it was an IVF baby as I was so upset. 'Why?' I asked. 'Is it not normal to cry over a naturally conceived child?' They had no answer. They didn't examine me; I was just told, 'There is nothing we can do. Let nature take its course. What will be, will be.' I was given an appointment for an emergency scan in a week's time and told to go home to bed.

The next day, a Sunday, the bleeding slowed down, and we left messages on numerous clinic answer machines begging for an appointment as soon as possible. The following morning, before 9 a.m., we got a call from a wonderful clinic telling us to come over and they would scan me. That was to be one of the longest journeys of my life.

We were called from the waiting area and into a small room. I was told to get on the bed, and the scanner was booted up. After what seemed like an eternity of silence, I finally willed up the courage to ask, 'Can you see the baby? Is all OK?' I didn't really need to ask. My baby was still; the only movement on the screen came from my body, not hers. My question was met with the worst answer: 'Zoe, I'm sorry to say there isn't a heartbeat.' I literally screamed . . . I then pleaded for a second scan, which she did. Then she went to get a consultant; he came in shaking his head saying the same words, ones that would become very familiar to us over the coming months: 'I'm so sorry.' We were quickly put in a tiny room, where we sobbed, wailed and clung to each other. We phoned our family, and hearing the words coming out of our own mouths, the nightmare of our reality dawned on us: our baby had died. She was still here with us, but we would never hold her hand, or rock her to sleep. 'What now?' we asked. We were told we could go the surgical route or the natural route. I chose the natural route, as the thought of going to a hospital where my baby would just be extracted from me seemed wrong. It was my baby, and I wanted to keep her with me for as long as possible.

What I wasn't prepared for was that the ordeal would go on for a week. A scan after a few days showed the baby had grown further, which is apparently totally normal, as the blood supply is still making the baby grow, but her heart remained still. No spark of life was visible: 'No, Zoe, sadly your baby hasn't miraculously come back to life. Yes, we know you had hoped it would happen.'

Was I wrong to hope this may be the case? That if I prayed non-stop, if I kept rubbing my stomach night and day somehow her heart would just start up again . . . I had been told by a nurse that there was one case of it somewhere in the world once, so was I misguided to believe I could be the second?

We returned home and the days passed, long and slow. Someone asked me how I could allow a dead baby to stay inside me. 'Because it's my baby', I said. Why one would presume that her death made her any less precious or me any less loving, I'm not sure, but for some carrying a dead baby within is creepy, morbid and wrong. To me, I was being her mother, keeping her safe in the place that had become her haven. I felt she was entitled to remain there until she decided to leave. It wasn't my place to suddenly evict her, and I was prepared to wait as long as needed for her to dictate the timing of our meeting.

A week to the day after her heartbeat stopped, labour started, and within twenty-four hours I had delivered my child.

For the next six weeks, my body raged with pregnancy hormones as it wrongly assumed I was still carrying a child, so all day and night sickness continued, along with the indigestion and headaches. What were once reassuring symbols of pregnancy were now horrendous reminders of what was no more. The oddest thing then started to occur, almost on a daily basis: complete strangers would randomly ask me if I had children. Each time it was like I was being thumped in the stomach. I instantly faced a dilemma of whether to protect the person's feelings who had just asked me this very innocent question, and just say, 'No, I haven't,' but by doing so, I would be denying my child's existence, or bravely say, 'I have, actually, but they died.' I tried both, and both felt wrong, and I quickly learned I was in a lose-lose situation, and I should just do whatever felt right at the time.

I was met with lots of well-meaning statements like 'Well, at least it proves you can conceive,' and 'Sometimes the womb just needs practice.' Thankfully the less sensitive statements were a minority, as I was blessed to have my husband – my hero – by my side, not always knowing what to say, but being wise enough to know that words often aren't needed, and that just to hold me would often be enough. And then there were my parents, who sat with us and filled endless buckets with their own tears, while helping empty ours. The rest of our family and friends were amazing, their support was tangible, and though most had no comprehension of what we were experiencing, they just made it clear to us that they were there, and that meant the world to us.

Some may think surely this extinguished the biological clock, but it didn't, it just increased the desire to have a baby; but the fear that I would never become a mum was overwhelming.

Two months later I lost my third baby via a miscarriage, but we kept this to ourselves, as we felt the family had gone through enough. As far as they knew, we had only ever lost one baby, and to tell them about this loss would lead to us admitting to them, and to ourselves, that this in fact was our third child to grace the heavenly gates.

Then we got pregnant again, and following a scary pregnancy, where we had fortnightly scans, we were finally handed our beautiful daughter, weighing six pounds fifteen ounces. The relief was profound, and there are no words to explain the elation of finally getting to hold and protect my tiny little girl.

We loved being parents so much; the thought of having another child was mentioned when she was one and a half, even though we had declared to all and sundry that we would be stopping at one. Nothing had prepared us for the amount of joy a little one can add to your life – there is nothing about being a mum I don't love – so we decided to try for a brother or sister for our daughter.

Naively, having carried a healthy, thriving child that went to full term, we believed our dealings with miscarriage and loss were in the past, and any further pregnancies would resemble that of our last one, rather than our first three. We were wrong.

We got pregnant, and all the initial scans were perfect, then on one of our appointments the scan showed our baby's heartbeat had simply stopped (again). Time went in slow motion when we were told. I literally couldn't speak. I wasn't prepared to tumble through that hidden trapdoor from expectant mother to miscarriage a fourth time. I misguidedly thought to lose a child when you already have one would hurt less, and in a way I was right, as you are not also grieving the fact that you may never be a mother to a living child (as you are already), but it hurts in a different way, as you can't help asking yourself, would this baby have laughed in the same way as our little girl? Would they talk in the same way? It's hard to explain, but for me it was definitely a different type of grief, but of course it was truly terrible.

In a bid to try to protect our little girl from seeing any upset, I only allowed myself to cry in private and forced myself to keep things as normal as possible for her. I opted to take the medical route this time, and within a couple of days I found myself in a hospital bed, filling in paperwork, sobbing after two questions were asked by the nurse: 'Would you like a post-mortem, and would you like the remains back?' Can any mother ever be prepared to answer such questions?

In medical terms those who die in utero within the first 24 weeks of life are termed as retained products of conception, so perhaps you should expect to be asked these questions while filling in a form. I am one of millions, however, who feel you should not. I know for some people these aren't babies; they are just a group of cells, and I respect that this is their opinion, but to me and my husband, it was our child, not just a potential person, but a person, and he deserved to be acknowledged as such.

We were blessed to get pregnant for a sixth time, and after telling the family around the Christmas tree on Christmas Eve, I went upstairs to find I had started to bleed. The bleeding continued for days, and when I finally managed to speak to a GP I was told I had definitely miscarried, and there was no need for a scan. That crushing sadness overtook me again, and those who have experienced this first-hand will know you literally have to remind yourself to breathe. Human functions just seem to disappear, as you feel you're free-falling over a cliff. I held on to the knowledge that to have my daughter would of course be enough, and that if we were never blessed with another child, we were one of the lucky couples who at least had the opportunity to raise one little girl. So we painted a smile on our faces and gave our daughter an amazing Christmas.

However, by 5 January I was feeling so ill I decided to go for a scan, in case I needed another operation, and to our surprise they could still see a sign of life. I was told this by no means meant all would be fine, but it was a good sign, and I should book another scan in a couple of weeks. During this time my sickness increased, and by the time I went for my next scan I was sicker than I had ever been while pregnant. The doctor could see two little lives on the screen, but one was much more developed than the other. We were told to be prepared to lose one twin, but the other seemed strong and healthy. Tragically we did indeed go on to lose one of the babies, but the other hung on, and we felt blessed to have one baby, but heartbroken for the baby we lost.

What followed was a minefield of a pregnancy. I had to have my gallbladder removed, I had liver problems, placenta previa, SPD, my placenta was stuck to the old C-section scar, then the final blow came when I developed obstetric cholestasis, but our little warrior braved it all! When she finally appeared in all her glory in August 2011 she was declared a miracle baby, and I don't think we have stopped smiling since.

'Was it all worth it?' some may ask. Of course! 'Do you wish you had detonated your biological clock as it caused you so much pain?' Absolutely not. I have two adorable little girls, whom I simply adore; they have made every single tear worth shedding. I'm so proud to be a mother, and I hope the trauma I have gone through makes me a better wife, mother and friend. My passion is to now raise my girls to love life and embrace every opportunity life hands to them; I also want to help others who have lost children.

What I have learned through this heartbreak is this: to me every child matters, however far in pregnancy a person is. I have also learned a lot about grief. Everyone is entitled to grieve differently. Some may not even feel a need to shed a tear, some may sob endlessly, and both are fine. For the heartbroken, however, acknowledging the loss is essential and it's imperative to both physical health and mental well-being to grieve. Life may never be normal again when you have been to such depths of darkness, but we can move forward, with as little scar tissue on the soul as possible, and saying goodbye was the key for me.

I will never forget the thousands of couples who are so desperate to have a child, and are still searching for the solution to their recurrent losses, or for some why that miracle of conception just doesn't happen. Whatever losses we have endured, we know we are truly, truly blessed to have two wonderful girls to raise and hold. For some people they are still waiting for their miracle to arrive.

20

The 'Rules' of Grief

We all grieve in our own unique way. There are no hard and fast rules to grief but there are subconscious chains of commands and instructions that we impose on ourselves that can shape the way we manage our grief, or fail to manage it, as the case can often be. A verbal example of a constructive instruction might be: 'I know I'll feel better once I've spoken about it', while a negative command might be: 'I'll never be able to forgive myself for arguing with him before he left the house.'

You may be wondering how such comments can carry so much weight. Beliefs of any nature are actually agreements we make with ourselves, contracts if you like that state what we think and feel about certain subjects, and if we continuously give ourselves the same command, we will inevitably grow to believe it's the truth, which, in the case of never being able to forgive yourself, can lead to all sorts of complications. And of course, our own version of the truth is not always entirely accurate because sometimes we make those agreements based on assumptions and a tendency to reach for the worst-case scenario, not realising that we can be responsible for making our journey through grief slightly more complicated than it already invariably is.

Language and how we use it is incredibly influential on how we see ourselves and interpret our lives. Some people are typically kinder to themselves with the words they choose, for example, 'I will be as honest as I can about how I feel', whereas some are incredibly harsh with their instructions and opt for more limiting versions, such as 'I can't see myself ever being happy again.'

The most important parts of these sentences are the verbs we use such as can't or won't. These are so rigid and limiting. How do we know we can't or we won't, until we try? The softer, more flexible presuppositions we could use are 'might' or 'could'.

Whether it's your language that is imposing the rules by which you grieve or your propensity to be quite closed and inflexible in the way you cope with difficult situations, the following case study illustrates the negative effects of imposing rules during grief.

Four years ago, James lost his mum to bowel cancer and his 10-year-old nephew to a brain aneurysm. There were barely weeks between the losses and James has had particular difficulty dealing with anniversaries or the marking of special occasions. The build-up tends to start at the beginning of December when he starts to feels down. He blows his fuse more often than usual and he has knots in his stomach, and at first he couldn't work out why. He came to realise it's because he has this run of anniversaries and birthdays to deal with and now he imposes a series of rules on himself.

His Rule 1 applies to the pre-Christmas period when he tells himself: 'I need to get it out the way and then I can feel more positive.' Rule 2 comes directly after Christmas when he marks his mum's birthday and then the anniversary of her death at the end of January with a family get-together and this allows him to think: 'Right, now the New Year starts here.'

After the event he describes his relief by thinking 'Right – it's done' (a slightly different version of Rule 2). When I ask James what he and his family do to mark these anniversaries, he tells me – Rule 3 – 'We don't talk about it, we just get together.' And after that, Rule

4 kicks in and he goes 'for long periods of time not thinking about my mother or my nephew unless it's convenient'.

Rules are always very obvious and noticeable; you don't need to speak to James for too long before you've heard them repeated a number of times. The use of the word 'convenient' is interesting. James said 'convenient moments are ones that are in my control like talking to you now and thinking of Mum when I look at the photo next to my bed. Inconvenient is when grief takes me by surprise and is not my choice.'

It is an unrealistic expectation to imagine that grief will fit in with when James feels it's a good time, and from my experience I suspect he is setting himself up for many 'inconvenient' moments.

Grief can be perceived in many ways. I happen to believe it works with or for us and actually plays a vital role in the internal recovery from a physical and visual attachment that has been lost. If grief didn't exist, what would stop James forgetting about his mum and nephew? Don't we need grief to remind us of what we've lost so we can just remember, even agonisingly? The absence of grief would surely mean that James might cease to remember his loved ones, something he absolutely did not want to do.

James realised that in order to remember them he was going to have to accept the reminders whether they were at convenient moments or not, or perceived to be in his control or not, because without grief's tap on the shoulder 'forgetting' would be the direction he would be drifting to.

What is strength in loss?

James described how he didn't like the idea of someone at work potentially asking him what he was doing on Mother's Day for fear of being 'reminded' that his mother had died. When I asked why, he answered that it was because he didn't like the idea of letting someone in to his pain and didn't want anyone feeling sorry for him, or for anyone to think he was weak.

I suggested that he could matter-of-factly tell a colleague who asked him such a question, 'On Mother's Day I'll be doing something for my mum, because she isn't here any more, sadly' rather than what I suspected he might do, which would be to say 'Er, nothing much', while looking down at his feet and shuffling awkwardly out of the conversation. He could see that my first response was much stronger. It required bravery and honesty and to look the colleague in the eye and state the facts, whereas the alternative, to avoid and deflect from saying what was really going on, was in fact a weaker strategy.

For every command or rule we impose there is an alternative. We chose the rules based on previous life experiences and also our expectations in our ability to cope with grief. Let me show you the options James had in his choices of language and supposed belief.

Rule 1: 'I need to get it out the way and then I can feel more positive.'

For starters, you don't get grief 'out of the way'. You get a car out of the way when it's blocking your driveway; you get your tax return 'out of the way' so you don't have a load of stress on your shoulders at the end of the financial year. Grief is something that remains with us, becomes part of our everyday and our life going forward, and what we discover when we learn to manage it is that we can live alongside grief.

Grief becomes part of our daily routine, so a kinder and more accurate response would be to say, 'I'm going to plan something for their anniversary that my loved one will be happy with and whatever emotion I feel on the day, I'll accept as being natural. I will feel more positive when I have expressed my feelings through talking, remembering or crying.'

Rule 2a: 'Right, now the New Year starts here.'

If James is happy to let everyone else in the world get a month's head start on the New Year, then that rule is OK. If, however, death has taught him that life is precious and every day should be made the most of, James might want to reclaim his December and January. Yes, he has some tricky dates to navigate, but when those dates become celebrations of what he had instead of inconvenient reminders of what he lost, it might start to feel less like a part of the year he wished didn't exist.

A healthier way to look at things would be: 'Now we've come through another batch of big occasions I know that we are remembering Mum and Harry the way they would like to be remembered. Because I'm being respectful to them I'm now glad to have the opportunity to release some grief with the people I share their memory with. There is no start and end to the times when I can miss them. Time goes on and so does my love for them.'

Rule 2b: 'Right – it's done.'

What's done? Having to remember because it's painful? It's never done. The more you share your loss openly and honestly, the less painful it becomes. Avoiding memories is a short-term solution to a long-term journey.

In the short term you may feel like you're outrunning grief but you're simply contributing to the additional issues that you'll need to recognise on top of your grief, sooner or later. Delay and denial also create other issues for those around us. Some need to act less naturally in order to enable your rigidity; some may feel unable to share their grief because you won't share yours and they have to suppress theirs in order to protect you.

We say, 'Right, that's done' when we have cleaned out the attic or braved the supermarket on a Saturday afternoon. Do we want our loved one to be thought of in that way?

The alternative thought here is: 'We are grateful to have had such an incredible person in our lives and their death gives us the reason to get together and share so many happy thoughts and memories about how they influenced our lives and truly made them better.'

Rule 3: 'We don't talk about it, we just get together.'
His family gives James support and there is still solidarity in silence, but a family that doesn't talk exists in a culture of suppression. One member may want to talk but doesn't for fear of upsetting the others and in the end it becomes 'the norm' for the family to deal with their losses without expressing their grief.

Getting together is a lovely gesture but not talking to each other about the 'elephant in the room' is like going to a football match and facing the back of the stand or going to a train station but not boarding a train. How would you feel if you were the person who had died and were looking down at that get-together? Would you be upset that nobody mentions anything about you? Personally, I would prefer to be remembered joyfully with lots of talking about how I touched the lives of the people I shared my journey with. The thought of my boys sitting in silence terrifies me!

I get it. James doesn't want to hurt someone or himself by mentioning the wrong thing. Can anything, anything at all actually come close to reciprocating the feeling of pain and trauma that he experienced when his mum and nephew died? No. James has done the hardest part and nothing will come close to that until he goes through it again. Remembering, however, needs to be seen as a privilege. James had his mother and nephew, and his love and respect for them should make it an absolute given that the very least he and his family does is talk about their existence. They can still live, in death.

Rule 4: 'I go for long periods of time not thinking about my mother or my nephew unless it's convenient.'
Convenience is the state of being able to proceed with something without difficulty. If you are expecting to proceed without difficulty following the death of someone very special to you, then you're seriously underestimating the challenge ahead.

Unrealistic expectations just set you up for failure. It's like trying to jump three double-decker buses on roller skates; not paying your bills and expecting your electricity to stay on; or not putting petrol in the car and expecting it to go on for ever and ever.

Do we want to go for long periods without thinking about our loved ones? What happens if we think about them little and often? Would we have the huge crashes if we didn't leave it for such long stretches? The ideal alternative to this rule would be: 'I think about my loss all the time; sometimes I create the thought and sometimes it just springs up on me. Either way it's up to me whether that memory is pleasure or pain, because I control the continuation of my thoughts, even if I didn't ask for it to be there. I understand that these waves may not come at the opportune moment and I might need to excuse myself from the office to catch my breath, but I'm being realistic by accepting that I don't have to be at my best all of the time. So, if I do feel the effects of grief, I'll let it come and let it pass and accept that this is part of my journey through loss.'

My rules surrounding grief have generally always been constructive and therefore helpful. My commands now I come to focus on them would typically be 'I will never forget all of the people I've lost or allow them to be forgotten. I must keep Jade's memory alive. Love will overcome every hurdle my children and I will ever face', to name but a few. I understand full well the power of my words and the responsibility I hold to condition myself to believe I can cope. In fact I didn't doubt that I would be able to get them through their childhood and into their adulthood. Whether that's confidence, blind optimism or just being hopeful (there's a long way to go still!) I don't know, but I accept that it's better to be positive than not. Even through the countless occasions when I've felt overwhelmed or out of my depth, things always seem to return to a peaceful calm, so I'd say it's worked for me up until now.

So what are your rules? What commands do you hear yourself stating on a regular basis? Here's a tough one: what are your children's rules? Do they have a positive or negative mantra to describe how their life is going to turn out from here? How can you help them to change it if that's what they need? Is there a quote that you can get framed that you want yourself or your child to see on a daily basis? Every time they see it, say it and condition themselves to believe that affirmation, they – or you – are a step closer to replacing a limiting belief with a constructive one.

I'm thinking of a particular quote for the boys that I have come to know is true: 'The greatest strengths can only be gained when we experience the very worst that life has to offer.' I also like something slightly simpler but no less poignant or true – 'You've gone through the worst. Now you deserve the very best that life has to offer.' What will your quote remind you of when you look at it every day?

21

The Trouble with Men

I have always received such warm acknowledgements about my efforts as a father, mainly from females who I suspect may feel a touch surprised by my ability as a man to cope with two children on my own. The world of parenting has changed for the better since the days when men were traditionally the breadwinners and I'd imagine if I have ever exceeded anyone's expectations it was probably more on account of their own experiences rather than what men are or aren't capable of.

I never questioned if I was going to be able to cope with them. I'd been a father for five years already at that point and considered myself particularly hands on from the start, so I wasn't fazed with the day-to-day aspects. As far as grief went, I had no idea what to expect but I always felt that I had the ability to learn quickly and adapt to my heightened responsibilities as I had so often already in my young life.

I totally concede, however, that men are less forthcoming in their emotional needs and this may present some with a real challenge when dealing with their own grief. Take Rio Ferdinand's documentary that highlighted his early struggles after losing his wife and being left with the sole care of his three children. He bravely admitted that his whole footballing career had been spent viewing emotion as weakness and I found it fascinating seeing a well-respected man in his late thirties start to realise that to be successful in his new reality he would have to become a very different version of himself. Change doesn't always come easily to men and Rio represented perfectly the fact that grief doesn't care who you are and what you've achieved; it is ruthless in its continuity and makes no exceptions. We have to adapt to it and not the other way around.

Prince Harry then disclosed quite brilliantly that he went twenty years before getting help to face up to his grief after losing his mum, Princess Diana, in 1997. Lots of highly regarded men speaking out about grief! I'm always curious to see how other men process their loss. Do we all face the same struggles, and are we worse off for living a stereotypical existence before our relationship with our softer side demands an acknowledgement?

I have a lovely next door neighbour called Dan. We've stopped and chatted in the way that most blokes usually might when crossing each other's paths outside their houses: talking about football, playing snooker against each other, that kind of thing. Then one evening we started discussing the book and how he was no stranger to the subject of death.

In conversation I noticed Dan was doing that thing most men do when discussing something personal: to label it 'a bit deep', to be almost apologetic that he was even sharing something personal, and verbally understating the emotional value of it all.

We were specifically talking about dementia and how his father died of it and how his stepfather is currently going through it, although he added he didn't have a particularly good relationship with either. He looked like, despite his best efforts to put on a brave exterior, that there was a story to share, so I invited him over a few days later for a cup of tea – and what a story it was.

Dan's first experience of grief was his grandad, who had a heart attack in 1993 when Dan was thirteen. Although he felt numb inside, Dan recalls his friends commenting on how he appeared to handle it in his true 'Ice man' like fashion. If he had any feelings about it he buried them deep down somewhere and doesn't remember grieving.

What he does remember was being left with his Nan in a room where people were coming to offer their condolences and him thinking, 'I've heard this story thirty times now.' He wanted to escape in that moment and regrets that he was subject to comforting his Nan when he probably didn't feel ready.

Due to issues at home with his stepdad he had lived with his grandparents for a large portion of his childhood, from ten onwards. His mother had pushed him aside in order to cater for the jealous, controlling demands of her new partner, Dan's stepdad. The notion as to why Dan would appear 'icy' was starting to take form. As far as his three parents were concerned, Dan had learnt that he wasn't important and that his feelings didn't matter.

One of Dan's earliest memories is from when he was around five or six years old, waiting by the window for his dad to pick him up and realising he wasn't coming that day and on numerous others. The male perspective on grief doesn't always need much encouragement, but if I ever wondered why Dan maybe wasn't particularly forthcoming I wasn't lacking in clues as to where that would have started.

Dan had attended between twelve and fourteen funerals in his childhood alone. These occasions served to reinforce his self-developed ability to tune out and switch off.

In 2000, Dan lost a father figure when his best friend Chris lost his dad unexpectedly. Dan loved this man; he had been the role model he desperately needed in the latter stages of his childhood and young adult life, but still Dan questioned jovially if it had affected him at the time; the barrier was still in full swing.

In 2006, Dan lost his father who had split with his mum when he was just one. He recounted how he didn't speak to him for five years leading up to his death, because he had called him fifty times leading up to that period and had decided he was going to stop allowing this man to hurt him by never responding.

More funerals were to follow. This time it would be his Nan's. In 2008, his 'second Mum' died and what was different about this one compared to any of the others was that he carried the coffin and doesn't remember one single thing about the whole occasion. He had completely shut down.

Was it the fact that he had a responsibility and played an active role that made him completely tune out?

In between this and the next death Dan would have to deal with, he had got together with his now wife, Emma, a girl he had known since he was seventeen, and in 2010 he became a father. Just how much difference to his typically male way of shutting down would having children make?

Of all the funerals Dan had to encounter (he has counted roughly twenty five in thirty nine years) the next at the age of thirty six was to be the hardest. In 2014, his cousin Ronnie, one of the most well-liked people in the area Dan grew up in, was taken by a brain tumour.

Again, Dan was carrying the coffin and this time it was the first burial he had seen which he had found far more traumatic. Dan admitted to melting on this occasion and questioned if it was the incredible sense of injustice that made the difference.

He thinks it's more likely that becoming a father 'forced' him to have feelings. That coupled with the fact that he was in a loving marriage gave him the safety and reassurance that he could actually wear his feelings instead of continuing the habits born out of a childhood of suppression.

Can you imagine all of this loss though? The confusion it would create emotionally? How would he possibly know who he was grieving for at any one time? I guess Dan made that simple by trying not to grieve at all but there was something new about him now. He now feared leaving his own child and it gave him a perspective on how valuable his life really is. He felt isolated by all of these deaths, like everyone is leaving him. It brought about a weight of responsibility, like he was the head of the family and needed to look after everyone.

Dan, like many bereaved individuals, found that he hated the idea of burdening people, so he bottled things up. Was he worried about his masculinity, before and after kids? Dan felt that when those older than you die you feel yourself stepping up a generation, which makes you feel closer to your time, even though Dan is not even forty years old yet.

I asked him how he was at discussing things with friends and he stated that after leaving my house he was going to see his friend to talk about his stepfather's dementia and the fact that there were some important decisions to be made, so you'd have to conclude that the 'ice man' was no more.

I love the idea that the love for your children can save you from yourself and your ways of coping that are meant to be temporary but are often accepted as just who we were born to be. It's all learnt. Dan was nicknamed the 'ice man' by his friends, so it became a persona. But you can see through the chapter how children, marriage, injustice, and a combination of the three, slowly lowered that defence and made him vulnerable, real and human again.

I don't know where this leaves us with our conversations over the garden fence. I feel like I know so much about him already!

There are many men like me out there who are going it alone with their children. Rob Tadman, 38, is bringing up his six-year-old daughter, Chloe, on his own after his wife Jo died from bowel cancer in 2014. I asked Rob, an old school friend, what he thought the typical male response was to anything as traumatic as grief. He thought the male outlook on grief was based around a man's response to many things in life and that it's quite an introverted view. He went on to summarise that men find it harder to open up about their feelings and emotions due to being less in touch with those feelings, and society's shaping of the male ego, how men communicate and the shortcomings of the stereotypical masculine outlook on life and how to deal with problems.

He recognises that he has had a fairly typical male way of dealing with grief by being far too insular and closed about personal issues and being afraid to express his true feelings as it often feels easier and less painful to bottle up problems rather than bare your soul and empty your heart to someone.

Men have many ways of avoiding talking about their feelings: changing the subject, or choosing various distractions such as drinking, sport, mindless chat and various other avoidance tactics, whether conscious or otherwise.

A better approach would be talking more. Rob thinks men are generally less mature in dealing with feelings and are sometimes backwards in asking for and accepting offers of help. In some ways this is like asking for directions when you are lost – men tend to ask for help as a last resort. This is potentially linked to pride, arrogance, ignorance and stubbornness, all of which are character traits that need to be left behind when dealing with grief and a major life change or personal crisis.

How does a man adapt?

Rob thinks he has started to move more towards a better approach of dealing with grief, mainly through accepting help, knowing his limits, talking more and accepting that he can't do the journey alone. Asking for help and reaching out has been one of his biggest breakthroughs as a person and as a father and has made the journey far more manageable and less daunting.

Rob thought that if he'd approached grief from a more constructive point of view he'd have let go of stubbornness straight away, listened to his heart and really put his own and his daughter's wellbeing before work and fear of being seen as a failure.

The truth behind the curtain . . .

Rob feels men could be perceived as coping better than they are purely through keeping a brave face and masking what's really happening on the inside, which is obviously counterproductive and avoids dealing with problems. Men are also typically bullish and stubborn and will more often than not race back to work far too quickly rather than take stock of a loss and work through feelings and issues.

What is the bravest thing you've done?

Rob has joined a widowed parents' group. He started six months after Jo's death when feeling very raw, with tears never far away. The group is all women but for Rob they are brought together with a common theme: they have all lost their partner to cancer and have children.

The group has offered him a regular outlet for his feelings and emotions and has given him the confidence to open up about everything, begin new friendships and widen his support network. The group has been incredibly powerful by showing that you're not alone in this journey where often you can feel completely isolated and incredibly lonely, even when surrounded by family and friends.

What he particularly found was that he needed people who really understood what it's like to be widowed and young. Your friends can give you all the support possible but the perspective of knowing what it's like to have gone through being a cancer carer is always missing.

Rob has also recently started some one-to-one counselling for both himself and for Chloe. Counselling is incredibly draining for him and after a short, usually very tearful, session it can leave him exhausted but elated that a burden has been shared and lifted from his shoulders.

How could you have made it easier?

Rob feels that by prioritising his mental health and well-being above more mundane chores that could have been delegated to his support network he would have been better off. Mental health and breaking through desperation by accepting help are fundamental to building a solid foundation for you and your children.

The best thing you grasped?

Rob accepted he was not a machine and began to slow down. One of his initial coping mechanisms was to keep busy – the clichéd classic dumb response to block things out with a whirlwind of unnecessary jobs, appointments, social engagements and lists! In the beginning he thought he'd hit the jackpot, just kept busy and hoped everything would be OK.

This eureka moment was pretty short-lived, though, and after racing through the first year in the wilderness of grief and loneliness he was left exhausted and longing to slow down and lead a much simpler life.

22

Motivating Yourself After a Death

There are very few things in life more likely to demotivate us than the death of someone we love. We may ask ourselves: 'What's the point? It's just not the same any more.' And indeed, what is the point of exercising, socialising, eating healthily, eating at all? What's the point in getting out of bed when the worst thing imaginable has happened?

There is always a point to carrying on, of course. You may have children who depend on you, a job that you have to sustain in order to keep your family alive, but how you carry on needs to come from inside you. You need to find the motivation to, say, go back to the gym or see your friends, and to do that, you need to identify and remove the obstacle that is blocking you from grieving, instead of wanting to grind to a complete halt.

Take Natasha, a 48-year-old travel agent, whose daughter Angie had committed suicide at the age of 26 after a long battle with mental health. Natasha told me how over the years everything possible had been done to help Angie, yet she had not wanted to embrace that help. Natasha believed that at the time of her death, Angie had not actually meant to kill herself and that she did so accidentally.

Since her daughter's suicide, Natasha had put on three stone in weight, had stopped going to the exercise boot camp she so enjoyed and was unable to get herself up in the morning. She had no focus and could barely get herself to work, the only place where she was able to find temporary distraction. 'I can't get over it,' she told me. 'I couldn't stop my only daughter from killing herself. Why would I want to carry on?'

Natasha was overwhelmed by feelings of guilt. She felt guilty for 'not acting soon enough', she felt guilty that she hadn't 'fixed everything' and she felt guilty that her daughter 'had been so unwell'. She was also angry. 'I'm angry at the NHS,' she told me. 'From their flawed procedures around mental health, the lack of support when Angie needed it and why there were no provisions for treatment on a Sunday. Angie's death was all so avoidable.'

'I should have been stronger,' she continued. 'I should have made her move back home. I should have made her want to find a solution. I should have changed her school years ago. I should have brought her up in a different area. I shouldn't have split from her father when she was younger. I shouldn't have worked so much. I should have stopped her from smoking dope.'

In voicing these regrets, Natasha was mixing up things that she could control, things only Angie could control and many 'what ifs?'. In my view, 'what ifs' amount to self-sabotage. To continually pore over the historic detail that might or might not have changed outcomes is something we can beat ourselves with repeatedly. Beat yourself if you like, but will it change anything to do so?

I asked Natasha why she felt so guilty when many of her reasons for doing so either belonged to her daughter or were hypothetical. How, I asked, did she think she could have been stronger? 'I should have made her see.' How do you make someone see something? Again, this was out of Natasha's control. I pressed her a little harder: 'What exactly can you give me that indicates you are in some way to blame for her death or events leading up to her death?'

To condense a longer coaching process that took place, now she had differentiated what she controlled from what she didn't, and had seen that the what if's were a way of her hurting herself, she couldn't think of a single thing that she had actually done to contribute directly to the outcome. Natasha concluded by stating, 'I couldn't have done any more than I did to help my daughter.'

We spoke about the day Angie killed herself. She had called Natasha in the morning and said she was having a bad day. Natasha told her she was going to get dressed and get over to her as soon as she could, which she did. They went to A & E together but Angie felt the receptionist was being rude and unhelpful, so she left without receiving any help. Back home Angie had a warm bath, which, unusually, didn't calm her down. Some hours later, as her behaviour became increasingly concerning, Angie called the crisis team. However, because it was a Sunday there was no way of admitting her. Later still, in a last-ditch attempt at getting help from the professionals she called the paramedics so they could admit her to psychiatric care.

Because of NHS mental health rules of admission, Natasha couldn't be with Angie when the paramedics arrived or they would just leave. Five minutes before their anticipated arrival Natasha left so Angie would get the outcome she had been attempting to get all day and be safely in the hands of the NHS.

When the paramedics arrived they waited outside for twenty minutes (Natasha has no explanation as to why they waited that long) before entering and when they rang the bell there was no answer. After they forced their way in they found Angie dead. Natasha insists that Angie was trying to ensure they would help her and not leave her there by simulating an act of harm. (I didn't want to press Natasha for the exact details of her death; it didn't feel appropriate to me at the time.)

'What more could you have done, Natasha?' I asked. 'Nothing,' she whispered, fighting back the tears.

A parent with a healthy child will feel some degree of guilt if their child has an accident or worse, dies, as we have an animalistic urge to protect our children. But in Natasha's case, she did the absolute best she could for Angie on the day of her death, leaving her precisely *so* she could get the help she needed. Natasha came round to accepting that she had done everything on the day and that she wasn't to blame for the circumstances of Angie's death, and, as difficult as it was for her to admit this to herself, she was able to see that Angie was responsible for her own death.

As a mother, Natasha had not wanted anyone to think badly of Angie, to think that she was responsible for her own death, and so, as many parents would, she had taken on full responsibility, telling herself that she had practically killed her own daughter, that Angie was blameless and that if she, Natasha, had lived the life of the what ifs, Angie would still be alive, possibly.

Now that she was able to see more clearly that Angie was responsible for her death, she felt better able to dismantle the brick wall that was stopping her from grieving safely. Only time would tell, and while nothing would take her grief away, now that she no longer needed to punish herself, she might, the next morning, be able to get out of bed or to think about going back to her boot camp and begin to manage her grief.

Is motivation conditional?

Motivation after a loss can be hard to find. You may not have the same issues of supposed responsibility as Natasha, but the death of a friend or family member may have you asking questions of life that didn't previously exist in your mind: What's the point? Why bother? It's completely Natashal to lose motivation for a period of time when you feel so flat after the bad news, but as you talk, express and understand your grief, your motivation for life or the aspects that were lost can return.

Following Natasha's example, her motivation returned because she gave it permission to. Are you allowing your life to continue or are you putting it on hold until you feel better? Have you downed tools? Are you waiting for someone to snap you out of it? Many of us could be containing our motivation to move forwards because we fear we may be judged by others around us for not reacting to loss in the right way or being seen to have recovered too quickly.

When is loss a motivating factor?

Michelle told me that the loss of her father fuelled her aspirations to finish her degree with a flourish: 'When I heard my dad's condition was terminal I wanted to defer my uni place but I didn't, and when he died it gave me the motivation to carry on, do well in my degree and make him proud. My results that year were surprisingly my best over the whole four years. I eventually passed with a 2:1 and know he was there in spirit at my graduation.'

This is a great example of how we can dedicate something meaningful to the memory of the person we have lost by doing something 'for them' or by putting in levels of effort that had not previously existed in an attempt to do something that would make them proud. It will differ from one person to another, though – someone else would have quit the degree feeling far too sad to think about furthering their education.

Theresa told me about a self-imposed rule that she had adopted after the death of her mother: 'When I lost my mum I wouldn't eat because I felt guilty because she couldn't. I lost my zest for life and just existed. After a period of time I realised how precious life is and now I live it to the fullest. If I want a tattoo I get it, if I want a holiday I go. I no longer care what people think; I live my life for me and my gorgeous mum.'

A period of time when your motivation leaves you is common and understandable. Theresa came to the golden conclusion that the most respectful thing you can take from the death of someone close is to live your life enough for the both of you. This is a powerful catalyst for levels of motivation not experienced by the individual before, but at what point can the death be given a constructive use? When does the switch flick from lacking motivation to having clarity and feeling purposeful?

Theresa told me about the moment she agreed life had to change, her switch-flicking moment:

'At the time I was in a nine-year relationship and I didn't realise how unhealthy it was until I lost my mum. Then one day I walked in my house and realised nothing was ever going to hurt me as much as it did losing my mum and I ended the relationship there and then. It was from that day I started to live, not just exist.'

So death can deliver the most incredible amount of insight and perspective, and if you're fortunate enough to be able to take the positives out of a negative end to a valuable life then that can give you the impetus to make big changes. Or you might be like Cheryl, making a very different agreement: 'I've lost all motivation. The only get-up I have is all for my daughter. If it's for me it takes weeks to prepare. I can't do anything at the last minute; I would have a panic attack. I have a three-year old who takes a lot of effort to get her out the door and it drains me, but I do it. She comes first . . . Before my dad died I worked full-time, cared for him and was a single parent too. Now I simply parent.'

You can tell by Cheryl's limiting statement about her ability to cope if anything were to happen last minute that her motivation is at a low, but then if we look closer you can see that her motivation is conditional: she finds the motivation to parent her daughter, but doesn't allocate any of that effort when it comes to herself.

Motivation can therefore be subject to the rules we impose following a loss – my daughter's life deserves to be cared for but mine does not. It really strikes me that motivation levels are dependent on the agreements we make with the absence of the person we've lost. Something about Cheryl's loss demotivated her to live, as though she didn't want to face life if it was without her dad, I'd love to know what she feels she would do if her daughter hadn't been born – what would her life's purpose be then?

Motivation seems to be a decision made by the individual. I heard another perspective from Martin: 'I used to be heavily career motivated, but that feels less important. I guess I have changed from live to work, to work to live. For the first couple of years after my wife's death my motivation was largely low. Now it is generally improving as I try to achieve things in my personal life, because I felt Jayne was taken young and it would be an insult not to make the most of my life. I have a bucket list; I am actively working on some of those things this year, such as learning the piano and to achieve a Guinness world record. These are long-term and take dedication, and my motivation is increasing all the time. These were always pipe dreams for me, but now I am actively pursuing them.'

When I asked Martin what the light bulb moment was for him he replied, 'I'd love to say some big dramatic event occurred but it didn't. It was months of wrestling with the questions "Why are we here?" and "What makes me happy?" – even "How do I make my kids happy?" The answer to that last question was key, that my kids had lost one parent and me feeling lost and demotivated about EVERYTHING was like them losing both parents, but I could do something about that. I could try to find something that enthused me about life. I had several false starts at fitness, piano, and anything that could get me motivated about life, but I think I am largely there now. Regaining motivation through grief is a rollercoaster and even yesterday I had a what's-the-point-in anything moment. But today I'm back and motivated again. Eventually dogged persistence has paid off.'

Finding your motivation to live is the biggest impact a loss can create, but it can also affect specific areas of a person's life, like their ability to eat and their ability to keep fit, as Moira once told me. 'After being super fit doing half a dozen-odd fitness classes each week, biking, walking, etc., when I found out my mum was terminally ill I lost all motivation to keep fit, I did nothing much. After Mum died I drank quite a bit and when I finally went back to work three months later I threw myself into work as it really helped, because I loved it and the people, but I still couldn't get motivated back into my exercise regime. I had life coaching with you, Jeff, and finally after a few sessions I found it again. Now I'm weight training three times a week with my personal trainer, walking and biking, and feel so much better. It was a long road. Mum died in January 2014 and it has only been since November last year I have fully got back to my routine.'

So in the wake of a death, life for those who that remain can take on new meaning, but it can take a while. It is almost certainly dependent upon your agreements with yourself: 'Life can't be the same because they are no longer here' or 'I'm going to achieve that goal because it's what my mum would have wanted me to do.' The perspective we hopefully gain from the death decides if we have learned anything about life, generally and personally.

The perspective I wish most for my children is that they use their loss as a catalyst for great things, dedicating achievements to their mum, creating additional layers of meaning to their actions. Loss can be a powerful motivating force or it can be the reason to stop caring, to do the minimum, to falter – but only if we allow it to be.

23

Before You Start Telling Everyone You Are Fine, Read This

My friend John told me how he had kept his fears, concerns and problems to himself, because he didn't want to pass them on to his partner Nikki, as she had a history of anxiety. Out of love for her, he felt that by not sharing his struggles this somehow protected her from the threat of 'catching' his anxiety and distress. He had worked for her family for fifteen years and he was overworked and underpaid, and he felt trapped and wanted a way out.

He felt he couldn't say anything directly to her family because they would potentially give Nikki hell and he didn't want to put her in that situation. So he just did what so many of us do. He kept going. Kept suppressing. Kept hoping. But nothing improved. He was in prison.

But it was a prison with an unlocked door and he was free to walk out at any point. He didn't, wouldn't, couldn't – for his wife's sake.

Communication is very often underestimated. Like John, we assume it'll make things worse to share something negative so we keep it to ourselves. It is possible that Nikki's anxiety was affected more by not knowing what her husband was dealing with: she could see that his stress levels were high, and she might have thought this was due to him worrying about her. All this guessing and assuming, because there was so little talking going on about what the underlying issues actually were. Until these two learned to talk without fear of repercussions, trusting in their ability to make things work, there was only ever going to be one result . . . more of the same.

John and Nikki are not part of a bereaved family. So what's the relevance, you ask?

In grief we make a very common mistake. Although this example does not revolve around bereavement it typifies this common mistake that makes our grief harder. Many of us would rather say 'I'm fine' when we are anything but. Are we trying to kid ourselves? Are we averse to receiving sympathy? Or are we just being 'traditional' in our approach and keeping our grief to ourselves?

The problem with saying 'I'm OK' repeatedly is that you don't help yourself. You don't allow yourself to get the support you need at a time of loss. You also don't allow the people around you, who are desperate to support you, the opportunity to feel like they are contributing to your care. If you *really* don't want any help – though few of us are in that category – that's one thing. But to need help and turn it away – why? Are we punishing ourselves? What for? Is there a rule that states that we have to do this the hard way?

This, in my view, is grief's version of self-sabotage and it usually stems from things way before grief took hold, patterns of behaviour we learned as children, from feelings of unimportance to 'not being worth it' and as a result, when it comes to grieving, we tell ourselves 'our feelings are not important', so we don't trouble others with the perceived triviality of such weaknesses. Why should we inconvenience people? They will think less of us if we bring them down with us.

It's here that a triangular effect completes itself. Like John, you may think your feelings are secondary to a greater risk, but in denying your supporting cast the opportunity to actually support you, this creates more stress for those you mean to protect, because they have to watch you suffer in silence while you deal with something badly, on your own.

The end product is that you have created a bigger problem by avoiding the one that you were dealing badly with in the first place – the complete opposite to what you aimed to achieve. It is not protecting them – quite the opposite! It just requires the courage to communicate.

When John and Nikki came to see me for some coaching, I asked Nikki if she would rather John leave his job and be without all of that stress and unhappiness while she dealt with the assumed comments of her family, or if she would prefer not to have to deal with their comments and criticisms but John would continue to spend his working life miserable, trapped and laden with stress.

The answer was completely obvious to Nikki. John's mental health came first and she didn't want her assumption of what might happen to come before something that was clearly taking its toll on her husband's health. John set a date to hand in his notice and a huge weight had been lifted as Nikki's approval gave him permission to take a very bold step, one that would benefit the family significantly even though there was a financial risk for them in doing so.

John may have felt as if he had been protecting Nikki, but by claiming to always be fine and choosing to suffer in silence he was actually living a lie. And he thought he was safe in that lie, that in avoiding the subject of his stress no one else would notice. But what he failed to see was that Nikki had to join him in that lie. She wasn't stupid or blind to her husband's stress but his denial affected her and in order to collude with him, she couldn't talk about certain things. By not talking about it, John was encouraging his family to be complicit in his stress and unhappiness. No matter how good his intentions were, the effects were damaging. Relating this to grief, if we don't communicate our woes we create a vacuum of negative effects that impact on those around us, the exact people we were 'helping' by not communicating with in the first place.

I've really learned of late how liberating and important it is to just say how you feel. I mean, we're worth that, right? There's you going through all of this grief and it's the hardest thing to tackle in your lifetime, so don't make it harder for yourself. Share, express, moan, shout! Especially when it's ugly. The uglier the better – you know why?

Because it's real. The truth. Reality.

I've watched too many people waste years and years of their life creating and sustaining a lie, and it's so sad to see others around them actually start to believe the lie too. The most satisfaction I get as a coach is when I can bring someone back in line with their reality, helping people back on their original path, shattering unhelpful, life-limiting lies as we go.

John was trapped not by his employers and not by Nikki's anxiety, but by his own choice to withhold and the false justifications for why he should sustain that decision. In your grief, don't create a lie based on avoidance of the facts. Don't sign yourself up to a long period, if not an entire lifetime, of living a diluted version of your life, a mere fraction of yourself. Confront bravely the weakness, sadness and suffering that you feel, knowing that it is temporary and something you will be able to manage.

Losing someone you love doesn't have to mean losing yourself. That part of grief is a choice you make. The greatest love you can ever show is to envelop the love and memories of that person within yourself to carry on the journey for the rest of your life.

Personally I have spent many years feeling as though I was a great communicator, but this was really brought into question recently when a relationship issue was understood to have existed for eighteen months, without my saying what needed to be said.

We can communicate brilliantly professionally but not apply that at home, and for what reason?

When you feel that barrier is up, does it stop you expressing what is behind it? Mine did. Sometimes we would rather blame others, point a finger in accusation instead of asking ourselves: 'What could I improve?' Or 'What am I doing to make the situation better?

Without communication, grief is condemned to silence, an internalisation of words and feelings that must be articulated or they will build and fester, creating harmful physical and mental repercussions. Be kind to yourself by being honest with others. Strive for a sense of reality, even if it hurts.

24

The Biggest Mistakes I've Made with my Children's Grief and the Things I Would Change . . .

I have looked after my children alone for eight years since Jade died in March 2009. They are turning into fine young gentlemen and they are a credit to themselves, their mother and me. They don't always get it right and neither do I. I have come to accept that it would be impossible for me to have done any of this without making mistakes, but I have always drawn comfort from the fact that there is no such thing as failure, just information that you can use to get it right next time.

There is a lot of trial and error in parenting generally and you have a few extra layers to contend with when you're bringing up bereaved children. Writing this book has given me so many ideas and access to so many inspirational bereaved parents that I have learned from, I'd be a fool not to apply these lessons to my own parenting.

I have a sense that the rest of the boys' childhood is going to flash by now that they've reached the ages of 12 and 14. I feel like I have much to do for their grief management before I see them walk out of my door and into their adult life.

It's good for all of us to review our performance in any respect, so why would we not do this as the guardians of bereaved children? I hope that by looking back honestly over the last eight years I can help you avoid the same mistakes but also motivate you to look at your own habits objectively and question what you might do differently.

1. I tried to please too much.

I think it's natural to feel sorry for our bereaved children and in doing so we may try to go a little further out of our way for them in order to make them happy. I allowed Bobby to go to a school in Brighton that Jade would have been anti and I justified it because it was close to our house and it was a performance academy and he was into performing. Subsequently he was given a very difficult time by one or two of his supposed new 'friends', he didn't participate in any of the school's drama activities and he was deeply unhappy during that year. We moved back to Essex unsettled as a result; another year and I feared I'd be messing up his GCSEs, so I played it safe, but it was all a bit too kamikaze.

In trying to give him what he wanted I went against my better judgment and while I enjoyed our year by the sea immensely for many other reasons, it was the wrong decision at the wrong stage in his education.

There are positives to be had from it. He has gone back to his original school and is doing very well for having learned a valuable lesson about the importance of being around people who accept and love you. Freddy was going to start Year 7 and move to a new school anyway, so the effects on him were limited.

I learned that doing what's for the best is far more important than trying to please by giving them what they want. I'm sure that when they're adults they'll thank me for these decisions even if it's hard to say no to a child who has experienced something so traumatic that you just want to say yes.

2. I took things personally.

I was warned that their grief would come out in anger and frustration and that it would most often land in my direction. I thought I was ready for that, and it was easier when they were little because their idea of anger was less verbal and more behavioural.

When they reached an age when they were able to release a missile launcher in the form of an articulate attack such as: 'I wish it was you that was dead', there's not a lot that can save you from being utterly knocked out by the ferocity of the blow.

Sometimes I fought back by joining them on their level, but even if I shouted or sent them to their room I regret every single time I took it personally, because every time I did that it stopped me from giving them what they needed from me in that moment.

What I wished I had always done, something I had achieved from time to time, was to consistently take everything they threw at me on the chin, give them some space to let the rage of grief wash over them and then go back to them to discuss their feelings when they had calmed down.

None of it was ever really to hurt me. It was to show me how hurt they were. Maybe this is the toughest thing I've had to face. It was always worse when it was done publicly in front of others. But this is what I signed up to. It's my responsibility as a father of bereaved children to catch their pain and recycle it into something constructive.

I'm better at that now. I think maturity plays a big part, and the gradual letting go of my ego has left more room for accepting that this is grief and this is parenting and it's not meant to always be a success, it's not always meant to be attractive, but it is always meant to have a purpose. For me, that purpose is to provide them with a punch bag when they need it and the reassuring words to make them feel listened to and acknowledged for whatever their outburst represents.

3. I stopped having fun.

How old do you feel when you try to explain to your children that once upon a time you were loads of fun? The truth is that six months before Jade died I had to get very real and I had to grow up a few extra notches overnight. I was 29, the boys moved in permanently and I immediately sacrificed the fun, replacing it with a need to cope and a desire to be on top of everything: the house, the boys' grief, my work, my relationship.

You get into new habits very quickly after a loss. These habits are valid and helpful but there comes a point when you have used them to achieve an objective that no longer applies. I was on top of things, I was absolutely coping, but I forgot to review the objective. I forgot to relax knowing that I'd answered many of my initial questions about how life was going to be, and so for a good seven years I was still treating the situation as I had in the first twelve months, and while forgivable, that was just unnecessary.

Writing this book has compounded my desire to make things far more fun. It doesn't mean the rules around what's expected of them both have to go; in fact fun and behaviour are not linked in the way we sometimes expect. When you're busy trying to cope you might think that fun with two siblings close in age leads to rivalry and bad behaviour, but the reality is if they feel like they're getting enough of the side of you that they want and enjoy, they are likely to be more content as a result.

I'm bringing back the wrestling on the living room carpet, bringing back the board games after dinner and making time for activities together that we have always enjoyed, except for the fact that I will be truly present in every moment with them instead of feeling like I am just facilitating their enjoyment.

4. I let some of my identity slip.
This has much to do with the rules I placed on myself in those six months before Jade's death. I immediately stopped going out,

playing golf, going on dates with a girl I was seeing at the time. Everything was about the boys. It had to be. But then I failed to ease up; I didn't recognise the point when it would have been acceptable for me to think of myself a little more.

I saw my new level of responsibility as being unattractive to some of my friends so I distanced myself. I wasn't getting involved any more. Instead of slowing it down a bit but still maintaining relationships, I took myself off completely, so I lost friends as a result, which is an unfortunate regret.

They always say that in parenting you should keep a sense of who you were before your children came along and not just completely morph into Mum or Dad, but I failed to keep a balance. I'm so grateful to the friends who have stuck with me and accepted that they wouldn't see or hear from me for long periods of time.

One of my best friends JJ once said: 'If it's not in front of you, you don't see it.' Never have more accurate words been spoken of me. I was fiercely focused on getting these two boys through childhood as relatively unscathed as I could manage.

Now as the children grow older and need or want me less due to their own social arrangements, it has given me the permission to reintroduce myself into some friendships. It has also given me the right to think of myself a little more, hence the redirecting of my career towards projects that I truly care about and derive great satisfaction from, such as coaching, writing this book and getting into football broadcasting.

It's so easy to lose sight of yourself. That said, I'm finding it's really easy to put myself back in view as long as I give myself the right permission and ask the right questions. Who am I and what do I want from life? Like everyone else, my two will grow up and go and do their own thing, and I don't want to feel in that moment that I'm a relative stranger to the person I once was before responsibility took over.

5. I didn't help them remember as much as I could.

How I'd love to say that we visited the grave every week or met up with one of Mummy's friends regularly so they could chat about their memories. The truth is, while we have spoken about Mummy a lot, I fear I didn't do enough in the earlier years to encapsulate their memories into pictures and letters that would freeze them for use later on in life.

I'm really happy that they can always talk about Mum, because remembering positively indicates that they're in a good place, but I think it's inherent within all of us parents to look back and see the things we could have done rather than the things we did.

What I'm looking to change now is the amount of time they spend with people who they would associate with their mum – people who have incredible memories of her that they can pass on to the boys. I also want to retrace many of their footsteps shared together. The boys often talk about a favourite holiday to Tobago with Mummy where she put out a fire and saved the day. I'm going to take them there. I also feel the time is nearly right for me to read their mum's book to them.

There are so many things we can all do to help our children remember. You just have to decide what's right at the time.

6. I moved too much.

This doesn't cause me as much angst as other areas but I'd like to have been a little more certain and measured about where we were going to live. I understand things change and I don't regret the Brighton move because it was such a cool place to live; I just had to learn the hard way that the most important thing is that your bereaved children are around other kids who love and accept them.

For your child to feel comfortable in where they live and who they live around provides the building blocks of their adult life.

Who are they going to have their first drink with? Who will they first go to a nightclub with? These are easier to answer if you've settled in one particular area but not so straightforward if you haven't.

I'm lucky that both the children have lots of good friends, but that wasn't the case for Bobby so much when we moved to Brighton. I took it for granted that they would both just fit in effortlessly, but at the age of 13 can anything of a social nature be taken for granted?

We've just bought a house in the area where all of their friends live and I'm now resolved that for the rest of their childhood, barring any arrival of a vast number of new children, this is the house that we will stay in. My anchor is firmly down, that is until they move out and no longer depend on me, and then I'll see where the wind takes me.

7. I cut too much slack.

I don't know if this is me or typical of all single parents, but I find myself on the softer side of some things that really require a tougher stance. I understand now more than ever that they are going to be men soon and I'll have needed to have ensured that they are prepared for real life, because that's my job, right?

I have always known that consistency is the key for kids; to know their boundaries and limits is to feel safe, something bereaved children especially need. So why is it that every now and again I'll go through a phase of doing too much for them and letting them slack off slightly, and then when they aren't treating their bedrooms very well and leaving things lying around that should be put away I get upset with them when it's me who let this happen?

Bobby is far more likely to be let off with something and I have no idea why. I find it much harder with him. Sometimes it's because we are similar so we clash more. Sometimes I think it's because he turns into his mum, and when that happens you really don't want to be on the wrong side of him. Mainly it's because he offers more resistance, which obviously requires more effort on my part to enforce whatever rule has been broken.

However, the fact that they have to do this all for themselves soon is really making me more insistent on their standards of behaviour and the stuff around the home, and they are much better for it. I'd like to have remained more consistent over the past eight years but then I think it's normal to blow hot and cold, especially when it's just you playing good cop, bad cop and every-thing-in-between cop.

8. I didn't make a scrapbook or a memory jar!

I can and will put this right very soon. I've been meaning to do it for ages. We certainly have the pictures of their mum to do it – one advantage of your mum being in the magazines a lot. I want them both to be able to go to the scrapbook when they're feeling sad and missing her.

I can be harsh on myself and say that is eight years of grieving that this book could have helped with, but I can also say they have a lifetime of enjoying this scrapbook ahead of them. Every time we realise there's something we haven't done for our children it's an opportunity to put it right and make things better. Writing this made me think how much fun it would be for the three of us to go through everything and do this!

To create the memory jar I'm going to ask lots of Jade's friends to send me memories that I can print out and put in a big bottle. I'll also have a party in the summer so people can come and write some-thing and pop it in. Sometimes we wonder whether our kids are thinking about their loss enough; these little projects give them the chance to show you without the need for a verbal clue because every time they go to the jar or the book, it means they've got that loved one on their mind.

9. I didn't put them in contact with other bereaved children enough.

Grief Encounter, the charity that has helped us so much, run regular events and weekend activities that give bereaved families the chance to be with one another, supporting and learning from each other as they go. When I look back I only took the boys to a handful of those occasions and they could have made so many friends of similar ages if we had attended more.

In future we will go more often. Maybe we will start something up in our local community reaching out to other bereaved children who live around us. Now the children are older I can see them enjoying the responsibility of looking after the younger children who are maybe less used to their new reality. Let's face it, it's a club no child wants to be a part of, but how rewarding will that be for the boys if they are able to use their experiences to benefit others?

Some of us will avoid looking back at past mistakes, but I'm happy to look at myself and hold my hands up to anything I may wish I'd done differently, so I've found writing this to be a helpful exercise. The clues as to which direction our paths should point in the future often lie in the regrets we hold on to from those days when the hindsight we have now wasn't available.

They say there is no such thing as a mistake, just data that we can use to help us generate a different outcome at the next attempt. I can't go back and perfect the past, but I'll take what was great about the last eight years and build on it. Every day is a chance to change something, to try a new approach, to find new ways to help the boys express their grief.

I'm always trying to learn and improve, overcome and empower. I know with the rate these boys are growing that their childhood will be gone in a flash and I'll be left to answer the question, did I do enough? I fear the answer being no, and I'll do anything to avoid that, which drives me on to be everything I can.

25

Young People and Bereavement

Some troubling facts and observations

1. In the UK, 1 in 29 children under the age of 16 will experience the death of a parent or sibling. – Grief Encounter UK
2. Bereavement is probably one of the hardest things to manage in life, yet while we teach our children about life, we don't usually teach them about death.
3. When a bereavement occurs, children can be propelled into adulthood, some without the actual skills to cope.
4. Children are expected to go back to school, college, their social activities and just 'get on with it'.
5. No government statistics are kept about bereaved children, although studies show that one third of bereaved children will experience emotional, physical and social difficulties following bereavement both in the short and long term.
6. Studies show that early intervention and long-term support will avoid future problems, yet there is little or no service provision for bereaved children in most parts of the country.
7. Children and young people will be emotionally and psychologically damaged following the death of a parent or sibling, yet our society continues to ignore this impact.

A bereaved young person's journey

Imagine reading at your desk right now, having just had your heart broken. Could you concentrate? Could you absorb knowledge when all you can think of is what is happening at home? Could you take on information about the outside world when all you can think about is the turmoil in your inner world? What are you to do with these feelings? You have not been taught how to manage these confusions.

Tears well up. Everybody crowds around you at break but all you want to do is cry. You can't do that as it's embarrassing and you may never stop. By next week they will forget to ask and how can anyone understand anyway?

You keep lots inside at home for fear of upsetting anyone. There have been enough tears. You just want to watch television in peace. Most of the stuff inside your head is too difficult to explain anyway. Things do get easier, but months on and little things can still really upset you.

Everyone else's life is the same, but yours has changed forever. It's not fair, you have done nothing wrong, yet the rest of the world is filled with happy families. You have become closer to your family, and with time, there's a sense of having weathered the storm. You wish it had never happened but you will always have a story to tell and a feeling of resilience.

Some of these behaviours are difficult to understand and manage, both for the young person and their family. At school, they really only learn about the outside world and very little about their inside world. At home, most of us are muddling our way through, but focusing on our emotional world can help change this.

Our bereaved young person's biggest fears

1. What if it happens again?
2. Who am I?
3. Being abandoned.
4. Social relationships.
5. Am I going to die?
6. Bullying – their obvious vulnerability identifiable to those looking for weakness.

Young people absolutely need:

1. Permission to grieve.
2. To know that grief will not be over in a day, week or month.
3. Those around them to be emotionally available.
4. To know they can survive the death of a parent or sibling.

Some small, daring but undeniable positives

1. To know that if you can survive the loss of a parent, it means you can survive pretty much anything.
2. Children are incredibly resilient.
3. To accept the privilege of life can make each day more valuable.

We cannot change what has happened, only the way we think and feel about those changes.

Who tells them about someone's impending or actual death?

Naturally, it may be helpful if this can be considered beforehand. This story will stay with them forever but can also be revisited later. Consider who your young person might like to hear it from best.

What do you tell them?

Be as honest as possible, accounting for factors such as age, family beliefs and culture. Most importantly, try to ensure you have time for the child to express their feelings and to ask questions.

When to tell them?

Young people who are involved in discussions fare better in the long term than those where family secrets overtake the truth. The earlier the better, as long as there are people to take care of the children once they know.

Where?

In a safe place with no distraction. Remember, they will remember this moment forever.

Children might also want to know . . .

The details of the illness and how the body has broken down.

The details of what has happened or will happen to the body with regards to the funeral or cremation.

Their involvement in the death rituals.

That life has left the dead person's body, separating the spiritual from the physical being.

For younger children that the dead person can no longer hear, see, think, feel and breathe.

That we really do not know what happens afterwards, although people may differ according to their religious beliefs. If no beliefs exist beforehand it can sometimes be an experience of death that helps us form them.

Summary

Grief is the deepest sadness anyone can feel.

All feelings are normal and OK. What matters is what you do with them.

Remember, they need to be told; they need to understand the reality of death to be able to mourn.

Young people may need permission to mourn.

The adults need to bear the awfulness.

The young people will be affected by the loss.

It is your adult instinct to protect your child; over-protectiveness may not serve them so well in the long term. Studies have shown that children who were involved in discussions about death had lower levels of anxiety.

Use active listening skills, which means to give the child your eyes and ears while having the conversation. Go down to their eye level so you are in complete rapport.

If we don't talk about death with our children,
where do you think they will pick things up from?

Talking about death in society today is similar to talk of a sexual nature in Victorian times – for adults only. Young people can have many fears and anxieties: that it may happen to them, or that it could happen to someone they care about.

Most people die in hospitals today. What do you think a bereaved child thinks about their cousin going to hospital for an X-ray? What attachments do you think it might trigger? What ultimately does hospital mean to them?

What do they take in about death from the news? Especially now, when even the daily news shows dead bodies, not to mention all of the social media access. Is school always a safe place? Some of the things we see on the news would suggest otherwise.

What do they think about nuclear power and global warming? How safe do they feel being a part of a modern civilisation that has to deal with the daily threat of terrorism, missile launches, icebergs melting, species being made extinct – all things they could see on the news or on the internet any day of the week. What does this do to their sense of belonging in a world that they might believe is falling apart? What do they imagine their future to be like?

What is the content of some of the computer games they play or hear about others playing? How does this affect a bereaved child?

What does school teach them about death?

What does life mean to them?

What do they think happens to us in the afterlife and what happens if this is contradicted by someone else's belief?

What are you as an adult teaching them about death?

Bereaved young people may become:

- Anxious
- Increasingly narcissistic
- Low in self-esteem
- Hopeless
- Distant
- More adult

- Rejecting of moral values
- Apparently untouched
- Inhibited in their learning at school
- More worried about their health
- Depressed
- Reliant on pain relief
- Happier
- Confused
- More aware of death and the fragility of life
- Less focused
- Fragmented
- More resilient
- Less curious and trusting
- Disturbed in their behaviour, for example, not wanting to go to school, fear of being bullied, stealing

When something bad happens, young people often:

- Avoid feelings
- Push their feelings away
- Hide their feelings
- Disguise their feelings
- Deny their feelings
- Cover their feelings

It may be that their feelings manifest somehow in different reactions. It may be that underneath some of these feelings are deep fears of abandonment and rejection. Usually there is a very scared and sad person. How can children cope? Usually, it is only when they have their feelings heard, acknowledged and understood by someone else that these feelings can be released and relieved.

Ten things you might encourage your young person to do when they are grieving

1. Recognise that they go through different stages. They will feel sad, then they won't believe it, then they will get angry about it, then they will begin to understand and start to feel better.
2. Encourage them to keep a scrapbook for their special person.
3. Help them to write things about their special person, poems or stories, to show other people how great they were.
4. Talk to you, their mum, dad or whoever about their feelings. Encourage them not to keep them to themselves.
5. They can write or draw postcards to tell everyone how they're feeling and what support they need from you.
6. Help them to find a suitable online resource. The internet can be a lonely and dangerous place for a young person, but it's likely that at some point they will go looking, so search for the right websites that fulfil the need for information, conversation and belonging together.
7. Encourage them to find a bereavement mentor if they have one at school to talk to.
8. Help them choose some books about losing someone.
9. Join a support group where other children are in the same position.
10. Suggest that they talk to their teacher about what to do if they are upset during class (time out, quiet place, library?).

And a final thought: try to remember that most people mean well. Help them to try to think of a kind way to answer when people say something they don't agree with or which hurts.

The complexities of language

Have you ever noticed that words can have very different meanings for others than they do for yourself? Imagine each word as a label that carries an agreement that you have made at some point in your past about what something is or means.

If ten people all attached four descriptive words to the meaning of any one word, for example 'strength', no two people would come up with the same four words. This is down to our personal experiences – our point of view is unique and individual.

There are some key words used to describe feelings in grief: bravery, crying, weakness, sadness, anxiety, safety, vulnerability . . . Just how sure are you that when your bereaved child mentions any of these words they actually denote the same specific meaning that you personally attach to the word?

To be as specific as you can, you need to ask good open questions to help the child refine what they mean by the word and then you will have a much greater understanding. My youngest son's key operating word is 'safety'. If I need to reassure him, I can tell him he is safe and he will feel better. What's your child's main requirement and how can you use words that are very important to them in order to make them feel supported and listened to?

Like many parents of a bereaved child, I wish nothing more than to know the innermost thoughts, feelings and fears of my babies. The truth is, I probably know no more than a fifth. My children are approaching the teenage stage, which means I'll be relatively in the dark anyway, and when you consider the fact that a fair amount of their socialising is done online I figure I'm going to have to really work hard to keep my channels of transparent communication with my children open and active. There is still much we parents can do to control their environment, such as how much news they consume, how much time they spend on their phones and how much on the computer playing shoot 'em ups.

Ideally I want to be the first person that they tell if something is troubling them, but I fear that on some occasions I'm likely to be the last. I can pre-empt my children's fears by assuming they exist and reassuring them on each one. I know for sure that they worry about something happening to me. Death will always be a topic for discussion that will help them in the future, because I'm sure of one thing after writing this book: that to know of death is to appreciate the value of life.

Guiding a young person through grief doesn't come with a handbook – well, until now! – but I hope you'll use this collection of useful points to regulate your expectations and avoid some harmful mistakes we the parents often make innocently along the way.

26

Mistakes We Make With Our Younger Children

There are ten main mistakes we make with our younger children in loss that we should all be aware of and try to address.

1. We fail to acknowledge and give recognition to their pain and vulnerability.
If you yourself are in denial, you will be reluctant to talk to your children about their loss, their feelings and their fears. You might even assume that they aren't actually upset. But grief is like electricity; you may not be able to see it, but it is all around you.

You can worry that you might 'hurt' your child by making them discuss their feelings, but the opposite is true. Unless we allow children to express their distress and confusion, these feelings will build inside them.

I regularly talk about Jade with the boys. Sometimes when we have a conversation they take on board what I'm saying, and sometimes I'm met with a look that tells me they are thinking and want to keep a thought to themselves. They know it's OK to do whatever they feel like, but equally they know that's it's not healthy to pretend nothing ever happened or that they are 'over it'.

How do we recognise what children are going through? How can you acknowledge and ease their innermost feelings of pain and vulnerability? Saying 'I can't imagine how you are feeling right now, but I'd like you to help me learn' is a start.

2. We don't contain their fears by rebuilding safe spaces.

The home must be a fortress for bereaved children, a place where they can express themselves without judgment. They need to be allowed to make everyday childish mistakes without the fear of criticism, and this should count for the school environment too. For a bereaved child, the world has become unbelievably scary and they need to learn how to trust so that an uncertain life can grow seeds of certainty once more.

Safety is also found in boundaries and consistency. Many parents are unsure how to, or even if they should, tell their bereaved child off. Over the last eight years I have made tons of mistakes, but I have also learned a considerable amount about the needs of a bereaved child, and most importantly, how to detect when grief is playing out and how to handle it differently to a bout of bad behaviour.

The two are fairly impossible to separate because the expression is the same, but I have learned over time to stay consistent in my approach to discipline. Usually when a child has calmed down and you have given them the opportunity to say why they were upset, you'll find out whether it was grief-induced or not, and if so I always make sure they get a cuddle afterwards so that they know it's OK to express their grief. I have always felt that if I denied my children the opportunity to express their anger or frustration it would just grow, or they would take it elsewhere and express it at school. I'd much prefer they did that at home.

The fact they are taking their anger and frustration out on those closest to them is the same as them saying 'I trust you with the worst of me. I feel close enough to share my insecurities with you and I'm comfortable to show you my grief because I know you will make me feel better.' You might never hear it communicated quite so eloquently, but that will always be the underlying message.

I don't ever like to allow my children to use their grief as an excuse for poor behaviour. It worried me that if I allowed them to play up, I would be creating an excuse to get out of taking responsibility for their actions, so that's why, regardless of the catalyst, when they were younger, I would take a toy or game away if there was sheer bad behaviour and made sure the boundaries were always consistently clear, be it about Mummy, hunger, tiredness or a mixture of the three.

3. We fail to give adequate opportunities to grieve and experience these intense emotions over time.

Children cannot be expected to create all of the opportunities to grieve by themselves. We have to help them along with this too; for example, when we visit the grave, release some balloons, or even more regularly, start a conversation with them about their loss.

Children can be given the opportunities to grieve by drawing pictures with you or writing about the person they've lost and I would suggest that anything they produce should be kept safe in order to provide memories when they are older. The question is, how many ways can you help them keep the doors of communication open? When was the last time you gave them an opportunity to talk about their loss?

But how do you get the right balance? Can you talk about their loss too much? Maybe so, and that's why putting a piece of paper and a few colouring pencils in front of them is quite different to saying 'I think we need to talk about your feelings.' The latter feels forced and the former is ultimately just saying let's do some drawing. Keep the right balance between the two.

4. We enable confusion and false hope instead of delivering the reality they need.

When your child has been bereaved, you may find yourself speaking in a sort of protective code, avoiding words like dead or dying, fluffing the situation up by using softer, less specific terms. The best thing we can do for our children is explain death as unashamedly real, as it actually is, because that way our children will know, in no uncertain terms, that what they are experiencing is not a nightmare, but their reality. The sooner they start to adjust to these difficult facts, the sooner they adjust to their new reality. As undesirable as it is, it's the only one they've got.

5. We don't show enough empathy and caring.

To mask our own inability to cope, we might demand unrealistic levels of emotional stability from our children so as not to expose our own fragile state. Imagine how a bereaved child feels, not being understood or feeling like nobody is listening?

To show empathy is to hear them without judging them for how they feel and to care is to give the opportunities for them to express their grief. Build a rapport with them by sitting at their level, facing them square on, making full eye contact with them so they absolutely feel you're taking in every single word they say.

6. We don't address the silence or find their language of grief.

Sometimes a child's silence can be so convenient to our panic that although we are suspicious of it, we naively take it to mean they must be alright. But just because they haven't said anything, doesn't mean they are not communicating.

Children may use different means to express how they feel and it's our job to be listening out for their messages so we can develop those conversations. It's more likely that a younger child will communicate through drawings than use speech to alert you to their emotions. Asking a child if they would like to draw a picture is the equivalent of asking an adult if they'd like to talk about their loss. It's going to generate the same outcome.

Be attuned to your children individually. You can almost guarantee the way they express themselves will differ from one child to the other. My eldest likes to talk and my youngest prefers to express himself through pictures.

7. We fail to understand the loss of identity that comes with the loss of a parent or sibling.

As a 37-year-old adult I concede that through having no relationship with my biological father I have been 'making it up' for most of my adult life for not having that role model or guide.

A bereaved child may feel like they have lost such a big part of themselves, they are no longer sure who or what they are. When so much has changed in such a short space of time, the absence of a key central figure, someone who that child thought of as a role model, a mirror image, the person they were most likely to emulate, can cause great self-doubt and low self-esteem now they suddenly don't have that person to look up to and follow.

Children will have grown used to hearing, 'Oh, you're just like your dad', or 'You and your brother are just like peas in a pod', and while these are harmless comparisons before the event, they can also consign a child to the belief that they are very little without the continued presence of the lost family member.

Maintaining pre-existing memories is vital, but in the denied absence of the yet-to-be-created memories that were cruelly made no longer possible, we have to teach our children about the person they lost in order for that notion of likeness between them to be extended long after death.

Making a scrapbook or photo album can be priceless for a bereaved child, a point of reference that will always be available to them, so they can express and connect in equal measure. That book won't just contain memories of their loved one and who they were, but equally who the child is too.

The process of making the scrapbook is as beneficial as the time spent looking through it. You can allow your child to choose what goes into this book – letters, pictures, scents, school reports – anything that feels like you're connecting with that person. Also, what should be put where and what is written next to it is down to the child, making it something they have put a lot of love and effort into, which only reinforces its value to the child.

8. We stop having fun.

Fun may seem like an insensitive idea when talking about grief, but what are we teaching our children if we are always so serious? There will be moments in your grief when you will laugh and you will feel happy too. Such emotions are far from disrespectful and are deeply necessary, and to be encouraged.

We are our children's shining examples, so if we can find humour we will give them permission to find their own as well. There is no reason why a bereaved child shouldn't smile or be happy about something, whether that relates to the person they've lost or not. Grief has many angles, but forbidding yourself or others to feel joy shouldn't be made to be one of them.

As a bereaved parent, one who is doing the job of two people, it's really easy to cling tightly to the need for order and routine. This desire to verify that we are coping from one day to the next can be the very thing that stops us from loosening up a little and creating opportunities for fun. Grieving is about a balance, and having a moment of laughter with your child is to be encouraged. You have to create lasting memories with them too.

9. We don't help them to remember and reconnect with the dead person; we encourage them to suppress or forget.

Again, if we have a desire to suppress our grief, if we can't talk about the person we have lost and we can't bear to mention their name, we are effectively consigning our children to a wall of silence, which creates a sad and harmful distance between their memories and themselves.

Memories can be forgotten over the years if they are not connected with and relived. They need to be topped up and played over in order to stay accessible and if, as time passes, your children start to *not* remember this will cause an element of distress. Remembering and learning about their deceased parent or sibling is to maintain a vital connection, and those memories will be cherished in later years.

This echoes the need for visual reminders like photos, quotes and even people they associate with the person they lost to appear around the home so you can initiate conversation and encourage your child to open up and share any concerns they might be having.

We should keep the conversation going long after we initially perceive a need for it. We shouldn't just be reacting to visible emotion but should remind ourselves that just because we don't hear or see them being upset it doesn't mean that isn't how they are feeling.

It is fairly reliable to assume that they will be thinking about the person they no longer physically have. In order to encourage others conversing with your child, you can let your friends and family know that when appropriate, your child would like to hear their memories of their parent or sibling too.

There is no limit to the number of associated people that you can ask to contribute to a memory book for the child so that they can read and gain comfort when they're older. You can even arrange a gathering for this specific purpose, to make the deceased person the subject, so stories and memories can be exchanged and a feeling of connection can be restored.

At all times we must ask, do our children know who their parent or sibling was? Are they learning new information about them from those who knew them best? Are we constantly allowing them to ask questions to fill in the gaps of their knowledge that they perceive they have?

10. We don't create a 'new kind of normal'.

A bereaved child's sense of normality will have been blown to bits by their loss. Everything will feel very abnormal and unsafe, so to build a new sense of normality is to enable the family to adjust to the new dimensions of the family home.

The mechanics of the family, the home and those around you will alter. It will need to. When something leaves a gap, a very large one at that, we subconsciously and collectively find ways to adapt to a new kind of normal. This won't be the one you wanted nor the one you asked for, but it is the future and you will need to embrace the subtle changes around you to help your children adapt.

The roles may change slightly, as may eventually the people around you. This process is about them finding out again what is safe and secure and rebuilding that perceived sense of safety. Adjustment plays a huge role and the belief and understanding that it will eventually become a different type of normal, one that becomes acceptable to all, is very important. Safety to a child is everything but you can multiply that substantially when you're talking about a bereaved child.

27

How a School Should Support Your Child

Having spent much time in the company of other parents with bereaved children, I have heard some troubling stories of how schools and individual teachers fail to recognise a bereaved child's needs. One father told me that his eight-year-old daughter was told off for crying as it had been two months since her mother had died; another told me that the teacher was so overcome with compassion for his son that she brought his mother's death up almost every time she saw him, causing him (and his friends) much embarrassment and unwanted attention. As in any case of grief, it's all about getting the tone right and striking the right balance, allowing the bereaved the space to talk if they want to but not forcing it on them.

Going back to school can be incredibly difficult after a loss and there are a number of things a school and individual teachers can do to help:

1. Provide outlets for communication in various forms.
If a child has lost a sibling or parent, they should feel enabled and supported to talk about that loss to a member of staff or to a trusted friend in private, or to a group of other bereaved pupils should this be something the school have actively put together with the permission of the parents of the pupils concerned.

As a parent of two bereaved children I would wholeheartedly endorse the involvement of either child in a group conversation at school, although I know this hasn't yet happened. I know my youngest would jump at the chance and I also fear my eldest would avoid it at all costs, but the conversation is there to be had and it should always be presented as an option. Whether it is taken up or not by the child is another matter.

We as responsible adults can wait for these things to be suggested by others, but I suspect that in most schools, if we ever really want to see something introduced that doesn't currently exist, we should take it upon ourselves to insist that the school support our children by whatever means they can. Schools should be working with organisations like Grief Encounter to gain training and workshops, and to have critical incident bereavement policies and procedures and school bereavement policies and procedures. The future aim should be for every school to have an appointed, paid, committed, professionally trained person responsible for bereavement.

2. Implement strategies for teachers to meet the bereaved child's needs.

Working in a better way with the child and family so the child doesn't have to be absent from school will help the child while at school and therefore improve rates of absenteeism.

For example, the management of work missed should be handled by an allocated person, and planned time be given for the exchange of information. This will reduce a child's worries about falling behind, give them space to process what's happened and help with concentration on their return to school.

Teachers should find a way for a child to communicate their feelings without the child worrying they are drawing unwanted attention to themselves. A useful technique for this is to give the child a signal – a particular pencil, or a surreptitious card that the child can use to communicate their need for some time out of the classroom. The teacher can then use some kind of excuse for the child to leave the classroom, such as, 'Can you go and get something from the staff on reception?', and the child can leave the class without drawing attention to their despair or need to be away from others, to go and speak to the person or teacher whose job it is to give pupils the space they require under such circumstances.

The time out strategy also allows for the ongoing work of the child. Once the dust has settled the bereavement is often forgotten about, yet the classroom can be a minefield of triggers. It could be in a religious education class, when talking about the meaning of life and what happens when you die. Or in an English or drama class, since literature is full of stories about death, killing and returning from the dead. Or more obvious times, such as the approach of Father's Day.

3. Formulate long-term strategies.
There are many charities and organisations such as Grief Encounter that offer schools the chance to provide bereaved pupils with individual counselling, group counselling, critical incident workshops for students and staff in the event of a loss to a student or teacher within the school community, staff training and education workshops about death and grieving.

It's alarming but true that there is absolutely no provision or legislation from the government to suggest that a school must meet the needs of bereaved children. There is simply no acknowledgement that bereaved children are a vulnerable group and that time and money are needed to provide simple steps towards caring, as well as to avoid future problems. Teachers need an awareness and interest, and to be prepared with resources and referral points. They can't just say, 'Please come and see me at any time.' It just doesn't work. At the end of the day, the class teacher is in the front line – they know the young person best – but they still have the class to run and education deadlines to meet.

4. Ensure an awareness of dates and special occasions.

Teachers should be aware of how to handle specific situations when parents are the subject of discussion or an activity. For example, a child who has lost a parent should not be avoided when it comes to writing Happy Mother's or Father's Day cards.

Teachers should ask the child privately if they would like to make the card for their parent or if there is someone else they would like to make the card for instead. My children have made cards for their mum in her absence with great pride and satisfaction. On other occasions they have made cards for their grandmothers or some-times even the mothers of some of their best friends.

Why shouldn't they write a card? It's an expression of their grief, a paying of respect and a beautiful way for them to feel connected to their parent. My boys will always have a mum. While she will no longer be with them physically she will always be their mum and she will therefore always be thought of with flowers and a card on that particular day.

Another longer-term strategy for teachers to help bereaved pupils would be to help to plan for calendar days like Mother's Day and the anniversaries when the loss can be exposed or avoided. The school should know exactly when these days are coming and should make provisions for support around those times so that the child knows they have been acknowledged.

5. Provide reassurance: you're not alone.

Children can feel less isolated by occasionally being in the company of other bereaved children, to form a private group that meets up at each child's discretion a certain number of times each term. They might wish to offer each other the value of their experiences. Maybe there is a child who has just lost a parent who may wish to listen to the thoughts of the child who has been bereaved for eight years. To give a child the opportunity to put their grief to good use by helping someone at the beginning of grief's journey can be particularly transforming.

I'm going to contact Freddy's school, who I know would be receptive to the idea, about my running a workshop with bereaved children in the school, led by Fred. I know he would love to take on that role, to be there for others, to coordinate a group of like-minded individuals, a source of recognition and praise that he desperately needs from school.

6. Take a teamwork approach.
Bereaved children can feel very lonely in the classroom and on the playground, and as parents cannot be with them while they are in that environment, the teachers within the school represent our eyes and ears. They are in a position to be the first to notice a worrying behaviour, then feed it back to a receptive and responsible parent so that there is a partnership that will invariably benefit all parties.

It's our job again as parents to ensure that we have a regular contact at their school who is feeding back to us everything we need to be aware of so we know what to talk to them about at home. We ideally want to work in partnership with the school to ensure our children have a suitable outlet in both environments so their education and social interaction are affected as little as possible during their transition through grief.

I have a great relationship with Freddy's head of year. I respect him for really caring about Freddy's development and I know he has his best interests at heart. I'd say this was one of the better examples of a parent–teacher relationship that you might find. He often delivers me bad news but he is always constructive in his response! I'm developing more of a relationship with Bobby's current head of year, but there is rarely any need for us to talk because Bobby seems very settled at school. I guess your relationship with those eyes and ears at school is only more familiar if there is constant need for communication, and it's fair to say I feel like I'm becoming very well acquainted with Freddy's teacher as there is always so much for us to discuss – good and bad, of course.

7. Know what to say, when and to whom.

Teachers also need to explain to the bereaved child's peer group how their friend may be feeling, both for the child's benefit and for the rest of the class, who will be aware that something bad has happened to their family but not know how to approach it. This can lead to that child being ostracised from certain groups, not because they aren't liked but because children find the situation too uncomfortable to tackle.

Firstly the teacher would need to ask the child if they would like them to say something on their behalf, and with the permission of the child, who might really want the teacher to speak for them on this one, they could then inform the class that the pupil would be happy for them to ask questions or that it is fine to talk normally to them without fear of saying the wrong thing and please don't avoid them because they really need people's friendship to make things easier at school.

Most bereaved children will feel very conscious that the class will be aware that something has happened and most will assume that it is glaringly obvious that what they are feeling on the inside is probably showing on the outside. I can see the opposite effects in both of my children. Freddy would have spoken about his mum, he probably would have shared the information before the teacher had needed to approach him anyway, because that's in his nature, to be open and emotionally honest. Bobby, on the other hand, would have wanted his friends to not know; he would have made himself fairly small in the class and just hoped that it all went under the radar. If I could go back eight years I'd tell his teacher to speak to the class so the option of hiding it wasn't available to him, because I think that he developed that ability to hide his grief in the school setting and I don't consider it to have necessarily helped.

You may feel uncomfortable with acting when your child is reluctant in this way. My instinct was to protect my then six-year-old from facing the discomfort of talking about Mum when he didn't feel ready. It's less about making him talk and more about ensuring that it isn't a kept secret, a subject that nobody should mention.

Teaching butterflies

Let me tell you about Freddy in the past. When he was nine years old his behaviour at school caused some concern among staff, and I was perplexed as to why when he walked through the school gates he played up, whereas at home he absolutely did not. I went in to talk to his teacher, Mrs Haswell, and instead of saying for the hundredth time that he behaved really well for me at home and accusing her of clearly talking about someone else's child at school, I decided to go in as a coach rather than a dad and help guide the conversation towards solution. I encouraged her to point out Freddy's good traits and asked how he could be encouraged further.

Mrs Haswell is one of the most open-minded teachers I'm ever likely to meet and there was a sense of renewed optimism about what she wanted to achieve and how she would go about getting it. The real magic happened halfway through when we were thinking about what sort of child Freddy was beneath the barrier he was hiding behind. In listing what lay behind the persona he adopted in class – joker, a desire to impress his classmates – she accurately named grief as a contender and so we opened up on his loss and what she knew of it.

I discovered that in the two months she had been at the school she had never discussed his mum with him. She had avoided the topic because she hadn't come across this type of challenge in her teaching career and not personally either, so she deemed it risky territory. She didn't want to do or say the wrong thing, which any teacher can be forgiven for thinking, due to the sensitive nature of the subject. Seeing as we were there to find solutions and agreeing grief would be a big part of the cause of his behaviour, she offered to go beyond her apprehension and have a conversation with him that day.

As it happened, later that morning in an RE lesson the subject coincidentally turned to the afterlife, and, without needing any cue, Freddy got up and spoke in front of the whole class about Jade and most poignantly, about how he sees her as a beautiful butterfly. Heart-melting stuff, and Mrs Haswell took this golden opportunity to congratulate Freddy on such a brave show of emotion. At this, something wonderful happened between teacher and pupil and an understanding was born, confirmed later when a loom-band bracelet appeared anonymously on her desk with a note proclaiming her to be the best teacher in the world. And Freddy ended that day, and the next, on Gold for his behaviour.

Mrs Haswell demonstrated how her willingness to lower Freddy's barrier by encouraging him to talk openly about his mum in class made all the difference to him, releasing the grief he was holding inside, and he was a different child almost immediately. She followed up by allowing Freddy to draw and colour in his butterfly, which

was then stuck up in class for all to see, a symbol of the new understanding my son and his teacher had found and, I think, a sign that
Freddy had let Mummy out of his pocket so she could float beautifully around in the environment where he most needed her to be
recognised. Children spend as much time at school as they do at
home. Mum is an open subject in our house but less so at school, so
it's important to have the recognition of a lost parent in that environment, the place he spends over half of his day.

By sheer coincidence, a butterfly landed on my window ledge the
very next morning, seconds after I had opened my eyes. Fred's face
lit up when I told him about my visitor, particularly when I described
its colouring; orange and brown just happened to be the colours he
had used for his butterfly at school. Priceless.

28

Life as a Single Parent After Loss

Not having someone to share the responsibility of bringing up our children, or making decisions, is something that still hits me eight years on. When you lose your partner or the children's other parent there are some things that are going to feel instantly harder in their absence.

Typically, in moments that require a big decision to be made you seek the opinion of your partner, but when there is no other opinion than your own you can feel the weight of each decision in a way that you hadn't before. The realisation that everything rests on your shoulders can be a very lonely place, but you can only ever try your best.

We can consider what the other parent might have wanted if it brings us comfort, but we mustn't give ourselves a hard time if we feel what we have decided may be contrary to the partner's assumed wishes.

The increased importance of maintaining boundaries

There is a forgivable tendency to allow your children to behave in a way that you would not previously have accepted, because you feel that given what they have just experienced they can't be told off for fear of upsetting them further.

The truth is, your child's world has drastically altered. They are in chaos internally and what they are absolutely desperate for (although they'll never verbalise this) is a clear sense of boundaries and the consistency that goes with it. In their new world of uncertainty this is at least one thing that they can feel safe with: that no means no and that you, the surviving parent, are in control.

Realistic expectations of your child's behaviour

While boundaries and consistency are paramount in parenting generally, irrespective of loss, it will help you to consider your expectations for their behaviour. For example, it would be foolish to assume that your child's behaviour won't be affected; a child cannot communicate their feelings verbally as well as an adult can, so they are going to tell you that they feel some pain by acting up.

When they start to misbehave it should be dealt with in the same way you have always dealt with it, but that's your clue to then know exactly what to follow it up with. You can't stop the emotion or the pain manifesting through their behaviour, so instead you must invite it out.

When the surface level issue has been dealt with, give your child the opportunity to talk about their loss and be available to listen intently, draw pictures of their loved one with them and discuss photos. If it leads to an outpouring of emotion, it may not feel like it but it's a good thing! You're not inflicting pain; you're extracting it.

How to help a child grieve

A big mistake we can make (I have made it hundreds of times) is to take something personally. We must remember it is the bereavement talking, but we all too often respond in the same tone, feeling like we are becoming victims of a cruel type of undeserved abuse.

As a surviving parent this is what we signed up to. We are the person they love most, sometimes all they have left, so if they can't take their unimaginable loss out on us, who can they take it out on? I have slowly learned to take it as it's intended – it's the anger and frustration generated by their sad circumstances that attacks and bullies you and may sometimes reduce you to tears. We have to remember where it comes from. They don't even know why they are acting that way; it simply emanates from the pit of their stomach, which is where we hold most of our fears and insecurities.

How to care for yourself while making the children your priority

Beware of being the parent who dedicates themselves so much to their children in their time of need (and far beyond) that you lose sight of who you are. You don't need to be a bereaved parent to fall into this habit, but if you are it certainly gives you far more of an excuse to do so.

The right perspective is this: if you are happy and fulfilled, the children see that as permission to be happy and fulfilled. If you're active and energetic, your children will see this as permission to mirror that behaviour. If you're honest and emotional, you're giving your bereaved child the greatest gift of all, to be allowed to follow your leadership and take that as permission to express their grief honestly and openly.

Be the role model they need, not just living your life but also showing them most importantly that it's OK to cry, to talk, to be sad, but equally, that it's OK to smile.

The importance of support and allowing it in

Lots of people bury their heads in the sand because they can't face seeing anyone as this means they will have to talk, and talking feels like the last thing they want to do in the circumstances. If I hadn't had my support network around me giving me the opportunity to talk about the boys, their progress, the difficulties and the way it was making me feel, I wouldn't have been quite so capable of giving them what they needed.

Make no mistake, you've got one of the hardest tasks ahead of you. It's hard enough being a single parent, let alone when you throw your own grief and the child's additional needs into the mix, but one day, as many parents of older bereaved children have told me, you will get a level of respect from your grown-up children that will elevate your sense of pride and achievement to an untouchable high. One of my clients once described it as 'losing a life and then saving two'.

I personally see my job as getting my boys through their education and childhood with very few things to repair, but with as many tools available to them as possible. Grief gives people layers of qualities such as understanding, the ability to be empathetic, an instinct to detect people's feelings and a greater sense of appreciation for how precious life is. It is my job to make my children fully aware of the skills they have acquired and to use them in a way that brings them comfort and meaning.

Looking after your needs too

You'd think that someone had told most parents of a bereaved child that they almost definitely no longer matter or cannot possibly entertain having some kind of life for themselves. Well, I'm going to break that misconception and share with you that I believe it's the example of you living your life after the loss that gives your children the permission to go and live theirs.

Many parents learn this after a few years of bringing up a bereaved child, but your children are likely to be so advanced in their emotional intelligence as they grow up that they will tailor their social habits around yours, so if you see yourself as a servant to their every need (or use their grief as an excuse to make yourself small) they will suitably reduce their ambitions and expectations of life too in order not to expose you, belittle you or make you feel left behind.

Be the engine in your children's life, not the handbrake.

The most common and again excusable reason for us to shut up shop is because we question our ability to cope. I did it. I shut down my social life almost immediately and sacrificed relationships with dearly missed friends who I was very close to. I was young, but then I'd probably do the same again now.

Coping mechanisms dictate how we react to stress and shock. Of course my kids clearly come before my social life, but if I'm honest I could have balanced things slightly better, and if I had done so, I might not have felt such an outsider. I take responsibility for that; it was a natural response and I'm doing plenty about it now.

Just remember your children will grow and they will become adults sooner than you care to admit. My boys will reach that stage in no time. Each time I look at them they get closer and closer to my height and it's just a matter of time before they overtake me. What will happen when they move out? Will I be lost? Will I know who I am? Thankfully I've got a good enough balance now, but I wouldn't be looking forward to them leaving me if I hadn't.

We must not feel guilty about being happy, active, satisfied and motivated. It's not disrespectful to the person you have lost; it's just respectful of yourself and the life you are still lucky to have. It's a crime that people are taken from us sometimes earlier than any of us plan for, but it's an even bigger crime to stop living while you still have the option.

29

Why We Maintain Contact With Certain People After Loss

After the loss of a partner it may become evident that some family members or friends were closer to them than to you, and over time you may see them drift away. Alternatively, while at first they have been helpful and part of your life following your partner's death, after a while you may decide that they aren't people you want in your life as you move forward.

Maintaining relationships with the people on your partner's side can be important for your children, though, and it is worth looking at the bigger picture and thinking long and hard before dismissing them from your life.

Making the effort to continue a dialogue with someone who wasn't that close to you personally may feel unnatural and in some respects unnecessary, but you may want to consider that they could have memories of your partner that you don't, which might be valuable to your children.

You don't have to have them round for dinner every night, but it is important to assign them a supporting role and establish some boundaries that are acceptable to you both, all the while keeping in mind that every memory could be of great comfort to your children. And maybe even, in time, to you.

Take it from someone who has brought two bereaved children up for the past eight years. You learn to be very grateful for those who could have been forgiven for drifting off but have stuck their head through the door from time to time. If someone loves or even takes an interest in the well-being of your children, then they are good people to have around for your children's benefit, if not for yours.

I recently took a step towards reconciling a contact on behalf of my children that I knew would happen one day, but not until it felt correct to do so. The boys have fond memories of their stepfather, Jack Tweed, who had a three-year relationship with Jade right up until her death.

After Jade died there was a sequence of unfortunate and ill-timed events in Jack's life that gave me cause for concern and it became apparent that he needed time to not just grieve but to let a few other things play out too. After a great deal of consideration, I managed to successfully ban all photographs of the children taken after the loss of their mum from being published, but at this point Jack's life was still of huge interest to the media. So, with the children's stability in mind, I felt it right to cool the relationship until things changed for the better.

Even before Jade's death I had always felt a great empathy for Jack. I had been through some of the struggles he was facing. To have a dramatic relationship with Jade in the full glare of the spotlight with the daily threat of journalists running stories that vilified and scorned him publicly for every mistake he made, or was alleged to have made, was not easy, and I knew exactly what that felt like and what he was going through.

To be the subject of public scrutiny on a regular basis can make you feel insular and self-hating and when you're tackling this in your very early twenties it's unlikely you have the tools to manage the pressure and scrutiny successfully. It has taken me a good few years to make peace with many of the effects my then chosen life-style brought about and I can only assume the same could be said for Jack.

When Jade became ill and was given six months to live, he was there for her and my children. He could have run away from the task but he took responsibility and gave Jade the support and care that she found hugely comforting. Jack married Jade, and in so doing selflessly signed over all rights to any of her estate so that everything would be left to the boys, and he didn't take a single penny for himself.

After a chance meeting with Jack while I was Christmas shopping, eight years after Jade's death, I asked him if he and his family would like to see the boys one Sunday afternoon. I knew for sure that the children would be happy to see him and open the door to memories of their mum, but it had, of course, to be right for Jack.

Fortunately everyone was happy to get together once more and the very next weekend we went to his parents, Mary and Andy's, and we had an enjoyable, happy afternoon that felt very relaxed for the boys. Jack comes from a wonderful family. He has an older sister Laura, who is married to a good friend of mine, and a younger brother Louis, who the boys adore. His mum and dad never showed anything other than love and acceptance to the boys and after that afternoon, I questioned myself for leaving it as long as I had but reassured myself that if everything felt OK for all involved now, there would be plenty of time for everyone to make up for lost time.

Why is it good for the boys to have their stepfather and his family back in their life?

1. A sense of identity
The boys were teleported back to their mother the instant they walked through the Tweeds' front door. Imagine it like a time machine – it was no coincidence that Freddy also called Jade's mum to tell her we were there and spent a good hour talking to her

on the phone. It was like he had travelled back in time and found himself with all the people who were around when he still had his mum.

The boys will never forget where they're from and although they've been with me for the majority of their lives, they'll always remember that this family played a huge part in their early years, so to have a connection with them is always to have a greater under-standing of their history and indeed their lives.

2. Priceless memories

Jack gave the boys some beautiful framed pictures of their mum that they had received as a wedding gift. They will cherish those pictures for the rest of their lives. I only have so many memories of Jade but the Tweeds had years of memories. Sharing them is a two-way thing – no doubt the entire Tweed family carried around their grief for Jade and being able to share memories brought smiles to their faces, and to see the way my boys reacted must have brought them real pleasure.

3. Love and support

Going forward, we may only see them a handful of times a year from now, or it may be more regularly, but regardless, for the chil-dren to know that they have another group of people out there who love and care for them is invaluable to their self-esteem and sense of security. It had been two thirds of their life ago since they had seen Jack and his family, yet within a heartbeat, they felt like family to them again.

4. A sense of belonging

The boys had a stepfather and never really felt like they didn't, even though there had been no contact since Jade's death. I have a stepfather; he isn't in my life but he is still my stepfather. It's not something that can be erased, even if there is little to no communication. To regain that piece of the jigsaw is to have a more complete sense of who they are and where they're from.

5. To give back
Jack's mother had told me that the boys' visit had triggered some unexpected emotion, especially in the week leading up to them coming round. I understood exactly what she meant. Being there took everyone back eight years and revived all the painful and happy memories we had of Jade and the time leading up to her death.

But no one more so than Jack. I could tell that he was going through a whole range of thoughts and feelings during the afternoon and I'm sure these continued long after we left. It so happens I don't just think Jack will be good for the boys at this stage of their childhood; I also believe they will be of benefit to him, and reuniting the children with him would have given Jade immense pleasure, something we all deeply desired.

Over to you . . .

Is there someone that your children would benefit from still having some contact with?

Was the drifting apart for reasons that were relevant then but are no longer valid now?

Did the loss of contact happen because it suited us more at the time than it actually suits the children now?

The memories of a lost relative are indeed a priceless commodity. Memories are like the currency of grief: the more you have, the better off you are. If your memory account is running low, find new lenders. Maybe these lenders are no longer in your life, but you can write to them in order to request a transfer of funds.

We recently visited Jade's grandad, before Christmas, and this was another vivid example of how a meeting took us back to the point of Jade being alive. Unfortunately, Bobby wasn't with us that day, but seeing Freddy made her grandad's day and probably a few more beyond that. Freddy enjoyed doing something that made him feel close to his mum, and also felt that he was doing something for her. I will make sure Bobby is with us next time, and when we head towards Bermondsey again they can both find solace in visiting a relative who meant a tremendous amount to their mum.

Both in this case and with Jack and his family, it was a perfect exchange. Everyone benefitted equally and everyone's management of their personal experience of grief was given some fuel to continue on.

Who will you visit? Who can you contact? Whose day will you make by taking yourself or your children to visit and share memories and being together, united and stronger for it?

30

I'm losing my Mum

I've known Conor ever since I met and became friends with him and his mum at a football camp that my children were attending in East London just over seven years ago. Conor, now 21, was one of the older children then, and my friends who were coaching all commented on what a great kid he was. Certainly my two had taken a shine to him.

What brought about the lasting friendship, though, was that when Dawn, his mother, came to collect Conor, Freddy just stopped and stared at her. She was wearing a headscarf because of her hair loss due to treatment and it would have been the first time he had seen someone wearing one since his mum.

For some fourteen years Conor has grown up knowing his mother has cancer. The majority of his childhood and early adult life has been spent worrying, dreading and expecting a certain day to come, because the last seven have been spent knowing there is apparently nothing the doctors can do to save her.

Dawn and Conor's father separated when Conor was just months old on the grounds of domestic violence and his dad has spent most of Conor's childhood in prison. They no longer have any contact. Conor's older brother Jaimie has since moved out, remaining close to them both, but Dawn's main support is her 80-year-old mum and indeed Conor himself.

The future isn't bright

Conor started by telling me that the hardest part is knowing the outcome. He would maybe rather not have known when he was younger because he has limited himself waiting for that day. In some ways he knows he is better off for his awareness. If she just disappeared one day, that would of course be far worse.

If his mum were healthy today he doesn't feel he would be the person he is, far from it. He would have done more, had more holidays, maybe worked abroad for a season, but not knowing when that day will come has stopped him. I wonder if 'it' has stopped him or if 'he' has stopped himself?

Holding back

His mother's ongoing cancer battle also stopped Conor from going for particular jobs. He went for a job he really wanted in the navy but purposely failed the test so he didn't have to leave his mum, knowing that she was terminal.

Talking about the biggest impact it has had, Conor said pensively that it has had most effect on the way he is around his mum. When they fall out he wants to resolve it straight away because he couldn't live with himself if she died after they'd argued, which in principle isn't necessarily a bad thing.

Building on that a little more, it does stop him from saying what he wants to say and he admits to verbally holding back. He has no idea when that day might be, so upsetting Mum is something he is particularly careful to avoid. The problem is, not communicating your true feelings leads to assumptions being made about how the other person views things, which can create more difficulty than it saves.

On the other hand, Conor says that his mum doesn't share much with him either. She'll only ever tell him anything about appointments and results the night before or at the last moment. She thinks he doesn't listen, according to him, but he takes everything in. He thinks she'll tell everyone else before him.

On reflection he feels she probably only does this because of his reserved reaction. Sometimes he doesn't respond at all, he pretends he hasn't heard, but he takes it all in. He is always very concerned but with his impassive exterior that must be hard for his mum to read. It certainly wouldn't encourage her.

If I'm not expressing it verbally,
where does that emotion go?

I wondered just where Conor has put everything for fourteen years. When he was younger he would spend hours on the computer, a big outlet for him and a form of escapism. Nowadays he goes out, he goes down the pub, and it takes his mind off it. He'll only open up to someone if he knows them well and believes they won't judge him. He is very conscious of how he might put everyone on a downer by talking about it.

We don't lose anything by telling the truth about our situation. Allowing people to support us requires us to give them the opportunity in the first place. They can't comment on what they don't know. We can gauge whether people are interested by giving them the headlines and if they ask questions they are worth your time. If they don't offer anything useful in reply, look uncomfortable or shuffle away, is that the kind of person we need to be talking with anyway?

We're not in the business of being liked by everyone; that's never the aim. Socially we are always striving to gravitate towards people who can offer us something useful at this difficult stage of our life, so a more honest response when someone asks how you are is vital.

Conor doesn't want people to feel sorry for him; he wants them to still see him for the wonderful kind lad his mum brought him up to be. Telling people the truth about how you feel doesn't make people take pity on you; I think the strength to discuss it actually earns people's respect, and if you share what you're going through there's a good chance they will share something with you too.

For allowing yourself to be 'vulnerable' you can access a deeper sense of friendship with someone. A relationship built on truth and depth, honesty and courage. As I say, some will walk away but we don't need fifty associates, we just need a few good mates.

Conspiracy theories

Conor knows only too well what path he is on. 'My mum is terminally ill. I can't change that. The only people that can do anything about it are the ones making the actual drugs for it. There is one out there, I'm sure there is, but it's all about money.'

This belief is influenced by people that he talks to, particularly a relative who was trying to find a cure, having suffered with cancer herself. He comments that people who are close to making discoveries always seem to end up going missing just before they make that breakthrough.

Conor feels disheartened by this and wonders if 'they' are going to let this drug become available in time to save his mum. In this respect he is not just waiting for the death of his mum to happen, something he has been told to expect for the last seven years, he is also agonisingly waiting for a miracle drug to come along that will give his mum a chance at life. The interesting layer here, though, is that Conor believes that drug already exists.

To not believe this theory would probably be easier. You'd be more accepting of the death as there would be nobody to blame – just the cancer itself. To feel that there is a possible cure out there can only heighten the frustration and mistrust in those who you'd like to think have the best interests of the human species in mind rather than a profit.

You hear people talking about the non-interruption of nature's way. Wouldn't it be awful if the lack of interest in curing the disease is part of a wider agenda to keep the Earth's population under control?

Just how much is each cancer patient worth to the pharmaceutical companies? What does the NHS spend on cancer every year? You have to assume the cure for cancer would cost someone a lot of money. Conor's conspiracy theories got me wondering just how many others agreed with him, that there is already a cure that is just not being released.

Why Mum's still here

Conor is certain that his mum's survival is down to positive thinking but she has also always sworn by turmeric and its ability to help contain the cancer. She stopped taking it for a period once and the cancer spread.

Conor also believes that her ability to control stress is another factor, although he actually counts himself as his mum's biggest stress in life. Is he going to get the right career? Will he be OK? That's her biggest concern. I recall her telling me she doesn't want to leave him until he 'grows up'.

Another life

I asked Conor what he would be doing if his mum wasn't ill. He said he'd be travelling the world, he would have taken more chances. He knows he is not giving the best of himself, but he also knows he'll be able to do it when he needs to. He added that he doesn't want to think about having a better working life because when he gets there, it'll be because his mum has died.

When he loses his mum, he said he will sit around and mope about but then remember what she wanted: for him to do something with his life and go and give it 150%. He'd want to enjoy his work. Take a job that he'd get up in the morning and be glad to be going to.

I asked Conor why he couldn't have that now and he said if he 'does something he likes' and she dies he would feel a lot worse. Conor is worried about 'tempting fate' – 'If I change something, something bad will happen.'

Conor told me about a message that came up on his phone about an article on the internet discussing a new treatment that has led to a terminal cancer patient being completely in remission. When I asked him what it said he told me that he didn't open it in case he lost it.

Such a revealing comment. The email completely mirrors how he feels about himself and his current life. Don't open it, it might kill his mum. Don't move, don't change a thing.

The rules of limitation

Conor told me that he couldn't stand the idea of not being there when it happens – as though he could change something if he was there. I saw an opportunity here based on the fact that Conor had just highlighted some unrealistic expectations that might give some insight into why he restricts himself so much.

We looked into how much control he had over when that moment would be and he realised that although he thinks he is with his mum as much as possible he actually only spends six hours a day by her side.

He conceded that he doesn't control the event, but that it would be more realistic to review the amount of time he spends with her when it is medically much more likely that she will die than seems to be the case right now.

While Dawn continues to be 'terminal' and has been for seven years and although you can never be certain, it doesn't appear that she is anywhere near done yet, so Conor could see that a more relaxed approach to how he spends his time is possible.

He has created a habit of working in the evenings because it leaves him available in the daytimes so he can keep himself close by his mum. When he comes home she is just getting into bed (she waits up) and when she goes to sleep he listens out for her breathing patterns, so he doesn't really sleep until four or five in the morning.

Unrealistic expectations

To expect yourself to be there when it happens and to imagine there's something you would be able to do is placing some pretty substantial pressure on yourself, none of which is realistic. This was compounded by his revealing that he thought there might be something he could say when death was imminent.

When we explored this a little Conor was able to refine exactly what these words are that he would like to give her in that moment. He would like to tell her when she is in those last moments that he wasn't really useless; he only did it so he could be there for her when she dies and that he is going to be alright.

The power of language

This statement: 'I've got to be there.' Something we have to learn is that sometimes we are simply helpless but by setting ourselves an absolute obligation that carries anything but certainty we are asking for a lifetime of regret. Conor had geared his whole life around being there in a moment that if he missed it, he would find very hard to forgive himself.

We looked at what we control and what we don't. Conor could see how he was indeed setting himself up to be very angry one day. We spoke of how he needed to give himself permission to not be there. To change his language to something kinder, more realistic, like 'I might not be there.'

Conor said something quite important: 'I control her health. In my mind I feel like I do.' He thinks he is keeping her here? We spent some time working through this alarming misconception. Conor felt as if he was controlling his mum's health by keeping himself miserable and disappointing her, which, if you've read about Dawn in Chapter 6, you'd realise was unbelievably accurate, given that they hadn't verbally communicated this. In Dawn's words, she couldn't leave Conor until she felt he had become a man.

Conor received that message somehow loud and clear and was doing everything he could subconsciously to keep his capabilities and maturity out of view, saving them for a day he hoped would never come.

Last words

I was still intrigued by why it was all about that moment, with Conor feeling he absolutely had to be there to tell his mum his prepared last words. I needed to show him the other option he had available to him. He needed to see how privileged he was to be in a position to be able to say those words at all, considering the people who aren't able to say goodbye to their loved one.

'What if you tell her tonight?' I suggested. 'Then there's no longer the need to "say something" because you've already said it. How about, "Mum, I'm scared of not being there." How long would she get to feel relieved and to act on that information?'

'She has years to feel better about it,' Conor said with eyebrows raised. I didn't say anything but I noted how subconsciously Conor let slip that he felt she still had years left of her life.

Conor had a slightly misinformed view of control. He had it the wrong way round. What he doesn't control he thinks he does (the time and the place) and the things he does control (telling her how he feels, not limiting himself) he neglects to see.

There is a strange irony here. The reason Conor's mum has earned so many additional years is because of her positivity; why does that not apply to what he is doing? I asked Conor what was more import-ant: his mum being happy in the time she has left OR her not being happy but Conor possibly being there in that moment? Conor replied, 'When you put it that way . . .'

If Mum is happier, she is less stressed. Less stressed buys time! Things were starting to take shape. He was acting out of fear. It's very understandable; most of us do exactly the same.

How long is a piece of string?

I wanted to focus on this thing Conor has with 'time'. Sitting across the table from him, I placed my left finger on the left edge of the table and my right finger on the right edge. Left represented when his mum was told there was nothing they could do; right repre-sented the day she would die.

I asked where we were on the scale today. Conor told me that realistically before today he would have said we were three quarters of the way towards that day happening. However, after today he said he believes his mum is actually no more than a quarter of the distance. We had miraculously granted her more time! 'You're right,' I said. 'You do control her life!'

I asked him seriously now, how has our conversation bought her time? Dawn hadn't been given time; the reality remained as it always was, unknown. Instead Conor recognised that he had to tell himself it was closer to justify his choices. How could he get away with limiting himself so much unless he subconsciously convinced himself that she was a lot closer than she actually was?

How long could it be? Conor, brightening up with every corner we were seemingly turning, said it could be another ten years! Another ten years of limiting yourself. And for what? He wasn't so sure any more. It didn't seem to matter so much now the fear had been reduced. He could have the work life that he would enjoy but it wouldn't come at anyone's expense – neither his mum's nor his own.

Conor was seeing the reasons why he needed to communicate with his mum. There was nothing he could say about today's realisations that would hurt her any more than the damage caused by his previous assumptions possibly already had. I asked Conor what he thought the value of what we'd learned today would be to his mum. Immeasurable, was his response.

We summarised how doing something that creates worry takes Mum closer to the right edge of the table. To take her further to the left edge is simply to communicate. To leave Conor with the future benefit of the scale we had created, I told him that if he ever felt like he needed to know where Mum was on the scale that day he could just ask her and she would tell him and there need never be an assumption about how she was feeling again. Truth may sometimes hurt but not knowing and guessing is worse.

Walking to the car on the way home from the cafe where we had breakfast together, Conor dared to start talking about a week's holiday in the summer that his cousin had put a deposit on and how he would like to go now. He asked me if I thought he was right to go.

I reminded him that he has many months to make that decision – you haven't left until you're on the aeroplane and they close the door. Assess where she is on 'the scale' a week before travel and make that decision much closer to the time. That seemed to be agreeable for Conor.

This was definitely progress and when I checked back in with Conor closer to the summer he had just finished paying off the deposit and was also planning a second trip to India to cycle for a charity later on in the year.

This story is an insight into how it feels for a teenager growing up in the anticipation of grief and the effects it can have on a young life. It also compounds the behaviours we display in order to avoid the looming subject of death and how without clear communication, precious time and understanding can be lost.

31

I'm Losing my Dad – a 12-Year-Old's View

Freddy has a good friend Charlie with whom he plays football. Charlie is a great kid – kind, genuine and loyal – and when Freddy told me his father's life is limited and he is going to die, I wanted him to know that Freddy and I were here for him.

Charlie comes from a loving and supportive family and his parents have been honest with him about his father's long and terminal illness. His commitment to football stems from enjoying the game but also being aware that he and his mother have to do things to maintain their own well-being. The family take it in turns to pick each other up when they are feeling down and Charlie is a mature boy, who functions well at school but of course is carrying an enormous weight on his young shoulders.

Life on a rollercoaster

Over the past few months Charlie's dad had been particularly sick and the family were preparing for the end. Some days he was a bit better, but mostly he was in decline, and Charlie described the rollercoaster of emotions, the ups and downs and the feeling of lurching towards a crash whenever he saw his mum's name flash up on his mobile. From one day to the next he wasn't sure what was going to happen and it made everyday things like homework and school feel trivial and inconsequential, although he also knew that these things gave him the safety of a routine and a sense of normality, even if this was forever on the edge of tipping over into the total unknown.

Facing reality

Charlie is often upbeat and positive and when we talked, he told us that his dad was getting 'a bit better' although there was a lot of 'unknown'. He used the word 'could' a number of times, as in he 'could' pass away instead of 'will' pass away, and this made me aware that in fact Charlie may not be as prepared for his dad to die as he bravely makes out. But then why would a 12-year-old child be expected to say 'will die' or 'when he dies' when talking about his dad who is still alive? This doesn't necessarily signal he thinks there is potential for a miraculous recovery, or that there is a false sense of hope, although it is something you would want to watch out for – more that the *certainty* that his father is going to die is far too big a thing for a 12-year-old to completely embrace. Where there is life, there is hope.

A child doesn't need to accept – and maybe won't be able to accept – a death of their parent before the death happens. This is quite impossible to achieve anyway, but it's an important point that we shouldn't allow our children to think that there is the potential for a miraculous recovery when the facts suggest otherwise, because while this is hard and feels maybe like you're hurting them with your insistence on facing reality, it reduces the confusion and shock they could feel as a result of being allowed to go into a false sense of hope.

Privacy

For Charlie, when he's in the outside world, he doesn't like to discuss his father's illness and impending death. Privacy is important to him and he keeps his feelings to himself at school. He doesn't want to risk someone saying something unpleasant or scary to him. Careless words in the playground can be damaging and while his close friends in and out of school know the situation, they respect his need to keep it private.

It isn't always easy to keep home and school life separate. Charlie likes to see his friends on the weekends and after school but he finds he gets embarrassed quite easily. Recently a friend of his came over and the door to his parents' bedroom was open; and he caught sight of Charlie's dad with his breathing mask on and Charlie was mortified, embarrassed and worried his friend wouldn't come back to his house.

Treading carefully

Charlie worries about his dad's moods and has to tread carefully in order not to upset him if he is having a bad day. He doesn't want to be responsible for getting him down 'and make him want to stop fighting'. For a teenager, worrying that his behaviour might make a difference to his dad's motivation to stay alive is an intolerable burden and I wanted to reassure Charlie that he was only a force of good for his dad and that both his parents appreciate and admire his perception and ability to ask the right questions. For me, these qualities are an indicator that Charlie will be better able to face what is coming than many others of his age.

His dad had been feeling well on his last birthday and in good spirits, and he told Charlie lots of stories about when he was young and Charlie loved hearing about his dad's life. But Charlie doesn't know how much he can ask his dad and is worried that if he asks him to remember too often, it will be like his dad will think he is near to dying. This is sensitive territory and an example of Charlie's mature and insightful sensitivity. I suggested he try to find out five new things a week about his dad by asking family and friends – and maybe every so often from his dad – and then gently, when he gauges the time to be right, bring one or two of them up with his dad, reassuring him that he doesn't need to talk about them if he doesn't want to.

If his dad is spending a lot of time in bed and is well enough to write or speak into a voice recorder, then Charlie could suggest to him that when he feels like it, he would love it if his dad could tell him some stories about what he was like at school, what he wanted to be when he grew up, who his heroes were, how he met Charlie's mother . . .

Shouldering the burden

Charlie is scared that after his dad dies, his mum will get depressed or run out of money. 'Anything can happen,' he told us. 'Once one thing happens, anything can happen.' Again, this is a huge thing for Charlie to be shouldering. It's one thing to be facing the death of his father and yet another to be worried about things falling apart after his death.

It's not uncommon for a 12-year-old boy who is losing, or has lost, his dad to elevate himself to the 'man of the house'. It was clear from his concerns that his parents needed to reassure him of their financial position and that he has to know that while he will inevitably need to help his mum, he will never, as her child, be responsible for her emotional well-being. He also, it appeared, needed his parents' permission to worry, as he told us that he sometimes feels that just thinking about his father's death might make it happen sooner.

Ways we can help our children in the face of the death of a parent

1. Replace memories with lessons.
If the ill parent can't create memories or share stories due to their mental state or ill health, enable your child to collect other people's memories, which will build a profile of who that parent was when they were younger and healthy. A learned memory is as much use as an experienced one.

2. Motivate the ill parent.
If the ill parent is capable but is lacking in the motivation to create memories or share stories I'd recommend writing them a letter, which would start something like this: 'Dear Dad. Please make some memories with me because what I'm left with is very important to me. Can you please tell me five stories a week about what you were like at school, what you enjoyed doing, what you wanted to be when you grew up, who were your heroes . . .'

3. Watch their terminology.
If it's going to happen don't allow them to say 'could' because they may be exercising a degree of denial that will make their comprehension of the event harder to process.

4. Give them permission to stay a child.
Let them know that they don't need to look after you but that they just need to be honest in their communicating how they really feel

and not be frightened to make mistakes in the way that they grieve, because we all do that regardless of age.

5. Make sure there isn't anything that the child is potentially going to try to take blame for.
The child may be worrying that they're not spending enough time with the ill parent, or doing something to upset them that could create a problem. You need to discuss realistic expectations with the child so they set a goal of exactly how much of anything they would like to do with or for that parent in the time they have in order to feel that they did what they could.

Obviously the amounts will vary dependent upon circumstances, but if we're talking weeks we would make it about words that need to be spoken rather than memories that are yet to be made. If a longer period seems available then it is about memories and communication of all that is important to that child, and you won't know what that is unless you have a good chat to them, like I did with Charlie.

6. Don't answer for them.
You may feel the urge to answer the difficult questions for them to save them from needing to face the facts. It's the process of talking about their feelings and sharing them that will determine their path through grief. You can answer the questions others are asking but you won't be able to answer the questions that they are asking themselves privately. Let them develop that ability to process all that comes with grief.

7. Don't assume it'll be easier for your child because of a long period of ill health.
If the parent has been ill for a long time you might find yourself thinking that maybe as a result the child's connection with that

parent might be less strong and that therefore the impact on that child might be lower.

That parent is half of where the child comes from and when the parent dies the child can lose half of their sense of identity. Regardless of closeness, or the number of times that parent was able to watch the child perform or play sport, the impact that their death will inflict is likely to be just as great.

If your child catches you lowering the other parent's role in front of them they will intuitively catch wind of this and interpret it as you implying that they shouldn't be as upset about it as they may want to feel.

8. Encourage them to share their problem.

Kids will avoid telling people things that they think they might get bullied for. In grief everyone will usually find out, so in preparation for everyone knowing it's worth thinking about allowing your child to get used to the idea of sharing with those they feel most comfortable with just so they can get a feel for how people might respond to them, treat them and support them.

Not telling anyone might contain the reality for as long as possible but it doesn't help them deal with the explosion of contact that follows the news getting out.

32

What We Need From Others: a Guide to Getting and Providing Support

Not knowing the right thing to say to someone is one of the reasons we avoid people in grief. We put ourselves under an amazing amount of pressure to find those magic healing words that will take away the pain and get frustrated when the perfectly constructed sentence just doesn't come to mind.

Unless you're a coach or counsellor who specifically deals with bereavement, just take the pressure away for a second. Your job just became a lot simpler: all a friend needs is to be listened to and to know that you're there for them.

So many people avoid a bereaved individual so they don't have to find the right words in an awkward conversation or run the risk of saying the wrong thing, but imagine how it feels to be going through that and to be avoided!

Bereaved individuals need to express their feelings, so if you're a really good friend give them the opportunity to do that; leave the judgment and opinions at home and just listen. Take it all in and if you're going to offer anything let it be a question so that your friend can continue to explore and unfold their emotions knowing that the more they talk, the better they will feel. The progress lies in their words, not yours.

You could sit with them in complete silence and that might be everything they need at that particular time – togetherness, companionship, unity and solidarity – so bear that in mind when you think you need to be able to come up with all the answers to a situation that actually carries no logical explanation at times.

'You're only as good as the company you keep' is a fairly accurate mantra for life but it really resonates in bereavement too. If you think you can deal with your loss quietly, privately and internally, you might find it will catch up with you at some stage. It's better out than in, as they say.

Part of our responsibility in loss is to give ourselves the best possible support network so that we have ample opportunity to express, share, scream, cry and sometimes laugh as well.

In an ideal world your support network is already in place, but maybe you're a fairly quiet and insular type, maybe you're the person everyone comes to with their problems, so you've never really shared your own? If you don't have a good group around you then you should look at the options available.

Charities such as Grief Encounter have counsellors and experts who can send you a range of help in a variety of forms.

Coaches and counsellors like myself can give you all the space and time you need to explore your feelings and help you progressively manage your grief as you face each new challenge that loss imposes.

Support groups in the community that get a group of you together at a coffee morning allow you to adjust to loss with the support of a group of individuals experiencing something similar to you. There's strength in numbers and just to know you're not on your own is a huge help.

To those offering support

Good and bad times to be supportive

Friends and family always require our support regardless of life-changing events such as loss, but if you're waiting for someone to blow a whistle to mark the appropriate point for when you should start communicating your desire to help, just imagine this. If they are feeling some distress or difficulty, they need support through that. How do you know they are having a tough time? Sometimes you don't. We can be very good at saying 'I'm OK' and sometimes keep ourselves so busy that not even we notice, but it's safe to say if they are grieving or anticipating a loss, they will be scared, anxious and upset, which is the equivalent of that whistle you were listening out for.

If they are losing someone gradually due to an illness, the grief starts before the physical loss, so your support can begin as early as a diagnosis or prognosis. If they have lost someone suddenly they will be in shock and suspended in disbelief; your presence will be noted although they won't necessarily know what kind of help they need.

How long should we continue to support them? There are different forms of support that are relevant for different stages of the grieving process. If you feel your friend or relative has found a good place don't assume that's your job done. At a later stage, support in the form of conversations about the person lost, or mentions at the very least, ensures that you're not only providing a sounding block but also keeping your friend in good habits. If they haven't spoken about that person for some time, check they haven't suppressed their grief by mentioning them and see how they respond. If it's an easy conversation you know they're in the right place; if they quickly change the subject they may need a good chat with you. At this point I'd ask them if they want to talk about it and it's up to them if they accept the invitation. I wouldn't push that any further and it may be a while before they come back to you, but you'll have left the door open to them putting their loss back in the open, which is important for them.

How can I support?

This depends on your relationship with the individual and the timing of your communication. Is your intention just to let them know you're thinking of them or do you want to be of some actual practical use? There is no bad way of contacting someone if you're trying to convey a message of support – text, phone call, letter, card – they'll all be appreciated. If you're hoping to do more than console through written or spoken word you might arrange a visit whereby you'll give them the opportunity to offload. Just knocking on the door to deliver some food shopping may be helpful in the days and weeks following the loss, though knocking with the intention of being invited in for tea might be reserved for those who know them best. How do you know you're not intruding? If they don't invite you in it might not be a good time and that's not something for you to take personally, but again, your intention to help will be noted and if they do need something you will be in their thoughts.

Presuming this is a close friend we're talking about, you should aim to lend them your ears as often as you can. Don't worry about making them feel better; this will happen naturally when they have taken your offer and have told you how they feel. Beyond this simple and effective objective you can go one step further and act as their stabilisers, which they may need while adjusting to the routine daily tasks that all of a sudden feel far less achievable than usual. There is also an art to knowing when to back off. It can become counterproductive if we are trying to force the subject on them. Let them dictate to you when and how often they want to go into the loss; you have to trust that when they're in a wave of grief you'll know about it and they'll know you know too. Supporting a close friend is really about being present, accessible and passive in a listening capacity.

It's possible that if you're waiting for your friend to ask for help you might be waiting quite a while, as a bereaved person is acutely aware of not wanting to burden others, seeing themselves as a drain on people's happiness and well-being. Sometimes you can say, 'Let me know if there's anything you need' until you're blue in the face, and while they might acknowledge your request, many bereaved people still won't reach out. To get the balance right is to concentrate on asking open questions either in person or via text. An open question in its simplest form such as 'How are you feeling today?' is an opportunity for the friend to explore how they are getting on in that moment. They might not feel the need to go into any elaborate detail; either way, the value here is that you gave them the platform to express their grief, and in the moments when you ask the right question at the right time that's when your listening skills will come into play.

Those daily responsibilities are also areas where you can lighten the load for your friend. Offer to do the school run for them. To cook dinner so they don't have to, have the children over for a sleepover or organise a play date instead. Anything that means the friend can spend more time adjusting rather than sinking into the overwhelming effects of loss is a worthwhile place for you to concentrate your efforts. If a supportive gesture is more your thing, making a donation to a relevant charity is a wonderful show of solidarity. How much is too much involvement? When I was first getting to grips with life as a single parent there wasn't any amount of effort made by those around me that I didn't want or need, and that's still the case today. I think too much help is when you're supporting someone for the wrong reasons: to be seen to be helping, to be in competition with others to see who can be the best friend to the mourner and using that loss as a reason to try to get closer to someone. These are all insincere forms of support that will be unhelpful to the person it's aimed at, and fairly transparent at that.

If the loss in question was experienced by a friend of your child then my advice here would be to let them find their own way to support their friend instead of giving them a list of instructions like send a card, text them twice a week, ask them how they are, etc. You'll find things are often less complicated among the younger generation and if we should be doing anything at all it would be to talk to our children about how they feel they can be the best support they can. They may astound you with their ability to show compassion and consideration, or alternatively you may discover that they back away from that friend because of the discomfort it creates in them. Either way it makes for a good conversation between you both, where you can support them in supporting others while learning a thing or two about your child in the process.

Lastly, if you feel yourself to be more of an acquaintance but have been touched by the loss of a friend of a friend, for example, then register your condolences and support by sending a card, supporting a charity close to their hearts or doing something thoughtful to help the family.

To those needing support

This grief you're experiencing doesn't go so well if you're not expressing your rollercoaster of emotions on a regular basis. Expression takes many forms, but the most effective way is to talk, which, unless you're going to talk to yourself in the mirror, requires you to have an outlet in the form of a partner, friend, relative, counsellor, coach, stranger, group member, teacher . . .

You don't need an army of people ready to help; a few good listeners will be sufficient. You'll know who you want to speak to because you'll feel comfortable enough to do so. It might be down to the individual and your history with them, it might be down to their personal experiences, or it might just be down to timing that you feel ready to be supported.

Just to warn you, here are some reasons you might not embrace your need for an outlet:

1. You feel so self-conscious that you're constantly going on about negative, boring feelings.
Here's the thing. Grief *is* negative. It's boring and it's unattractive but it's real, and that's what friends are for. If you struggle with this, why don't you identify who it is you can talk to and rotate them so you're giving each friend the minimum amount of bother and you don't exhaust one in particular? You should also make sure you speak to them when you feel surprisingly upbeat so that they're getting the balance of you.

2. You're suppressing your emotions, which you somehow confuse for being 'strong'.
Oh dear, it's like being a Victorian: we don't talk about it and if we ignore it, it'll go away. Who needs friends when you've got the ability to bottle things up? The irony is when your 'internal bottle' is full it's going to spill and you'll be needing your friends to help you then, only you'll have pushed them away so much they may be less willing.

3. They'll say the wrong thing and it will make you angry or upset. The problem with these outlets is that they not only have the ears that we fundamentally require, but they also have mouths and brains, which means they are likely to actually put their experiences and opinions across in ways that we don't particularly want.

Some opinions are relevant, some less helpful, some tell stories that act for them as an exchange: 'You show me your grief and I'll show you mine.' In these conversations it's your responsibility to set the rules for what is allowed and what isn't. If you're speaking to a person who has recently lost someone it would be unrealistic of you to expect them to not share back with you.

Find someone who knows that all you need is their ears and their hugs and a nice cup of tea if that's your idea of comfort. Make sure you understand, however, that the reason certain words or phrases feel like a sore spot for you is not because that person is insensitive but because there are meanings behind the words that you have not yet dealt with.

4. But I don't want to cry! Crying is the ultimate expression of the way you feel on the inside and some people are desperate not to reveal their feelings after suffering a loss. Those in denial of grief know this only too well, so in order to maintain and protect that position they avoid anyone who asks them how they feel because a genuine question delivered with love and concern can undo months of hard work!

I've seen grown men cry over a football result, people cry at sad moments on the TV, people cry when they are at the funeral of someone they just about knew, yet, when they lose someone who they have known all their life, someone who meant the world to them and was a significant influence on the person they are today, they fight back those tears at all costs.

All of a sudden crying is to be avoided. But why? Because it is a threat to the control we feel we have over this transitional period of uncertainty. And yet, we only gain control when we allow ourselves to cry. So if you have that friend who you're comfortable enough to cry in front of, you're in good hands.

Some don't feel it appropriate to cry in front of their children, thinking it will upset them and therefore it's unhelpful. You need to consider who sets the guidelines for their children in grief. If you can cry, what does it give them permission to do? If you don't show them that being emotional is natural and healthy, you'll be contributing to their emotional suppression as well as your own. Just remember, crying is an expression of pain, which is always beneficial.

What's in it for them?

The most overlooked fact here is that there will always be certain friends and family members who really want to support us; in fact they may feel like they need to support us or they'll be dealing with their own sense of guilt that they're not doing enough.

Friends who really care in our moments of need are absolutely priceless and sadly rare. If you were in hospital, who would come and visit you? Or who would help hold the fort back at home? The people who come to your aid and are ready to listen deserve to be given the opportunity to do just that.

Some of you may be thinking: but I'm bereaved, so isn't it all about what I want? Well, yes, it is about your needs, but there are the needs you're aware of and those you may be unaware of, which talking will help express. Letting people in on what's going on inside you will strengthen and deepen your relationship with them, which is great in the long term for both of you.

Friendships are tested by the challenge of providing support when it's not all dinner parties, drinks, shopping and football. When you are grieving, you may even lose a few friends, as testified to by a client who had five close friends who she thought were always going to be in her life. They went out, had fun, partied, were 'her girls'. But when her father died and she called one of them to tell her what had happened, the friend replied that she didn't have time to listen as she was in Tesco doing her shopping. Things got worse than that and she soon realised that one or two of them were not 'her girls' after all.

Their reactions really unsettled her, and after talking through why and what she had expected from these friends and what it meant to her that her expectations hadn't been met, she concluded, 'You can't soar like an eagle when you're flying with turkeys' – confirmation that she was coming to accept that as sore as it was, for her long-term benefit this had been a good thing. They had let her down when she needed them the most, so had they ever been particularly good friends after all? It is a great shame it took the death of her father to show her this, but there is very often no better perspective to be gained than from a loss.

We've all heard of the term fair-weather friends, and if we aren't willing to be there when a friend has bad news then what is the friendship anyway? I personally relish the chance to show my solidarity with friends who have had bad times, even more so if I've gone through that experience myself. It not only contributes to the equality of our friendship but also shows them that I'm more than there for them too.

I think the bigger picture to this is that the quality of our lives sometimes depends upon those who that we have a shared experience with and we are better people for selflessly helping each other along the way. You don't need to have experienced loss to help someone else through it, though. The true definition of friendship is when you are willing to sit and be present and listen to anything that's thrown your way.

You may not think it now, but one day you'll be very grateful that you shared your pain with someone. Pain is the fuel that creates the best possible friendships. Life isn't always glamorous, loss is part of our journey and we simply need people to help us recover.

33

The Significance of Last Words in Grief

The impact of the words spoken in the final moments of life should never be underestimated. Not by the person saying them or the person on the receiving end. The power they possess can be immense and, dependent on their intention, nothing short of life-altering.

The final words spoken between two people before an expected loss can be consciously delivered with meaning and purpose or they can be accidental, delivered without knowledge that they will in fact be their last. Regardless of how and when, they can be etched in the memory for a lifetime.

Perspective

We really should learn from the distress of those who were not able to say goodbye to their loved ones, that whenever we part company with someone we love, there is a chance that we may not see them again. Thankfully that isn't going to be the case very often, but it should make us stop and think about how we treat others and want to be treated ourselves.

How would you feel if that last conversation had been an argument and harsh words had been spoken? You could work towards eliminating the prospect of guilt and regret by ensuring that, irrespective of the prevailing mood or situation, your parting comments are always as loving as can be.

Words delivered from the deathbed

Thankfully, I have come across many who have been fortunate enough to know that, at the end, their loved one said something they had longed to hear – expressions of love, gratitude, praise, recognition, validation or approval that was long overdue, all of which had a wonderful releasing effect.

Some, however, have been given a limiting instruction such as, 'Stick with John, he's a good man', based on the deceased's opinion or wishes. It's very hard to actually go against the wishes of someone we are losing, or have lost, but what happens when their wishes are not in line with our own? Are you strong enough to defy the unrealistic or unreasonable nature of their words or will you do what they say regardless of the cost?

In this situation, you need to ask yourself, whose life is it? How much more life-affirming it is if they offer you reassurance, guidance and love in those final moments. Yet in contrast, how crippling and stifling, to know that you have to do something you don't necessarily want or believe in, in order not to disrespect your loved one's dying wishes.

If someone does give you an instruction you don't want to carry out, it's important to remember why they would make that request in the first place. Sometimes it's based on either limited knowledge, a lack of facts or their own point of view, which may carry traditional values, ones that differ from your own. If you feel bound to carry out those wishes, ask yourself if you would have felt the same if they had asked you when they were in good health – what would your response have been then? Speak to other family members about it. Perhaps it took one family member to cast the spell, and it will take a few others to break it.

Unspoken words are just as bad

Over the years, I have encountered many people who regret wasting the opportunities they had to tell their dying loved ones exactly how they felt. 'Why didn't I just tell them that I loved them? . . . Why didn't I tell them that I forgave them?'

So many of us fail to ask our loved ones the difficult questions about our past, seeking information they have that we need, instead preferring to leave those we leave behind or those who leave us with harmful assumptions. Facts set you free, no matter how hard they are to hear or say, so leave as few assumptions behind as you can.

Self-imposed rules

Our use of language is one of the main things that predetermines exactly how our journey through bereavement will take shape. We often, in life in general, overlook the responsibility we have to be kind to ourselves in the way that we talk to ourselves.

How often do you praise yourself, give yourself a pat on the back or allow yourself to feel proud and recognise a job well done? Maybe your natural tendency is to criticise yourself, berate yourself for feeling or acting a certain way? Your internal dialogue is a big part of that. Turn the volume up and have a listen . . . How kind are you to you?

These predetermined habits will play a big role in how you grieve. If you are kind to yourself, you will, on the whole, deal with grief and grief alone. If you are unkind you may find it harder to deal with your grief due to the added complications of a few self-imposed ingredients and obstacles.

Our internal dialogue is our way of programming ourselves to live and cope with the way our life experience and upbringing has conditioned us to feel. If you have low self-esteem, you may be more likely to take the responsibility and blame for things that don't necessarily belong to you and, as a consequence, will be more likely to feel guilt and regret than someone who is less willing to use these areas as sticks to beat themselves with.

Our issues that have existed before our grief came along will invariably combine to create a version of grief that is unique to us. We all have hang-ups from childhood – relationships, school experiences and so on – and I mention this to make you aware that there will be a combination of factors playing out and 'grief' will not just be about the loss of that loved one.

When our turn comes

If you know you are going to die, I believe you have to make absolutely sure that you leave a gift, a bunch of flowers in the form of a well-thought out formation of words. It could be in the form of a letter, in case when it comes to it you are unable to speak or give voice to what you want to say. What are those things you might never be able to say, or haven't expressed for a long time, that you know would mean so much to the people you are leaving behind?

Think of each of your closest loved ones and how you can best

deliver them the compliments, praise, reassurance, encouragement, forgiveness, explanation, apology and clarification that
will be felt, absorbed and replayed a thousand times after you've
left.

And – just a thought – even if you don't have a life-limiting illness
and you're not expecting to die anytime soon, is it such a bad habit
for us to ensure that we give all of the above on a regular basis
anyway? When you think about it, why should all of that be saved
up until our final days?

The words we avoid

How many people absolutely avoid the words 'dead' and 'death'?
Why do we find it so difficult to use the words that actually describe
the very thing we are consumed by?

What happens if we do say 'death, dying, dead, deceased'? Do we
think we are being harsh? Disrespectful? Insensitive? Frightening?
Rude? It might feel a little abrasive, shocking or upsetting at first,
but when we use accurate terms, we can help eliminate the potential
for denial or delusion. By using them, we also give others around us
the permission to use them. Our children, for example, will be under
no illusion exactly what is happening or will be, and by being accurate in our wording, we are promoting facts and not giving rise to
debilitating assumptions.

We are a death-denying society, which doesn't help us in grief.
Use whichever terms you feel comfortable with, but at least consider
why you might not use certain words and whether that helps or
hinders you or those around you as a result.

Outdated terms

There are some terms used to describe grief and our journey towards death that could do with some updating. I often hear people referencing their journey through grief as 'getting over it'. Maybe this is just my view, but I think it isn't entirely helpful. We 'get over' obstacles but grief is absolutely not something you can just jump over and overcome indefinitely.

I prefer to think that we learn to 'manage our grief' and learn to live with it. If we weren't so busy using such unspecific terms, such as grief, we wouldn't be so vague about what we need to do with it. The word 'grief' is, in my opinion, such a soft term, a nominalisation, so hard to pin down as to what it actually means or encompasses, that it doesn't upset us. If grief were a person, he or she would be by our side forever. I believe that grief is a human reflex that reminds us to think about the people we have lost.

And in this capacity, why would we not want to have a prolonged relationship with grief? Not just any old relationship. Most of us tend to get off to a rocky start with our grief, and many of us try to shake it off, but it just won't leave us alone. I have tried to make my relationship with it a good one. I reached a point when I accepted its presence and now I see that without grief, I may not have been able to look back and remember so much.

The word 'terminal' has traditionally been linked to illness when describing someone who has been given a prognosis of limited life expectancy. But 'terminal' is a final and definite word, as if everything is going to stop very suddenly and very soon, and some interpret it as meaning the individual now has a death sentence. This certainly isn't the case for everyone and some people outlive their prognosis by a long way.

I've no doubt that people accept their prognosis so completely that they plan their life not according to their own expectations but to those of the doctor who has just plucked a figure out of the air, no doubt based on experience and averages – but you're not the same as the others; you're unique, you're you.

A better term than 'terminal illness' is 'life-limiting illness', which while also suggesting that life is going to end sooner than wanted doesn't imply that you're on a head-on collision course with death. It also lends itself to an undisclosed period of time, so hope should not be abandoned and neither should life.

And how should we look at the term 'dying'? You could argue that the act of dying is actually the moment we draw our last breath, so that at any point leading up to that moment, no matter what is going on with our bodies, we are very much alive. But if that doesn't work for you, then how about this: life has an expectancy, a period of privileged exclusivity that is gifted to you by your parents. Could it also be said that from the moment we are born we are then on a timer? Who wears the stopwatch is anyone's guess but if life is certain to end from the moment it starts, are we therefore dying from the moment we begin our existence?

Maybe we're alive right up until those last seconds, because you're either alive or dead and there is no in-between.

34

Grief and Social Media

We are still very much a death-denying society. We don't like to acknowledge it, we fear it and we don't especially like to talk about it, but it's very interesting to consider how social media has changed the way we grieve today. You could assume that increased ways of communicating can help us grieve, but having such a public way of expressing our grief can be both good and bad. In terms of when we are needed to support friends and family in their grief, social media can remove barriers and help us find ways of offering the words and sentiments we might find difficult to deliver face-to-face. It can also help us stay in touch with bereaved friends and family who we may not live near or who, for reasons of work or other commitments, we may not be able to help in person on a day-to-day basis.

I've heard it said that using social media is like screaming into an empty room – a way to express what's on your mind and how much it hurts without actually saying it in person. But is it empty? Facebook is full of your friends and relatives and Twitter may be more anonymous, a place you may feel less judged by those closest to you, but it is still a place where you get heard. In my opinion, expressing your grief on social media can be a positive thing and part of how you manage your grief, so long as it doesn't become the only point of expression.

Posting about your grief, however, can have negative consequences for you if you wear your grief like a badge. Having it at the
top of your profile may give the impression that this is what defines
you. It is important for your own mental health that you make sure
you are still the person you were from before your loss and that the
pain you're dealing with is a part of what you are experiencing now
and will come to manage, however much it has come to dominate
your life. While posting something on grief may signal that this is
what is consuming you, actually having your grief as part of your
profile may signal that this is who you have become and can have
negative consequences – for example, your friends feeling that
whatever they respond to your posts, they ultimately can't bring
your loved one back, so what use are they to even try to comfort
you? It's all about balance and moderation, and ultimately, while
social media can play a useful and restorative part in helping us
manage our grief, nothing, in my view, substitutes for real-life
interaction.

So what are the pros and cons of using social media in grief?

1. Social media and its many short cuts.
One post on Facebook or Twitter can take the place of fifty or more
conversations. You may have dreaded the thought of telling people
over and over again about a death or how you are coping and social
media gives you the opportunity to tell people all at once. Why say
it yourself when you can tweet a beautiful quote that says it for you?
Posting on social media has its definite advantages but I don't think
it should ever be done to the exclusion of actually talking to your
friends and family in person. Maybe when you next post a message
about your grief, leave out a few people and call them. You can go
for so long without seeing someone in real life and get used to

'seeing' them every day on their feeds. Social media can mean you are observing a life instead of interacting with it on any particular level and can be a lonely world to inhabit, with everyone else seemingly having a good time. Making sure you actually see some of your friends for a cup of tea and a chat will enable you to get the balance of the real and hyper-real right.

Posting tributes about your loved one can be very cathartic and allows a wide group of your friends and family to get to know them and share their memories. Make sure, if your children or other family members don't have access to your account, that you share any meaningful tributes with them.

2. The uses of groups and forums.

I liken posting to fishing. You cast a very big net with social media and while you know you won't catch every fish in the lake, you don't really need all of them. In reality, you just need the one to feel like you got a reaction or that you 'caught something'. Be aware, though, that the fish can get wise to your strategy and potentially start to ignore the bait or inhabit the shaded areas of the lake when you're around. I'd suggest that while the reason you're fishing is clear, you should evaluate whether the big net is always necessary or whether there is a particular person or group that will respond when you aim your landing net in their specific direction.

One of the best aspects of social media is that by posting or searching, you can find others in a similar position to you, likeminded people – those who are grieving for, say, the loss of a child or parent – and these people can become your support and advice group. Nobody quite understands the complications of your specific type of loss better than those who have walked a mile in your shoes and being able, at the press of a button, to access them and share your experience and feelings is invaluable. People actually make lasting friendships on these groups because they have supported each other through a journey that encountered incredibly tough times, forging bonds that surpass many friendships you've had in the past.

Do make sure, however, that the group is 'real' and that you are safe. Make sure you don't 'get lost' in the group. Choosing to express your grief exclusively to strangers while ignoring your friends and family's support may have negative ramifications. It's great that your Facebook friends know how you are but your closest relatives may need you too.

The most obvious potential danger of online activity comes with meeting up with people in real life. Bereaved people are often seen as vulnerable targets, so always ensure you have the assurances that you're meeting the person you think you are.

3. The meaning of the communication is how it is received, not how it is spoken.
Sometimes posting something about grief is a very definite cry for help. However, putting it out there that you're feeling down and need some support can potentially upset others who are grieving for the same person.

I would argue that sharing something is a really positive step, and if it's not going to cause great distress to others, it will be of immense benefit to you. It shouldn't stop there, though, and once you've shared how you are feeling, you should also look at why you have shared it and what your desired outcome is. While you could just be letting everyone know where you are, you might also be crying for help, in which case you should state clearly in your post what it is you require, so that you get that help. We often look to social media to air our issues, not realising that it can actually mean we don't always get quite the support we need. Yes, 'support' could be achieved when you get those 140 crying face emojis and lots of comments to say 'If you need anything, shout' but how many of those comments actually amount to something real when you try to take it further?

Dropping hints that your busy friends may not pick up on might lead to you feeling resentful or upset they haven't recognised your needs, or might make them feel you are somehow challenging them to prove their friendship. Social media is a great form of communication, but as in face-to-face conversation, the things that are left unsaid can often cause problems.

Similarly, if you don't get the reaction you are hoping for, it's not always because people are ignoring you or don't want to help. Your friends may want to know you're OK but they care about their own state of mind too and if they feel like your posts are having a negative effect on their well-being, bringing up painful memories or reactions for them, then they might not be able to respond in the way you are hoping for.

4. Access to memories.
Social media can now deliver archived pictures or posts from the past, precious memories in the form of anchors that can cheer you up on a bad day. If you think there may be a picture lurking in the background that would cause you some distress after your loss you may wish to seek advice on how to turn that function off. In the event of someone's death anyone can request that the account be 'memorialised', which turns the profile into a page that friends and relatives can share memories on. Family members or executors can now ask for a page or account to be deleted, but documentation would need to be provided. It's becoming increasingly common for wills to nominate a 'digital executor' who will be responsible for the distribution or deletion of emails, social media messages, text

messages, etc. There is also an app connected to Facebook called 'If I die' that you can use to manage your social profiles and to create videos and messages that will be posted across your platforms when you die.

Some of you may not want access to your loved one's social media accounts. If memories are the currency of grief we should try to find a way to extract what we want from these platforms and leave the rest behind. It's an interesting thought, though, that these pages may become the modern-day version of the grave, where society now goes to mourn.

5. Comforting stories.

It can bring you great comfort when people from far and wide are able to share memories of your loved ones and can really make you appreciate how many people loved and cared for them. This is especially the case with children. Having received this idea on one of my many social media research sprees, I have set an account up for my boys so that personally invited people can post memories of their mum for them to read now and for the rest of their lives.

6. Special occasions.

Mother's Day, Father's Day – any special occasion can hurt like hell, even after many years. The good side is that on special days – anniversaries, birthdays or maybe just because you're missing your loved one – you can put out a little post on social media and take great comfort in actually typing a message just for them and sending it out into the great wide world.

Conversely, being on social media at certain times when it is awash with pictures and posts from others, celebrating their living relatives, can be difficult and you need to impose some sort of self-censorship if seeing them causes you grief or envy. Anticipate those days and maybe once you have posted something to your loved one, take time off social media. There's always tomorrow!

Reviewing social media and grief:

1. Social media gives you access to a larger community of support but a balance between online and physical one-to-one communication should be sought.

2. Manage your likely outcomes by being clear on your daily objective. Do you want to share, to befriend, to meet or to find? Maybe you want to be liked or acknowledged? Have a clear idea of how you want social media to work for you so you can control it instead of it controlling you. After all, it's a tool, not a lifestyle.

3. Be mindful of how positive or negative an influence social media is on your state of mind. Is it helping or hindering your alignment with grief? Do you need to spend less time on it or maybe reconsider your objectives?

4. You may experience a social pressure to express your grief online because of how others in your circle are discussing theirs. You have the right to choose how, when and where you explore your own feelings of grief and you shouldn't need to conform to others.

5. A question to help you identify what the right expression of grief is for you. Mourner A stands at the back of the church at the funeral and says very little but is physically present. Mourner B doesn't attend the funeral but sends the tweet that is retweeted and seen by many. Who is grieving the most?

6. Facebook, with 1 billion detailed, self-submitted user profiles, was created to connect the living. But it has become the world's largest site of memorials for the dead. Facebook contains the profiles of about 30 million people who have died. The existence of a social media afterlife is one way we are using the latest technology to deal with a timeless fact of life.

35

Where Do They Go?

Is the end the end or just the next step in our existence? You decide!

While many believe in a 'heaven', others in reincarnation or that we become ghosts, there are many who feel that once we die, that's it; there isn't anything left for us beyond that fateful day. Some of us are religious, some more spiritually inclined, some atheist, and while there are many different ideas, explanations and guesses as to what happens when we go, just how important is it for us to have a belief – and what if we don't?

A personal belief, be it religious, spiritual or something other, can give us direction and bring comfort in an otherwise rudderless situation and we should feel free to let our hearts and imaginations run wild. Seeing as there are no definitive answers, if it brings us comfort to believe something about the person we've lost and where they are now, who is to disagree? I talked to a woman who told me she believed in 'heaven because I like to think my loved ones are together; reincarnation because I truly believe my sister has come back to visit her children as a butterfly on several occasions; and ghosts, as I've seen a ghost while on an early shift at work.'

I'm of a spiritual disposition and reincarnation makes more sense to me than heaven. I'm content with knowing that if I'm a good person, I'll have as much chance of ending up in the best place or reincarnated happily and that's good enough for me. Not that I give the afterlife a great deal of thought as I'm too busy living – I have plenty of time to find out later, I'm sure!

I did a social media survey asking people to offer their views on what becomes of us. After seeing the results and receiving hundreds of comments, many of which I developed into conversations to explore their views further, a few things became clear.

People like to think there is something there when we die.
Most people who responded wanted to believe there was something there after death. Some of the reasons were: this makes people feel better about the way they live their lives; that life has a greater purpose if there is something afterwards and that when they die they will be accepted and welcomed somewhere, by someone.

A faith in something – religious, spiritual, whatever – creates belief and from belief grows comfort and hope. If it comforts you to believe that you will be met by your god, or that you will be reborn or that you can go back and haunt someone who has upset you, or guard over someone you love, then that's not just going to help your acceptance of death, but it may also help you to grieve for someone close to you who dies.

Angela lost her dad eleven years ago. He died in a hospice and '. . . the day after he died my sister saw a robin on her window ledge at home and she has seen it every year since. When our mum went into the same hospice eight weeks ago the nurse commented that the robin who usually came visiting hadn't been seen all summer but five days later, when Mum died, there it was on the window ledge. The other day my five-year-old granddaughter Ellie was at my house and in the garden there were two robins, one big and strong and the other small and cute. Ellie shouted: "I think Great Nanny is in the garden but she's with another robin!" My dad was six foot tall and my mum was five foot!'

Similarly, Lisa finds great comfort in her belief that there is life after death and that our loved ones live on and are together. 'My personal belief is that we are here to learn lessons. Those of us that have lived a troubled life and learn enough live on a higher spiritual plane and those who fail to learn from their experiences may come back time and time again through reincarnation. I know not everyone will agree with my ideas but I've had far too much proof from my loved ones that they are still around. This is a huge comfort to me.'

Finding comfort is the main ingredient towards acceptance and I can't emphasise enough how important acceptance is to managing our grief and finding peace within ourselves for the day that will come to us all. If, when you lose someone or think about your own death, you feel they or you will be 'in a better place', or will be 'with Mum or Dad now', or 'out of pain' then these comforting beliefs will enable you to draw strength and hope in times of distress.

Even if you think that when we die nothing happens, or have a cynical approach, as one of my respondents put it: 'Heaven is just a belief for people who cannot come to terms with the fact that they won't see their loved ones again', then that does actually constitute a belief, just not necessarily a belief that makes the afterlife in any way attractive. Some people said they didn't ever think about it and didn't really know what they thought; they were too busy making the very most of life. Perhaps they are even thinking that having any expectations for what happens after might make them less motivated to make the most of this life while they still have it, as if there's a complacency in imagining you get another crack at it.

We like the idea of being able to meet people we have lost.

Several people expressed the view that when we die we are reunited with people we have lost. What a beautiful idea, the thought that we can go and spend time with our grandparents, parents, friends or relatives generally and hold them once more. This is certainly a belief that will help manage grief, to feel that our connection with our loved ones remains intact. So long as we aren't holding on to the notion that death isn't final, an avoidance of the reality that a loved one has in fact gone, then the idea of being reunited is comforting.

We like the idea that those we have lost are around us.
One person who responded to my survey really touched me and made me see things differently.

Martin, who lost his wife Jayne, told me: 'Everyone is entitled to their own opinions but I'm a scientist, I like evidence, so I am an atheist. We are made of matter and energy. Every atom in our body was forged in the heart of a star and when we die those atoms still exist and are reused in say plants, rocks or other animals. I would like to think that some of Jayne's atoms will one day re-emerge as a butterfly. When I think of the energy that was Jayne and apply the first law of thermodynamics that no energy is created and none is lost, I can believe that every bit of heat from Jayne's body, every sound wave, every bit of reflected light that emitted from Jayne still exists, forever travelling through the stars, being reused. Maybe in a million years some of that energy will be part of a new star with planets and life around it. But for now I know that it's out there, travelling around the Earth and beyond, and so is she. She has left an impression on the universe and without her it would look remarkably different. The universe is beautiful and every happy accident that is life is a wonderful addition and every death heralds new life eventually. I guess in a way I do believe in reincarnation, not the mystical variety but the scientifically proven method. Physics can be lyrical, romantic and beautiful too.'

We listen to mediums.
So many people started their replies with: 'A medium once told me...' Clairvoyants or mediums can be a major comfort and validate some people's belief in the afterlife. Obviously psychics aren't for everyone but if they can bring comfort to some, communicating calming messages from their loved ones, letting them know they are OK wherever they are, then this can help with the grieving process.

We're not always sure if we want people looking down at us.
I had a good conversation with a lady who just wanted to believe that we cease to exist, that a peace descends when we die, because she didn't want her loved ones to be looking down worrying about anything in this world. She obviously thought looking down would bring concern rather than joy, and so an interesting discussion ensued about her personal situation.

I agree with her in the sense that I too wouldn't want to look down on my loved ones if I was witnessing difficulties and I was powerless to do anything about it. This might stop me from enjoying my eternal rest!

Some of us prefer not to think about it.
Many of us fear death and many of us don't like to think about it. OK, so death isn't a cheery subject, but it's going to happen to us all and probably a few people we love before we die too. It's a reality, an indisputable fact, so what purpose does it serve avoiding or ignoring the question of what happens after we die?

I'm not saying that you need to think about death every day or anywhere near that, but I feel strongly that it shouldn't be a taboo subject that we can't talk about. If we all felt a little more comfortable with facing our deaths or the inevitable death of loved ones, maybe we could all tackle grief a little better. It would certainly help one of my respondents, who wrote about fearing death: 'To be honest, this is the one topic I try desperately not to think about as it really scares the you-know-what out of me. I'm near enough having a panic attack writing this!'

A fear of death can sometimes be attributed to a dissatisfaction with one's life so far. If you haven't achieved everything you want yet then naturally your outlook on death is going to be filled with fear and trepidation. Death can be a reminder that we still have much to achieve. It can also be a reminder that every moment we have is precious. Maybe the way to confront death is to do our best to ensure we go with a heart full of love and a head full of memories and this goal should form the basis for the way we live each day.

36

Burial or Cremation: Where Do We Want to End Up?

We have a big decision to make in life as to where we would like our families to come and pay their respects when we are dead. It's not just about where we want our ashes to be scattered or our bodies to be buried, but also about what our bereaved family and friends will find most beneficial and convenient in their need to feel connected to us in grief.

The grave: a place to grieve or a tie for those left behind?

My children and I feel close to Jade by visiting her grave, or 'Mummy's special place' as it is affectionately known. Mourners typically go to graves because they like to 'show' their loved one that they are thinking of them and respect them, or maybe sometimes to release a build-up of guilt that they haven't done something for them for a while.

Depending on your beliefs about what happens after death, you may feel the visit isn't about your loved one but something you do for yourself. Of course, visiting the grave shouldn't be the only time or place that you allow yourself to remember your loved one, or the only place where you allow yourself to express emotion about your loss. And anyway, graves don't have to be a place of sadness. From when they were little, my children have always happily run around, playing together around Jade's grave, something that she would have wished for. The boys take flowers and over the years the drawings have turned into letters or cards and we sit on the bench that overlooks the grave in such a beautiful country setting.

What will happen if we don't go often? You may already be remembering that person, talking about them and expressing how you feel about their absence, so what does visiting a grave do that those important factors do not?

Let's think about it from the departed's point of view. If that was you, would you be happy that your loved ones were remembering you and talking about you from time to time or would it only count if they were standing talking about you in the exact place that you were buried? I personally wouldn't want my children tied to having to visit a specific place. I'd probably opt to send them on an adventure and challenge them to take my ashes to a place we have visited and loved together, or a place of great emotional value I have been to over the years like the Lake District. If I was feeling cruel I'd want them to scatter some on the island of Yaukuve in the South Pacific where I lived for three months while filming *Shipwrecked* in 2002, although I've just looked it up and it's now a six-star resort called Kokomo Island, so I don't think they'll be too put out by my request!

We mustn't get hung up on tradition and the importance of 'being seen to be grieving', conforming to expectations. People put incredible amounts of stress upon themselves to 'get to the grave' and if they haven't been, they feel they haven't cared for their loved one, failing to take into account the fact that they have remembered and spoken of them on countless occasions. A headstone and the area in front of it can represent as little or as much as you and your family like. If you think that placing fresh flowers on your loved one's grave every week or once a month is important to you, a way for you to mark your loved one's passing and to feel close to them, and it isn't an obligation that burdens you or your family, then that's all that matters.

And if you prefer to spend your time remembering your loved one in a variety of ways that renew your connection to them, but spend little time at the cemetery, that's fine too. If, however, it bothers you when you do go and it's not very well maintained, do prepare yourself for the slight pang of guilt you may feel. The grave can become perceived in the same way as if it were that person's 'house', and if it is covered in moss and the flowers are all dead it might feel like you're letting that person down. But you can quickly restore it.

Whatever you decide is the right balance between visiting and not, a simple plan made between those who care enough to maintain the resting place will be enough to keep the grounds to your personal level of expectation while avoiding a needless case of 'grave guilt'.

The ashes – grieving remotely

For many the choice of burial or cremation is about what you want to happen to your body in death. I'd like to challenge everyone instead to think about what they leave behind with either choice.

To be buried is to provide all of those who will miss you with a central and definite location for them to focus their grief and pay their respects. With cremation and the various options that the scattering or re-forming of the remains provides, the ashes are a way of creating meaningful opportunities such as keeping them at home or placing them in several locations that potentially enable a person to feel that graveside connection far more often. This can be a lot less limiting to when we feel we can grieve than if we are of the opinion that we only feel connected when near the grave or the ashes.

There are pros and cons to either and people often don't know what to do with the ashes until they've been sitting on the mantel-piece for some time. I know, from my mum's experiences of having Grandad's ashes at home with her for the past eight years, that if you are of a denying disposition then you can very well hold on to your grief just as much as you're hanging on to those remains.

More and more people are choosing cremation as a final dispos-ition method, for numerous reasons:

1. Cost
Cremation generally costs 40–50% less than traditional ground burial. It doesn't require a grave or headstone, many families skip embalming and cremation urns are generally cheaper than caskets.

2. Simplicity
Cremation can remove the need for the more elaborate burial cere-mony involving a casket, viewings, pall bearers, etc. An urn is smaller and therefore much easier to handle than a full-sized casket.

3. Flexibility
As mentioned above, an urn is much smaller than a casket and therefore very easy to transport and/or store at home. Cremation also frees up the timeframe, so you can hold on to the remains indef-initely until you and your family arrange burial, scattering, or some other method of disposition.

4. Environmental concerns
Traditional burial takes up space in the earth and often involves heavy doses of chemicals (when the body is embalmed). There is some debate as to the benefits of cremation, but generally it is considered more 'green' and eco-friendly. Cremation does take its

toll with carbon emissions, but as equipment and technology improve, the impact on the environment is lessening. If concentrated amounts of ashes are placed on grass it can cause a 'burning', a similar effect to putting on too much fertiliser, so ashes need to be spread out, and if you are putting them in the soil you need to dig them in to prevent concentrated matter in one place. Once spread out it appears that ashes will have no impact, although large amounts in sensitive ecosystems such as at the top of a mountain may alter the natural ecology. So if you're planning to take your loved one's ashes to Kilimanjaro, try to avoid doing it at the summit!

5. Less tradition, more personal

While family and religious traditions are still very important to people, there is a general trend away from tradition for the sake of tradition. Instead, families are increasingly preferring to celebrate their loved ones in unique and personal ways. Cremation offers the flexibility for loved ones to design a completely one-of-a-kind memorial and disposition. Scattering ashes is a popular choice, and this can be done in a myriad of ways: at sea, in your backyard, from a helicopter, planted as a memorial tree, shot off in fireworks, and so on. You can also have the flexibility of scattering the ashes in multiple places. These days, there are all sorts of commercial enterprises offering ash-scattering services, for example, on to a vineyard so your loved one can contribute to next year's wine, or if you fancy something further afield, there is a company that can shoot your ashes into space.

Your ashes can be made into jewellery, a tattoo, a frisbee, stained or blown glass, and in one offering, you can place them upon the water, set them alight and adrift, then as the fire ebbs away the ashes sink gracefully below the water on a Viking longboat urn. Any of those take your fancy?

6. Claustrophobia

The idea of being buried awakes deep-seated fears in many people: 'I'm too claustrophobic to be buried.' People may also find the idea of their remains being scattered into the open air or sea to be liberating.

7. Mobility

If you move around a bit, or an eventual move away following a loss might be on the cards, then cremation can free you up as you are not tied to a cemetery, feeling that you have to tend to the grave that you might end up living miles from. You may also eventually become too old to maintain your partner's grave.

8. Being near loved ones

Since cemeteries are pretty packed these days, you can often have an urn buried alongside an already-departed loved one. This can solve the difficulties and trauma of being told there is 'no room' for your loved one.

There is an increasingly popular option of a woodland burial, which offers somewhere more natural to hold a funeral and remember a loved one. Woodland sites are often set within acres of countryside, amidst the peace and tranquillity of trees and flowers, providing a natural alternative to the traditional cemetery or graveyard. Most woodland burial grounds offer burial plots, but ashes can also be buried or scattered within the grounds.

Instead of a traditional headstone, graves are marked by the planting of a memorial tree or the placing of a simple (often biodegradable) plaque. There is a focus on preserving the natural beauty of the woodland environment and encouraging native wild-life and flowers.

I personally like the idea of being permanently reacquainted with a place I love and felt a huge spiritual connection to, a place where I watched the sunrise on countless occasions. Even the thought of my sons taking me there gives me great satisfaction – and that's the question we all need to answer: where is that place for you that when you think of being scattered or buried there fills you with a great sense of peace and calm? If nowhere springs to mind hopefully you've still got lots of time to find it. I think it's worth the effort. We're going to spend a lot of time there, after all!

37

The Mistakes We Make in Loss

You may have experienced several losses in your life and cumulatively, each time one happens you gain experience and know a little more about what to expect. But when you are exposed to loss for the first time, it's like going back to school to learn about a subject you know nothing about. If we are no spring chickens when this happens, we can find learning difficult.

Everything that has ever happened to you in life – trauma, heartbreak, your achievements and successes, strengths and weaknesses – will play a part in how you process death and how you choose to respond to the influence of grief. Your journey will be unique because of the variables involved, so don't get too concerned if you don't seem to be doing as well as others around you. It's not just about how equipped you are, how resourceful you are or how honestly you allow yourself to grieve, but as much to do with the relationship you had with your loved one, the role they played in your life and how intrinsic they were to your sense of security, your reason for being, your purpose in life.

We are born with an ability to survive, to repair and to adapt, and the process of bereavement works both for and against these natural abilities, dependent upon our reaction to the pain and confusion that grief will contain. We are all destined to make mistakes in grief; there is no perfect path, no set of rules or experts to tell us when and how to feel.

Without mistakes, there can be no progress that springs from the strength and courage to persevere. Grief is initially a cruel and unpredictable presence that we try to deceive, dodge, deny and distract. When we make mistakes and identify a different approach to generate a better result, it allows us to understand that grief is like a shadow we must learn to manage and accept and that an awful amount of energy will be wasted if we try to run away from something that is attached to us.

When we enter a relationship with grief, the actions that elicit an unfavourable outcome will dinimish. I'm grateful for the mistakes I made (and continue to make) after Jade's death. They make me look out and beyond into the distance, and in doing so I'm finding the answers and ways to move forwards.

My first mistake was to allow Bobby to stop his counselling sessions at the age of six. The children's bereavement charity Grief Encounter provided a weekly counselling session for both boys and while Freddy loved his time to speak openly about his loss, Bobby wasn't so sure.

I didn't want to put him through something that seemingly added to the pain of losing his mum so soon after her death, so I pulled the plug. What I should have done was to ask whether it was the process of discussion that he disliked, or the indignity and embarrassment of being taken out of class midway through a lesson to go to see the counsellor who visited him at school. He has always loathed being embarrassed and even back then he didn't like the idea that everyone knew why he was leaving the room.

If I had set up the sessions to happen at home, after school, first thing in the morning, at the weekend, even, maybe he would have enjoyed them. Freddy undeniably benefitted from his numerous counselling sessions and Bobby might have got rid of some of the suppressed anger that I still sometimes see in him.

There's no sell-by date on counselling or any type of therapy for children or adults and as I write this, I realise that to repair the gap in Bobby's development and hopefully eradicate some of the guilt I feel for this mistake, I should try to introduce the counselling again right now.

My second biggest mistake was that I under-estimated the impact grief would have on the boys' behaviour and there were many occasions in the past when I took their upsetting behaviour very personally, causing me great upset.

No parent knows what to expect when they become the all and everything in the worst of circumstances. Naively, I felt like my relationship with my children was so close that I would be able to do a great job of mopping up all of the sadness and tears, but I didn't account for the untamable effects of anger. There were times when I was nothing short of verbally abused, to the extent that my existence was wished away in return for their mother's. Poor children that they would feel such emotional desperation, but also what a privilege for me that they trusted and loved me enough to share their frustration with me, on me, to me, whatever. I would love to go back and adopt the approach that eight years of grieving and bringing them up has given me, especially the ability to see beyond the words and judge only the meaning from which they came.

Nothing good ever came from reacting in kind, as with any parenting dilemma. They may have got what they thought they were looking for in the form of an irate, devastated, scared, deflated father, but what they were craving and will always require from me is for me to be that example, the adult who doesn't judge the noise, who allows the irrelevant to pass by, while analysing their emotional requirements, delivering what they need in the form of space, patience, cuddles or the right words and actions.

Switching off our innate reaction to negativity from our own children is difficult, but with a conscious, mindful and pragmatic approach, holding on to the desire to be as effective for them in our parenting as we humanly can, we may not get it right every time but we can make progress towards being more in control when they are anything but.

My third mistake is a natural and common one, but I wonder how many of us distance ourselves from friends? I saw my sudden overload of responsibility as possibly unattractive and being too complicated to many of those in my social circle, though I have to make clear that this was my insecurity as opposed to something they gave me any reason to believe.

It isn't practical to maintain the same social activities when you go from having the boys three nights a week to seven nights a week, so I can see why I did pull back, but eight years later I'm only just waking up to the fact that I can do something about it.

I'm lucky that the majority of my friends appear to have understood my absence for long periods, but I do feel sad about the friends I was close to who are no longer in my life. Irrespective of my bereavement, losing friends when you go from mid-twenties to mid-thirties is par for the course as people settle down or move away, and there is still time to pick up old friendships. Guilt played a big part in my bereavement and I just couldn't bear the thought of not being there enough for the boys.

I'm just grateful that now the boys are older and have their own ideas of what they want to do in their spare time and at weekends it is easier for me to grow socially again, and I'm happier as a result. In fact, I'm not just more content, I'm actually much more patient and effective in my handling of all of the adolescent issues that I'm constantly faced with. I always felt a balance between my parental duties and the responsibilities I have to myself to continue to provide for my family, to keep myself healthy, and to keep my social life active, is key to a successful home and it's proving invaluable now.

The number one problem in grief is found in individuals who think that grief does not apply to them.

I had a client who saw me ten years after her loss – she had 'successfully' managed to go a whole decade without confronting the loss of her mother. Did it mean that after such a long period of time there was no grief to deal with any more? Not a chance. That grief had been festering away causing other issues, creating excessive emotion that was of course always attributed to being the fault of something or someone else.

So what happened when she began to face up to facts? Well, when the sale of her business went through (the main reason she was able to mask her grief because it kept her so busy), she was hit by a backlog of emotion that took her straight back to square one. Now you may argue 'at least she got away with it for ten years' but then I wonder what the last ten years would have looked like if she had learned to manage her grief?

What decisions would she have made differently? What would she look like physically? Grief being bottled up is like the collection of a big black cloud that just sits within you waiting patiently until it is recognised and expressed.

Secondly, the failure to see when an issue generated before the loss combines with the bereavement can have a catastrophic effect. I had a client who was in an abusive relationship and went on to lose his father; the combination of the two created quite a psychological and emotional tangle that affected his life in a series of negative ways.

The benefit of coaching for this individual was that the two factors could be separated and understood. Working on the existing issue from his younger years completely changed the face of his perspective towards his father's loss, and after many hours spent unravelling things we were left with a person with a completely different and healthier view of himself.

Here's a collection of other people's confessed mistakes. See how many you can avoid!

Steph: 'I supported those around me without dealing with my own grief; still don't think I have properly.'

This is something we must take responsibility for and, frankly, thinking that putting everyone else around us first somehow bypasses our own experience of grief is a natural but ineffective way of cheating the inevitable. Besides, those around us cannot truly begin to manage their grief until everyone around them is on the same page. This approach just delays the healing process, but is sadly a common defence mechanism designed to avoid and deflect.

Catherine: 'I think the first mistake for me is the saying that time's a great healer. It's really not! You'll always feel the pain of your loss forever more, you just deal with it differently.'

This is one of those clichés that get bandied about that we don't really understand and take very literally. From my own understanding, time doesn't heal us, we do. If we do a good job of managing our grief, in time we will feel better, but time elapsing doesn't take care of this process. There has to be a conscious effort to express our emotions, to be resourceful in giving ourselves the space we need and placing realistic expectations upon ourselves as to how we may perform differently as a result of our loss.

Victoria: 'I was thinking that going away to different countries and away from reminders will cure the pain. It doesn't really . . .'

Why would the pain go away? It lives within us. It's in our hearts and our heads and every inch of our being. Sure, we can run and distract ourselves all we like but we can't avoid the process. Holidays are great, time to be still, to sit with your emotions, but to distract? Just imagine when you're looking at that beautiful sunset, the first thing you'll think is, I wish that person was here to share it with, and then you're off.

There is an element of validity in Victoria's sentiment, which is that the triggers she refers to – the objects or places that remind her of the loved one she lost – and the things that she is running from will of course be easily avoided by distancing herself from them. What we have to appreciate is that avoidance is not helpful. It might mean you don't have to deal with something immediately but your grief will always be sitting there waiting for you when you return home, and it is very patient and very good at waiting.

Those objects and places that remind you of your loved one can initially be felt to be a negative. The truth is, when we are in a more accepting position those objects and places that we try to avoid soon became priceless as they become a means to elicit memories of people we love. Remembering is good, and inevitable. If you're going to remove anything, make it the items that elicit negative memories, but keep the things that bring comfort and take you somewhere happy.

Ryan: 'I ignore it and tell everyone I'm fine. I know it's a bad idea, but . . .' Ryan is absolutely right. It's a bad idea. Grief is like a big black cloud that follows us around floating gloomily above our heads for all to see. We can try to ignore it but when we lie in our beds at night, in those quiet moments, there it is, staring you smack in the face and it's not moving – well, not until you start to tell people the truth or actually start by telling yourself the truth.

To be honest with yourself and others is far from a weakness. Strength in bereavement is not to suppress your emotions so as to appear of a 'normal' state of mind; it's the absolute opposite! Weakness is suppression and strength is the courage to express.

Both paths lead to very different destinations. Denial, be it external or internal, is like being on the M25: you may feel like you're moving forwards but you'll always end up back at the toll crossing.

Linda: 'I lost friends through grief. I didn't tell them how I was feeling, so they didn't understand. My mistake was/is isolation.'

This is desperately sad. Is there anything sadder than losing someone you love? I think there is. Losing someone you love and then coping in such an unnecessarily destructive manner that we then push away or cut off the vital love and support that was available to us. It's like being shot and then refusing to go to hospital – two separate matters crucially merged together, making what I would describe as a 'Grissue', when grief is followed by an unhealthy response that creates a bigger issue. I always say that we need to let people in, to afford ourselves the support, the hugs and the conversation that we benefit from hugely in desperate times, but through coaching bereaved clients I know how easy it is for people to create a parallel existence just slightly removed from the actual reality.

We take drastic steps to remove anything from our life that could make us face up to facts. We avoid people, we don't go to certain places and we convince ourselves that everything is OK, but it isn't. We take these highly time-consuming and energy-sapping steps simply so we can continue to live the lie and prolong the chase, but we always get caught in the end.

If blessed with great friends, let them listen; if blessed with a wonderful family, let them hold you; if blessed with an understanding boss, let them give you time; if blessed with the internet, find a group where you'll be understood; if you're blessed with your health, look after your mind.

Accepting your loss may be a struggle but it takes only a second to make that decision; repairing the years of unfamiliarity between you and good friends takes a long time if you're even able to fix it at all.

Catherine: 'Even though my husband and I have been together since we were seventeen, I thought my grief took precedence over his grief when my sister died, like I had the monopoly on it, but really she was as much part of his life as mine and I was being selfish!'

I think Catherine required her husband's love and support to an extent that because of his own grief he couldn't initially provide and the disappointment, confusion, rejection and possibly abandonment generated may have fuelled the pulling rank described above.

'Grief Offs' are an unfortunate affair in loss. 'My grief's bigger than yours!' Everyone deserves the sympathy of others, yet some can look for a little extra believing that they were closer and therefore must be hurting more. There is no competition in grief; we must all support one another. We all feel it differently, and who are we to decide how someone else should feel about their or someone else's loss?

It's a great thing in this example that Catherine's husband embraced his sister-in-law in life to the extent that he truly felt her loss. They must have had a great relationship and isn't that what we all want for our partners to develop with our siblings? Hopefully Catherine realised this soon enough and they have continued to support one another ever since.

Charlotte: 'My biggest mistake (still is!) is I pride myself on being pretty tough in life and therefore I don't really like to share how I feel unless it's positive! This results in big moments in my life being filled with a lonely longing for my mum that I tell no one about . . .

Charlotte's fear of showing her grief or distress at losing her mother is all too common.

When we allow fear to succeed, we are not simply avoiding the inconvenience of the emotions attached to the trauma of grief;

we are actually reshaping ourselves to reflect what is essentially a lie.

The misconception that being tough is not sharing how we feel is in fact the polar opposite. It has been easier for you to suppress, in the short term at least. It would have been 'tough' of you to confront your emotions and allow yourself the routine indignity and help-lessness of loss.

The long-term ramifications of 'the lie' are extensive. When we are not truthful to ourselves about our grief, we construct the foundations of our life from that moment and relationships, opinions, attitudes and actions thereafter have to perpetuate the lie.

The behaviour of avoidance is easily formed and the truth (I'm grieving!) is easily forgotten. Before you know it, you've lost sight of what's real and what's precariously being held in place to protect yourself from having to admit that somewhere deep inside of you is a collection of something you've long since denied, which is literally about to burst.

It is never too late to reverse the effects. You can always stop running and hiding, which are so incredibly tiring for us to maintain!

You may have built a new identity on top of the loss, something you pursued to 'be safe', but you can peel this away if you wish by cour-ageously announcing yourself ready and intent on recognising your true feelings, not just to yourself but to those around you, who will no doubt embrace the opportunity to support you.

The biggest mistakes we make in loss, in a nutshell.

1. Unrealistic expectations about how quickly or how well we're likely to cope. Set the bar low, in fact leave the bar behind. Be ready

and willing to just experience it as it hits you. How can you possibly know what to expect if you've never been there before? It's like going to a remote Chinese town and thinking you'll know your way around.

2. Failure to communicate with those who are willing to support. You need to talk and they are willing to listen – a perfect partnership, so don't waste it. Your grief collects in your body like steam in a pressure cooker. If you don't let the pressure out in a controlled way by talking, crying, shouting when you need to let go, it will overwhelm you.

3. Rushing into things too early may have a counterproductive effect. New relationships, counselling, work are all good things eventually, but give yourself some time to find your feet, to check in with your feelings and allow grief to introduce itself to you before you start dating and finding answers. After you've started grieving things are more likely to fall into place.

4. Running and hiding from the sadness of grief is a natural response. Some get as far as the front door, some get to the end of the street, some make it to the next town, but very few ever make it across the borders without the echo of a memory of the person they've lost calling them back. And the ones that do? They might be there physically but mentally they've left something behind that they can't reclaim until they give themselves up to grief and go back to the reality of bereavement.

5. Whacking blame and guilt on yourself in order to mourn a loss and find your bearings in the sadness of it all is dangerous to your long-term well-being and relationship with grief. Seek therapy if

this is you, because heaping blame on your shoulders is very bad news.

The point most important to retain is that there are no such things as mistakes, especially in such an interpretable and creative experience as parenting. There are just actions that didn't produce the required outcome. Fortunately they can be changed, altered or learned from in order to produce a far more positive result next time. To make a 'mistake' is forgivable, in fact it's quite useful, but to repeat the exact actions or behaviours that continue to deliver us the exact same outcome is less so.

Imagine yourself playing darts, standing in exactly the same position, throwing the dart with exactly the same force and angle only to hit the outside of the board each time. What would you do? You would adjust your aim, change the direction, the height and the speed at which you released the dart. This would almost certainly get a different outcome and if it went in the right place, you'd try to do it exactly the same next time, wouldn't you?

38

When Grief Combines with Pre-existing Issues

Grief is hard enough but some people are always going to find it harder than others. How does someone, for example, with anxiety cope with bereavement? How does a person who has experienced abuse react to loss compared to someone who has experienced stability, support and positive relationships? If you're bereaved, what negative experience in your life could be interlocking with your grief to create additional layers?

Just about every conceivable reaction in the midst of loss can be attributed partially to something unrelated to the bereavement, and it's also common for people to unduly apportion blame and guilt to themselves as a result of previous experiences. It is helpful to raise your awareness of the possibility of past influences and have a good look at what combination of events in your life might be relevant to your grief. Doing so can lead to the relinquishing of undue responsibility, an unblocking of your sense of deserving and an ability to forgive – all of which would benefit just about anyone.

Imagine all the feelings relating to your loss to be like a cocktail. You might think that the only ingredient is grief itself, but on closer inspection it may be that grief is just one of several, with regret, acceptance, sadness, guilt and all sorts of past experiences mixed in together. In the case of Sam, a 41-year-old single mother of one, grief combined with a lot of complicated feelings born out of a difficult family history.

After decades of battling alcoholism, Sam's father committed suicide by throwing himself in front of a train. He hadn't been a good father to Sam and for most of her life she had been prevented from raising the issues of his drinking and absent parenting. His alcoholism was a subject her family did not communicate well on, if at all.

Sam felt her mother enabled her father's drinking and held her mother to blame, not just for her father's suicide, but also the circumstances that led to it. Her relationship with her mother was complicated further because Sam and her daughter currently lived with her. Sam was preoccupied by thoughts that she could have had a better father and he could have had a better life if things had been different.

This longing for 'what could have been' was not necessarily born out of grief. She felt abandoned, not by the fact that he had died, but because of his original choice of lifestyle that led to him being in the clutches of addiction and her mother's choice to be complicit.

To help Sam differentiate the components of her supposed grief, we did some work on putting a percentage to her feelings. She identified that when she was around her mum she felt 80% upset but when she wasn't, her general feelings for her loss were between 10% and 20%. These figures showed clearly that there was much more in the mix here than simply grief. Her bad feelings when in the company of her mother broke down into four main components: grief, anger, sadness and regret.

At times, grief can be pinpointed to how, when and why you are missing someone. Sam reckoned her level of grief in this respect was only around 10% as she felt she hadn't had much of a father to miss. He hadn't been around for her and had spent large parts of his life drunk.

Sam's anger, however, was far higher and she put a 40% value on it. She was angry that her mother had funded her father's alcoholism; she was angry at her mother's infatuation and obsession with her dad; and she was angry that her mother had not, in Sam's opinion, done enough to prevent her father's drinking (which had led to his suicide) or to protect her daughter.

Sam's feeling of regret, something that is commonly mistaken for grief, was at 20% and this was about 'what could have been'. What if her family had been able to help her father beat his alcoholism? She had told me that before her father ended his life he had called her mother and she had spent fifteen minutes on the phone to him. Sam will never know how that conversation went but she only knows that it wasn't enough to stop him. What if the phone call had produced a different result?

Sadness was also a component of Sam's feelings. She put this at 10% and attributed it to how things had played out when her father had thrown himself on the train tracks. Dealing with the police, feelings of how the train driver must have felt, telling people, the inquest, sadness for her daughter that she had to be a part of all this and sadness when she learned from the professionals who helped her how common suicide is.

It is important to differentiate between sadness and regret. Regret is for things that didn't happen, what could have been – if Sam's father had been a better father and hadn't been an alcoholic – and sadness is based on the reality of the experience – the tragedy of her father's suicide. Regret can be more destructive than sadness because it comes from our imagination and can take us to places in our own thoughts that make things harder for ourselves.

When it is isolated as a self-prescribed and fully self-controlled factor, regret can be reduced when we ask ourselves subjectively: 'What can I do to change the past?' We have an obligation to be kind to ourselves, and placing our focus on what we do control is part of this. To spend any length of time wanting something you can't have is to torture and punish yourself, and for what gain?

The way to reduce a regret is to do something in the present or future that appropriately fills the void created in the past. If you regret not spending enough time with that person, make more effort with existing relatives so the pattern isn't repeated. If you regret the health implications suffered by a relative in the past, take extra care of your own health and then in a small way you have created a positive reaction to a negative experience.

Living with her mother was far from ideal for Sam, but because of the recent breakdown of her relationship, she was for the time being dependent on her mother providing a roof over her and her daughter's heads. Both she and her mother worked, so they weren't spending all their time together, and when Sam wasn't with her mother the feelings associated with her grief diminished and were relatively manageable. But even if Sam had been able to move out, this would have been a short-term avoidance of what were long-term, deep-rooted issues that needed to be addressed. It became clear that Sam didn't even know if her mother loved her. She couldn't remember the last time she'd expressed her love or pride in her daughter, and this was extremely hurtful for Sam.

The main thing on Sam's mind was how she could better understand her mother. Why couldn't her mother acknowledge Sam's achievements? Why couldn't she ever show any interest or tell her daughter that she was proud of her? Why did Sam feel her mother judged her and why, asked Sam, '. . . do I allow her negative remarks to influence me and hold me back?'

Her mother had in fact asked Sam to move out before the next school holiday, telling her she didn't like her granddaughter being around so much. In the face of such hurtful hostility, I asked Sam what was preventing her from moving out. She said that as she was self-employed, the pressure of having to pay rent from week to week on top of providing for her daughter would be a real 'leap of faith' but then when she heard herself say that, immediately recognised that this supposed risk 'could be the kick up the arse I need'.

In order to help Sam understand her mother's behaviour, I asked her if she would answer questions taking on the role of her mother – a perspective-shifting technique that, in my experience, never fails to help. It's always hard to assume someone else's identity at first but Sam warmed to it pretty quickly.

Sam (or Barbara) told me about her childhood and how her grandfather was a highly successful builder, so her family had been able to afford foreign holidays, which in the fifties really meant you were doing well. She had a settled, privileged childhood with no apparent drama to speak of, though she harboured rebellious thoughts.

It wasn't until she was 17 that she met Sam's dad in a pub. He was quite a drinker even then and 'Barbara' explained that she may have been attracted to him because of her wish to rebel against her parents. Sam's dad was married, so the whole thing felt illicit and exciting and provided Barbara with plenty to stick her rebellious teeth into.

Their relationship continued in secret for some time and Sam's father's alcoholism was evident throughout. The relationship was unsustainable and Barbara split from Sam's father some years later. He then went on to get married and had three children and then a further two with his second wife. It wasn't until a few weeks after she died that he came back to Barbara. And she was more than happy – even with his five kids – to take him back. All five kids moved in as well, and Barbara played her part in raising them.

Barbara did not cope well with having so many stepchildren and the stepchildren did not cope well with having Barbara in their lives.

Later on, the contact between her and all of the stepchildren would cease entirely, but at this stage she had them all under her roof. Sam was Barbara's first and only child and she pretty much handed her over to her parents as she had to cope with all the stepchildren and an alcoholic man with whom she had always been infatuated. Life for Barbara was undoubtedly tough.

I 'brought' Sam back into the room and asked her what hearing herself tell her mother's story like that told her about the way her mother is now. She told me that, as uncomfortable as it was, she could see why her mother had become the version of herself that was unable to praise her or enjoy a good relationship with her grand-daughter, and that her experience of rebelling against a stable and protected childhood to end up effectively giving her only child over to her own parents, while parenting the five stepchildren of the alcoholic man she had always loved, had damaged her immeasurably.

Sam added that we had omitted a key element in understanding her mother and this was the guilt she was carrying over the day of her husband's death. Their fifteen-minute phone conversation that day had not prevented him from going on to jump in front of a train. Sam had had to find out about it from the police reports as her mother had not told her and refused to talk about it.

When people have a huge sense of suppressed guilt it can lead to the building of a brick wall, which they hide behind in order to protect themselves from facing the reality of the harm their actions may have caused, and to give them room to justify their actions to themselves. In Barbara's case, her apparent dislike of Sam and disapproval of Sam's daughter was what she was holding on to in order to continue blocking out her own pain. In inventing grievances, she could justify to herself that others were doing wrong to her and never have to face the truths and hurt of her own life. But even in her actions she was showing contradictory behaviour – having her daughter and granddaughter live with her (she could, presumably, have refused) while being aloof, cold and inconsiderate in her actions and words.

We don't always need to hear an acknowledgement or apology from the person who causes us the most pain, or that they understand where their negative behaviour comes from, though that would always be preferable. To understand their pain and to feel their sadness can somewhat reduce the impact of the blow each time you hope for something positive from them, a glimmer of connection and light despite a lifetime of emotional darkness. Sam had achieved the realisation that Barbara didn't show her love, not because it wasn't there (even though it's safe to say it might be so buried under the weight of her pain that she no longer knew how to access it herself) but because her doing so would have been to undermine the adopted beliefs that kept her safe and protected from a less than desirable life.

The question for Sam was whether she wanted to press her mother for her version of the truth and possibly set her free by giving her the opportunity to talk. It was no longer a question of whether or not Sam would be moving out, but how far she was prepared to go in talking to her mother.

Grief can open a door to many underlying emotions and set you on a journey of discovery both in understanding others and exploring issues or answering questions you never knew existed.

I asked Sam how she would feel if her mother died and she had never got around to raising any of these issues with her. And then the reverse: how would she feel if her mother died and she had raised some or all of the issues with her? Might this change the way she grieved for her father – and her mother?

Sam was waiting for her mum to share her thoughts and feelings with her even though she knew there was very little chance of her doing so. It was possible that waiting for her mum to come good as a parent and to liberate Sam with her words was in many respects holding Sam back, but she chose to wait nonetheless.

What did she think she would get from waiting for the emotion, the reassurances that would never come? Hope may be alive in her heart but she wouldn't seem to be getting anywhere. Should she give up on the prospect of hearing and feeling the truth and release in her mother's voice and actually getting somewhere, or should she continue to stand still, allowing life to go on by, ever hoping, ever waiting, ever growing older?

On catching up with Sam a few months after we spoke she informed me she hadn't raised the subject with her mum, mainly because she didn't want to be dragged into something negative. She thought that if she focused on the past then it would send her down a rabbit hole that she would rather steer clear of. Not to ignore it or brush it under the carpet, but accept that she couldn't change the past but could now actually recognise that her upbringing had made her a far stronger and more capable person.

The most significant change was not in her relationship with her mum but that her other daughter, Chloe, 16 years old, had been home for half-term a few weeks earlier and had told her that she wanted to come back to live with Sam full-time. She had been living with her dad in Ireland to pursue a better education. So, Chloe would be moving in with her mum imminently! Which meant she now had to get a move on with the house hunting.

Ask yourself these questions:
Does the way you are handling grief echo a way that you have coped with something in the past? For example, if you feel you are avoiding grief, have you avoided tackling things head on before in relationships? In employment? In parenting?

Is your current behaviour in relation to grief and grief only? Or do you feel like there are other factors from your past that have surfaced since your loss?

As an exercise, imagine that you are staring at a pint glass and try to establish what the different ingredients are in your cocktail of grief – OK, I know you're too sophisticated to drink a cocktail from a pint glass, but . . . How much of that drink is relevant to the loss? How much of it was already sitting in the glass before you lost somebody? And does that measure ever actually subside? Or are you very good at keeping yourself topped up?

As an interesting addition to this line of enquiry – who tops it up? Is it you or is it somebody else?

If you communicated more, what would happen to the amount of liquid in your glass? Would you like to be left with just grief? Or are you happy that other issues combine so that grief is harder to define exactly?

The overriding point is that we want to feel like we are in a position to manage our grief, but how can we possibly manage something that is undefined? In order to best manage our grief, we should be mindful not to cope with our loss in a similar way, using a similar coping mechanism, to ones that have probably been in place for some time. This is incredibly difficult to do if unchallenged, but with additional focus on the way we respond to grief, to words from others, to reminders of our loss, we should ask ourselves, 'Are these responses constructive, or do they potentially do more harm than good?' If you want to understand anything, be it grief or any other unrelated issues from the past, the only real way to achieve improvements is to talk, either to professionals or to family members and friends. Having the space to discuss our innermost feelings gives us the opportunity to make sense, to gain clarity, to find new perspectives that can reduce the effects of negative experiences from the past.

39

When Losing One
Means Losing Many

My family has experienced its fair share of loss and the adjustments required following a death were not only focused on the person no longer with us, but also the difficulties that arose when parts of our family separated as a result.

Some people are the very substance that hold a family together and it isn't until they are gone that you can see the role that they played, and relationships begin to feel less relevant when the reason for their unity is no longer there.

When my much-adored grandmother died, I learned how central she was to my whole family. She had been the one who brought the family together for so long and in her absence we all rallied around my grandad so the family remained together. But on his passing, the glue came unstuck and while there were no arguments or fallings-out, everyone just went their own way. It was the same when I lost my Auntie Jackie. My cousin and I sort of went our separate ways and lost each other, not intentionally and not because we didn't love each other. It was the fact that the dynamics shifted and the years went by, and before we knew it, we were relative strangers.

Looking back, I realise that while my grandparents or my Auntie Jackie were alive it was easier to maintain relationships with my extended family, but there was no reason why, following their deaths, we couldn't have adapted and maintained those connections. If you don't want to completely lose touch it simply requires effort, but you should also know when to let go if the effort isn't reciprocated, as some people deal with grief differently to others.

It's hard for someone who is totally accepting of the nature of the loss to travel alongside someone in life who is in complete denial. One can talk about the loss and the other can't, so we often gravitate to those that have similar coping mechanisms and I'd say this accounts for more non-contentious drifts than anything else.

Drifting apart

My family have drifted in the absence of a central figure, a leader if you like, who will arrange gatherings either to remember our dead relatives or because we are a family and should be seeing more of each other anyway. When their anniversaries or birthdays come around it's not something that we get together for. I wonder if this is because as a group there is more internalising of grief going on than there is expression? I suddenly feel guilty because I can't remember my nan's date of birth or the days some of my family died, and because they were people who played such a huge role in the more positive aspects of my childhood and young adult life, I need to realise that there is no reason why that instigator, the person who arranges something next time around, can't be me.

Focusing on my own family for a moment again, it's hard not to believe that my children have lost out as a result of the lack of closeness in the extended family. Even though they didn't meet my nan, who died in 2001, a few years before their births, or my grandad, who lost his life when Bobby was five and Freddy four, some of my happier childhood memories were being surrounded by family and sadly, my children haven't really experienced that particularly often.

It makes me reflect for a moment on how wonderfully different it would be for those dearly missed relatives to still be here. How the boys would have enjoyed staying at the cottage in Bracknell, Berkshire with their great-grandmother Pamela, the card games, the open fire, badminton in the garden, the usual ritual of going to a car boot sale first thing in the morning to see what comics I could find, and the influence she would have had on their education. Then there is the extended family they would have known via my nan's second husband Bill, a family I sadly no longer see either.

They would also have loved visiting my wonderful Grandad Jack in Hornchurch – his love of watching a good film, his constant use of inappropriate comments and jokes. He would have always spoiled them with things only a grandparent would think to buy and maybe taken them over the road to the social club where I spent many Saturday nights playing pool and running around. He would have loved their company, because he lived on his own and really enjoyed it when people visited him.

My Auntie Jackie, who died not long after Bobby was born, would have been one of the greatest assets in their life, as she was in mine. A really tough East Ender, she said it how it was but she would have organised us and boosted their courage and confidence, and her house would have been our second home, because she was so much fun – always something happening, plans being made. She was simply so full of life, all of the time. It would also have also meant my cousin would have been in their life. I have never once imagined what life would have been like for my children if those three had still been around, and it's as desperately sad as it is comforting and satisfying to play that movie in my imagination. I suddenly feel closer to my grief for all three of them for doing so. I so wish they were here – how much better things would be.

Contentious family issues

A divide can also occur when, following a loss, opinions on what's right and what isn't differ. There is very little quite as contentious as moving on in love after the loss of a partner, and nothing says 'I'm moving on' quite as much as when someone new is moving in.

Take Ross, a guy in his early forties with two young children, whose wife Claire died after a short illness. He was a good husband, caring for her with devotion and love while also looking after their children, and Claire's family could not have asked for more from him. After Claire's death his wife's parents shared in the care of their grandchildren and Ross got on well with his in-laws.

Eighteen months after Claire died, Ross met Kirsty and started seeing her, and found himself falling in love after a few months of dating. It soon became clear she wasn't going anywhere and that they might build a life together. Acutely aware that others might find this difficult, Ross was sensitive as to how he told them about Kirsty.

He had been careful as to when and how he introduced the children to Kirsty and they had started to respond well to her. First he told his children that there was someone he wanted them to meet. He waited several weeks before introducing her, having of course told her about them right from the off. It was when he knew that this was going to be more than a casual friendship that he arranged for them to meet each other. Then, as a dutiful and caring son-in-law, he told Claire's parents about Kirsty. He told them he had been seeing her for a while, that he thought this was something that could last and that the children had met her and seemed to like her, though no one was rushing anything.

So far so good. What Ross didn't expect, however, was how livid his in-laws were. So livid in fact that his father-in-law attacked him verbally in front of the children and proceeded, over the coming weeks, among other calculated lies, to drip-feed them harmful speculation as to how quickly their dad had moved on, causing them confusion and upsetting Ross, who quite understandably didn't want his children being looked after by Claire's parents.

Having been exposed now to many examples of children being caught up in the contentiousness of grief, I can tell you that this behaviour by Ross's in-laws is not entirely unusual. It can be the result of all sorts of unexplored emotions, or a case of one person in this new and bewildering set-up being able to move forwards and allowing themselves to be happier earlier than others think appropriate. In Ross's case, his grieving in-laws were undoubtedly still devastated, unable to fully accept their daughter's death, so the fact that her husband had found someone else just compounded the reality that she was no longer alive, something they did not want to be reminded of.

Instead of taking their time to get their heads around the new relationship – talking to Ross about Kirsty, encouraging the children to get to know her and voice any concerns they may have to them or their father and not to worry if they didn't feel able to love or even like Kirsty at first – they criticised and bemoaned her at every opportunity, not only creating a huge problem for the new couple, but confusing two grieving and unsure children.

The loss of their mother at such a young age – Molly was eight and Tom was six – was without a doubt going to have an effect on them both then and going forward, but losing a parent at a young age does not necessarily need to be the downfall of children's lives.

However, as you can see here, there was a need to tread carefully. In Molly and Tom's case, losing their mother was upsetting enough, and however carefully Ross handled it, the appearance of Kirsty on the scene would inevitably be unsettling for a while, so the additional layer of unnecessary drama stirred up by their grandparents was bound to create many issues for them to have to unravel, both at the time and later in their adolescent and adult lives.

If Ross had talked to me about how to approach his situation, I would have advised him – ages before he had anyone in mind – to have asked his in-laws how long after Claire's death would be appropriate, in their view, for him to start dating again. If Claire herself had given him a timeline then all well and good, but if she hadn't then Ross was heading for a difficult discussion.

Some parents or in-laws respond well. I've known of cases where they put their own feelings aside as they can see this is what their bereaved son- or daughter-in-law might need in order to start rebuilding their lives, and they give their blessing and embrace the new partner. Not in Ross's case. If, when he talked to his in-laws, they had said something totally unreasonable like five years – or never – then he could have explained to them how he felt about that and they could have come to some understanding. Maybe then they would have said that they didn't want to know anything about his love life until someone significant came along. Maybe they would have told him that whoever it was would be hard for them to accept as in their eyes their daughter was the only rightful mother of their grandchildren.

But involving them in something so intimate would have made them feel empowered, as if they had a bit of control at a time when they might still be feeling helpless in preventing their daughter's death. Despite their wishes that Ross didn't date, in time they might have come around to this very natural fact of life, and their reaction to Kirsty eighteen months down the line would have been very different.

For what it's worth, in my view, Molly and Tom's grandparents, as two adults, even if they were bereft and lost, should have played this differently and recognised that the children depended on their guidance and that being furious and weaving a web of lies was not going to help anyone. They reacted as if Ross had cheated on their daughter, as if he had substituted her for someone else and as if he were the one responsible for sending her away.

But Ross hadn't sent her away. He hadn't cheated on her. He had loved her, did everything he could for her and what's more, had provided his children with the stability and support they needed after the death of their mother. He had waited a year and a half after Claire's death to start dating again, a respectful amount of time by anyone's standards.

It is clear here that his in-laws were still struggling a year and a half after the loss of their daughter and maybe in their eyes, any time was too soon for Ross to be dating again. They were perhaps too blinded by grief and irrationality to understand that if Ross had continued on by himself, without having another chance at love, he would have been lonely and unhappy and eventually unable to provide such a supportive foundation for his children.

The damaging 'domino effect' created by an absence is not exclusive to family members. Sometimes there are social ramifications in grief when someone feels ready to start dating after the loss of their partner. This can often create irreparable damage if the choices people make in loss defy the moral parameters of those around them.

Social abandonment

Martin, a widower who also has two children, lost his wife Jayne to cancer. Like many single parents, he was finding it hard to adapt to his new reality. Martin had allowed the feeling of being overwhelmed to take over, until he realised that it would be an insult to Jayne if he allowed his life to waste away in her absence. He had seen her suffer for eighteen months and after five months of being alone, he decided out of a strong desire to return to some sort of normality that, more for adult company than anything else, he was ready to go on a date.

'Bereavement is one of the few times in life when people judge whether it is appropriate for you to be in a relationship,' Martin told me. He recalled how he had been on a second date when his friends called him to instruct him he needed to come and pick his children up at once. They gave no reason and when Martin arrived, the kids seemed fine and perplexed as to why he was there. There was no doubt in Martin's mind that his friends had deliberately sabotaged his date because they strongly disapproved.

Not long after he became aware of a rumour that was going around the parents at the school gates – that Martin had in fact started seeing the woman he was dating before Jayne had even died. He felt people were cutting him off, avoiding him and talking about him behind his back and he felt belittled and judged. He felt socially ostracised, unable to invite anyone round or pick up the phone to friends.

The rumour had been started by one woman in particular and I was interested to know what the reality was, as opposed to what Martin imagined was being said behind his back in the school play-ground and among his social circle. When we unpicked who in real-ity had actually cut Martin off, he realised that while he had actually fallen out with a few couples, which upset him, there were others in the circle who he probably would have lost touch with anyway, and that the only reason he thought he wanted to see them was because while they were still present in his life, they induced fond memories of a time when Jayne had still been alive, memories that lived with him and still felt alive and vibrant. But the fact was that Jayne had been the instigator of their time together and now that she was no longer alive, Martin would have drifted from them anyway. These people were not the loss he was mourning.

In talking to Martin it became clear that the fact he felt betrayed was an enormous issue for him. His dad had walked out when he was young and had never returned. Abandonment and betrayal were clearly the link and it was less of a mystery as to why Martin would instinctively withdraw socially after his loss. He had learned that it is safer to rely on nobody rather than taking the risk of allowing himself to be supported by others.

Martin had told me that he had 'lost his world' when Jayne died and spoke of how his work life was restricted, and he quickly realised that was nothing to do with the hearsay either. He then discussed the heightening of his responsibility at home and in general and again realised that was nothing to do with the gossip.

When I had pointed out that his house, their pets, their family, their schools, their neighbourhood, their car, his love for Middlesbrough FC had all remained present, he realised his world was far from lost.

He knew what was coming by the time he also realised that the fact that his role in life had changed so much was absolutely nothing to do with the terrible friend he once trusted but had everything to do with Jayne. I asked him to change his statement to something more realistic, to which he responded, 'I've been cut off from three couples and my Jayne is lost.'

Quite a difference, and another great example of how our carelessly misplaced assessments of certain circumstances can create beliefs that are far from realistic and therefore entirely detrimental to some aspect of our grief. What have you conditioned yourself to believe about your loss/life?

It was getting clearer that while Martin hadn't initiated the cutting off, he certainly saw it through. I suspected there might already be a coping mechanism there that he had used before he even encountered the loss of his wife. Betrayal was a really hard word for Martin to say but he hadn't been betrayed by anyone important enough to create such a pained expression.

Martin confirmed, telling me about the fact that his Dad walked out when he was young and never returned. Abandonment and betrayal were clearly the link and it was less of a mystery as to why Martin would instinctively withdraw socially after his loss. He had learnt that it is safer to rely on nobody rather than taking the risk of allowing himself to be supported by others. What a stream of realisation for Martin. It sounds painful, but exposure to reality can be such a relief. His trust was not broken; it was still his to share with whomever he pleased. He was only ever as cut off or isolated as he made himself. He didn't need to keep himself safe – he had lost his wife, the worst had already happened! As a coping mechanism it was entirely relevant when his dad let him down, but now? It was like stirring his tea with a fork.

Martin had confused his grief with other issues, but with him firmly in the picture again we started looking at ways he could take his head out of the sand and stop hiding himself and his children from people who could support them and enrich their lives, which regardless of their loss were very much for the living.

Martin identified five steps that represented a complete reversal of the strategy he had been unwittingly adopting and agreed to take action that very day:

1. He was going to stop keeping people he trusted at arm's length. He was going to invite two friends down to Kent from London who that he hadn't seen for years.

2. He was going to make new friends at his daughter's school by inviting her friend and the friend's parents round for drinks at his house one evening.

3. He would do the same for his son – slightly awkward in that three of his son's friends would be banned, not through their own fault

but the fact that their parents were the couples in question that Martin mistook as representing society!

4. He would go to salsa again with his girlfriend (the same woman he dated when the gossip began), which would be a good way for them to meet new friends.

5. He was going to invite the ex-husband of the rumour-starting troublemaker out for a beer. (They were now divorced after he had learned of her affair.) He and Martin had got on well before that started and this represented a bold effort to reclaim a piece of his old social life.

We had spoken earlier about celebrating anniversaries and Martin had told me that all of the anniversaries were in a difficult two-month period. His biggest concern was that he had made them very personal and he wanted to make them bigger and more inclusive. It's amazing how we drop clues into what we say. I asked him why he thought he had minimised the interaction at the anniversaries and birthdays, and he just smiled. I left with a good feeling that Jayne's next anniversary will be celebrated by many, although not all will be welcome.

Family and friends can drift away after a loss. It's not always necessarily due to a falling out but just where the mechanics of the family structure have to adapt to the absence of a sometimes integral part of the group. Things do not fall into place automatically, either; it requires some manual effort from those involved to keep friends and social circles together. In problematic social restructuring, while we may battle against the dispersal of friends, on most occasions, the ones who don't drift are the ones we should really care about, but when a family divides, there is no limit to the ongoing repercussions a family feud can create.

40

How Grief Might Affect Your Job

When we lose someone our work life can be affected as a result. It's not just that might we need some time off but we may also struggle to perform to our usual standards. This could cause some insecurity around your position. Some employers are likely to be more understanding than others, but you give yourself the best possible chance of protecting your relationship with them when you communicate your bereavement as early as possible.

Employers' views vary significantly and one's sympathy will not match another's, but it's always important to be truthful to yourself about how mentally and physically present you are able to be in your role after your loss and whether it is safe or productive for you and your employer, until such time that you are able to function to a reasonable level again.

Some bereaved people will approach this differently to others. Some actually find the idea of going to work disrespectful, as if it represents moving on too soon; some use work as a distraction to stop them from thinking about their loss; and some do not feel 'up to it' for varying lengths of time.

The goalposts have moved and a big mistake would be to insist to your employers that it won't affect your role. In some cases it can actually make you more productive because of the distraction value of your work, but that will come at a personal cost, when you return home from work to find grief waiting for you in the quiet moments when the day slows itself.

Do you want to be left with this job after you have learned to manage your loss? If you communicate honestly to your employers about when you feel you need space and when you are fit to perform they will most likely see no reason to be anything other than supportive.

Your employers should provide some support so that if you have a wave of grief and you feel work is the last place you can bear to be, then because you have warned them that this may happen from time to time they will have put something in place to cover you. If you haven't forewarned them they might be slightly less supportive if it's a last-minute phone call to say you're staying at home that day.

In the early days of your bereavement, it is good for your employer to:

1. Offer their condolences to you.

2. Ensure that you know you are not expected to work on the day the death has taken place. You need to hear that work comes second and that you must take what time out is needed.

3. Begin a dialogue with you, asking how you would like to stay in contact. Is phone or email contact preferred? Are there particular times to avoid? They should also be aware that in the first few days, you may not wish to speak to anyone as you may be in shock.

4. Ask how much information you wish your co-workers to have about the death and remember that this information is private under data protection legislation and to stick strictly to the facts.

5. Consider what action needs to be taken if the death is in the media; particularly if the press contact the workplace or approach co-workers for interview.

6. Ask if you wish to be contacted by colleagues.

7. Be conscious of any days you need to fulfil religious or cultural expectations such as mourning rituals.

8. Be open to revising and reviewing the situation with you. A conversation about when you think you'll be going back may not be appropriate in the first days of bereavement. However, it is important they start a dialogue with you that will allow an open discussion around how you are coping, their policy on bereavement, when you might be ready to return to work, and any adjustments that might help with this (for example, a phased return).

They need to remember that every bereavement is different: you may feel able to return to work very soon after, or you may need more time. The relationship with the person who died and the circumstances of the death will both have an impact on your needs, particularly if the death was sudden or traumatic.

A case study

I wanted to know first-hand what it was like to be someone staring the death of a loved one in the face knowing that it would have a detrimental impact on their work life as well as everything else.

The people involved

I met Jenny Swift, 58 and a full-time civil servant, to discuss her concerns about her work following the sad news that the father of her child was becoming very ill. Jenny has given fourteen years of service in her current job and endured a messy separation from Michael, her ex-husband, in 2013.

They have a son, George, aged 12. Michael has regular access to his son and is a good, attentive father.

In September 2016 Michael was diagnosed with a rare and aggressive form of prostate cancer and due to the damaging effect of the chemotherapy he is having no further treatment at present.

In the background

Jenny's family are livid that she is helping Michael in any way, shape or form since his behaviour surrounding the split. They witnessed her go through hell; she was on anti-depressants and signed off from work for a month.

Jenny is taking Michael to hospital appointments, collecting medication for him and doing his washing and ironing, all of which she does for George's sake, so that he knows his mum did as much for his father as possible and ultimately so that there are no regrets when it is too late and people are held accountable for their actions.

Jenny also adds that he would otherwise be isolated, lonely and progressively less able to cope, which is something she doesn't want him to suffer or for George to see. She also very much hopes that if it were the other way round someone would step in to support her too.

Work

Recently Jenny took Michael to get some results. On her return to work her manager warned her that she would be receiving a stern email about her erratic timekeeping. This manager also said that she thought it questionable that Jenny would want to care for her ex-husband, as if it would be OK if he was her current husband but not now he was an ex.

The manager was not taking into account the fact that what Jenny was doing was incredibly selfless, an act of forgiveness towards Michael and an act of extreme love towards George, who is soon to have his world turned inside out.

Jenny told me that she made up every single hour that she used to care for her ex-husband by working as late into the night as was required. She is incredibly conscientious and ensures not just that her time is accounted for but also that her workload is always completed so that there is as little reason as possible for her employers to feel disgruntled.

There is one part of Jenny's role that can't be fulfilled outside of office hours but she knows that there are many other colleagues at work who can cover this specific task.

Questions to answer now

Jenny admits that she has no idea how much time Michael has medically. She doesn't know how much care he will require, whether he will go into a hospice, or whether he will move back in with Jenny and their son. If the latter were to happen, she doesn't know how she will manage with work and him to care for.

And when it happens?

Will she work? Will she stay at the same place? Will she take something less pressurised? Does she have to be at home when George gets home from school? How will she cope financially and will he continue going to school immediately after? I wanted to help her settle her mind and answer some of her own questions, so we started with the next step.

Options

Jenny may not know what is the best thing to do, but she can always look at the options she has available to her. Obviously her employers will have a big say in future developments, but to look at what might be possible, even if she knows it's not so desirable, will help her to make the best possible choice.

1. Go part-time? Jenny could go part-time and have three days at work and three days at home.

2. Leave? Jenny could manage with her current savings for around a year.

3. Take early retirement? Jenny is less than two years away from the retirement age of 60 but could take early retirement. There are people in the workplace who have retired but are still working on a part-time basis.

4. Take a less pressurised role? Jenny could take an easier post. It would likely be more of an admin role.

Considerations/Priorities

We discussed the factors that would be most influential in deciding her best course of action. For Jenny, they are:

1. Financial benefit. Jenny has to ensure that she is able to pay the bills. It isn't about earning the maximum, but it about maintaining a suitable income, however possible.

2. George's benefit. Her son needs to be better off for whatever decision is made.

3. Creation of time. Any decision made needs to suit Jenny from a time perspective. She may need to be looking after Michael and George while maintaining that income. She needs more time at home.

4 .Protecting her mental well-being. Jenny does not want to take an option that put her mental well-being at risk again.

The simple strategy here would be to focus on each option individually and check its merits against her main considerations.

To go part-time means that financially Jenny would be secure. Not as secure as she is now but then she knows that she will have to earn less; it's just a case of how much less and by what means.

George would benefit from having his mum around more and it would give her the time to care for Michael. As a result, Jenny's mental well-being would be protected by the fact that she would still be working and renewing some purpose outside of the situation at home, which is important in pursuit of some balance.

To leave would create financial uncertainty. Maybe George would like his mum around all day every day, but then again, maybe she could be around too much? Jenny fears that this would be counter-productive, and the pressure created by the uncertainty might tip her into depression again, which would stop her from being on top form for George when he loses his dad.

Early retirement and working part-time would give Jenny some freedom and flexibility. Her sense of purpose outside of the house remains intact and it may be the way to get the income/time balance as well matched as possible.

Jenny realised she would need to find out what her pension entitlement was if she retired now or at the age of 60. Both outcomes would affect her differently but she would need to ascertain the rules in order to fully understand her options.

Taking a less pressurised role would require taking a hit financially but she wouldn't gain any additional time as a result. It would just mean that she didn't have to think so much when she was sitting at her desk. Jenny realised that to her this would be boring, but most importantly it wouldn't benefit George or the time she was able to spend at home.

From taking these simple steps she was able to see that there were two emerging front runners: early retirement and going part-time.

I then asked Jenny about her next steps. She understood that it was not a given that opportunities for part-time employment or early retirement currently existed so she would need to speak to the HR department at work.

She also identified that going part-time would possibly leave more in the pension fund for later but wasn't sure how much of a financial benefit it would be to work an extra two years before retiring. Again, assuming that both options were available from the workplace perspective, this might just be the detail that sends her one way or the other.

Jenny and I discussed who she would speak to and what she would say. She had identified that the only other people in the workplace who had suffered a loss were part-time and so she couldn't really gauge how work would deal with her.

The next thing for Jenny to decide was how much of her private life to disclose in that initial meeting with HR. She quickly realised that in order for work to support her in the best possible way she would have to be honest and open.

In taking it one step at a time and discussing what a favourable and disappointing outcome would look and sound like, Jenny saw that it would be best for her to send an initial email to HR but to copy in the area manager just so everyone was made aware of the circumstances.

As a self-professed 'people pleaser' Jenny worried that this was a little bit too much fuss at first, but when we reviewed the nature of her enquiry she felt that if there was ever a subject that gave you the right to copy in people at a higher level then this was it.

I would imagine that it also motivates the person in HR to do a more efficient job. Lastly, Jenny committed to sending that email at 11 a.m. the next day.

She declared with some satisfaction just a day or two later that the area business manager had replied almost instantly. The manager had suggested a further option of temporary adjustment to her hours before making any permanent changes and personally requested that the HR person meet with her to discuss it.

Jenny felt this was 'amazing' and constituted the perfect response. Was it so difficult, though? It depends on a few traits to your personality that you may have developed long before you took the job. Is it amazing or is it someone doing their job, showing compassion and looking after their colleagues? The hardest part of this for Jenny was the asking of the question. We must never be backwards in coming forwards with questions that we are entitled to ask, but which we often neglect to pose because the fear of a negative response is just too much of a threat.

A month later and Jenny updated me on her 'good progress'. She had agreed that she wouldn't work on Wednesdays from May for a three-month trial period so she could watch her son play matches in the afternoons, create a healthy balance by doing some form of fitness in the morning and take her ex-husband to his hospital appointments, which tended to mainly happen mid-week. They had also proposed a review after three months and probably partial retirement at that stage.

Summary

Let's go over the priorities here. You could do more harm than good hanging on to a job at the cost of your on-going mental health, so if you continue working straight after your loss and you are not coping, either within your role, or you're collapsing into a heap when you get back to the safety of your home, then it is absolutely a good time for you to speak to your GP, your family and your employers – in that order.

Losing your income will be an absolute 'no-no' for most of us, but reporting your loss doesn't need to cost you that if you tell them as early as possible and give them as much information as is appropriate. You're more likely to incur that fate if you try and keep your personal situation from them, because then what other explanation can there be for your potential inability to perform, poor timekeeping or erratic moods and behaviours?

There are laws to protect employees experiencing bereavement and you'll find some great advice on the www.acas.org.uk website.

This book is a guide and whilst I hope this chapter is helpful, you should always obtain independent legal advice.

41

Words That Might Upset Someone Who is in Mourning

It's easy to say the wrong thing to a bereaved individual. After a loss or at a specific time during the process such as the funeral, we often feel the need to say something about the death to comfort the family, and no matter how much time we have to prepare for that exchange there are so many ways that it can go wrong, but only so many ways that it can deliver the desired effect.

Here's a collection of phrases that a vast number of bereaved contributors have shared with me. These comments have offended someone, causing the opposite reaction in them to the one the speaker was probably hoping to create. Some words are not insensitive on the speaker's part but are more indicative of an issue for the receiver, either caused by the grief or something pre-existing. Some phrases, however, are proven to invariably cause some degree of upset to those recently bereaved.

Either way, the effectiveness of the communication should be measured by the way it's received and not the way it's spoken. So if you're going to a funeral or are likely to see someone recently bereaved, use this interesting look at the thoughts and feelings of those grieving the loss of a loved one and consider yourself better equipped to support them verbally, either in passing or on a more continuous basis if they are a big part of your life.

The mild ones

'I lost someone too.'

This presumes that by offering something in common with the mourner it will help to take away the pain that person is going through. OK, so you know how they are feeling because you have also lost someone and you've established that, so that means you'll know exactly what to do now. What are you going to follow up with? We shouldn't use someone's immediate grief as a vehicle to express our own. Make it all about them in the moment or we are no support at all.

'If there's anything I can do, let me know.'

What's wrong with that, you ask? You're close but not close enough. Do you really think someone who has just had their world turned upside down will be in a position to draw up a list of things they need to do to keep everything ticking over? No. They need to down tools completely and you, as a friend, need to use some initiative and just do something without waiting to be asked.

'Passed away.'

I've used this term a few times during the writing of this book, but to some anything other than the word 'dead' is somehow questionable, as if it tiptoes around the facts. Those who see fault in this phrase are people who need a degree of realness maintained around them. If you don't know the mourner particularly well you won't know if they are adopting this approach. Just be mindful that some don't like this term.

'Lost their battle.'

This seems to upset those grieving for a loved one who has died from cancer, as it suggests that they were in some way weak-minded and as a result were defeated. It doesn't personally offend me or my children, but it was certainly something that has caused some thought from others. The people who I have lost to cancer were in no way defeated, nor were they weak, and they faced the disease heroically with every ounce of will and determination that they had available to them. So if we're not going to use a term that sounds like they went 'toe to toe' with something and they lost, what could we use?

Imagine if someone with cancer could choose to actually fight their illness in a boxing ring. Do you think they would ever stop? What kind of opponent is cancer anyway? The illness doesn't overcome the body because it's strong and a great fighter; it gets into places that it can't be extracted from, in order to survive. It's a sneaky and immoral disease. It throws the first punch or indeed a whole string of them before you've even heard the bell go. If all was fair, it would have no chance against someone if they were truly fighting for their life.

'I'm sorry.'

This is not an expression I would have queried personally, but if someone takes offence at it I feel I must include it and seek to understand why. When you say you're sorry it's a throwaway remark. Respectful, nice, but throwaway, the underlying message being that if someone is desperate for help and you are offering a sorry, then you aren't really much use to them. 'I'm sorry' also implies it's your fault in some way, which it clearly isn't. What if you say: 'I am sorry that you are grieving?' This implies the speaker regrets what has happened to the mourner. Which makes much more sense.

'I'm sorry for your loss.'

Again, this isn't going to strike some as insensitive but it came up quite a few times when I reached out to my groups and social media platforms. It's the same as above with the added annoyance that you're saying that they 'lost' someone. Technically they have lost someone from their life but we don't usually add that part, so the interpretation that people dislike is the suggestion that person is hiding, misplaced or temporarily unavailable.

People coming to terms with the death of a loved one may not want to be teased with words that make the event appear inconclusive. The people who don't like the word 'loss' need you to be definite and accurate in your wording because anything short of that makes them feel like you're maybe pretending it hasn't happened.

'I'm thinking of you.'

People often don't want to be thought about, they want someone to wrap them in a big hug and make them feel safe. Sit with them, make them a cuppa, hold them as they sob their heart out. Thinking about them just doesn't cut it. Again, words but not action.

The marginally insensitive

'You've got to move on.'

We move on from a question we can't answer in a pub quiz. You move on from a job you don't like. You most certainly do not move on when something as difficult as the death of someone you care about interrupts life as you know it. When you think of it visually, moving on from the memory of a person is like walking away from them and leaving them behind. This just isn't how grief works. They will be with you always, so 'moving on' feels wholly inaccurate as a term.

'They'd want you to be happy.'

Yes, they would, but they would also want you to have the right to feel whatever comes naturally to you and at the moment you're actually doing the opposite. Happiness is a place you will inevitably get to one day, but today, the moment that you're experiencing, you don't want to be told your loved one would want you to be happy when you are sad and confused, because it implies the speaker is maybe disapproving of your mindset.

'Be strong.'

Here's one that I definitely understand. Being strong in grief is the opposite to the way this throwaway instruction is intended. People say 'be strong' when what they actually mean is 'stop being emotional' because they don't know how to cope with that and they'd rather you said nothing about your grief.

Strength in grief is to allow yourself to feel, say and do whatever feels natural anytime, any place, and if that means sobbing your heart out, then it is strong of you to allow yourself to do that. Weakness, in case you are wondering, is suppression – not allowing yourself to feel, say or do whatever comes naturally, denying your physical and mental self the freedom to express itself, for which the consequences are damaging.

The awfully insensitive

'Time's a healer.'

Time. The biggest misunderstanding in grief. It's not how long you've been on the horse but if you can get the animal to move forwards or not! Seriously, time is just a secondary consequence. Time doesn't heal anything, we heal ourselves, and a comment that assumes you don't need to do anything but let the days, weeks and months pass by is unhelpful and inaccurate.

'They're better off.'

Better off than who? If you're referring to the fact the deceased may have gone through some illness or disease that led to their death, then I can see where you may be coming from, but be prepared that the family member or person you're speaking to would still rather they were here, if there was even a remote chance that their health could improve. This is your opinion, so be mindful that it may not be one the mourner or their family shares.

'Chin up.'

OK. So we keep our chin up when the person we took out for a date doesn't reply to our texts, if we have an injury or if we have a bit of bad luck. We do NOT keep our chin up when we lose someone that we love, a real-life human being! See your chin? It's attached to your neck and you need to wind it back in if this is the best you can do in attempting to comfort someone.

'Everything happens for a reason.'

Oh, does it? Will your philosophical approach help you when you experience something like the poor person you're attempting to talk out of their feelings of immense pain? Probably not. OK, you mean well, but while the cosmic forces or gods you imply have acted with specific purpose to rob them of their loved one for a 'greater cause' might make sense and be a comfort to you, it probably won't to them. Use with caution.

'At least it was quick.'

Be careful, because whether it was quick or slow, it's still death, right? Again, that's your opinion. Maybe in your mind dying quickly and relatively painlessly might be exactly what you want but why should we assume that this is either agreeable or comforting to the mourner? We tell people how they should feel too often; let them tell you whether they took solace from the speed of the transition from being here to simply not.

'Pull yourself together.'

Straight out of the old school. If there's something that is emotionally challenging for us to witness we take the easy route and dismiss it as a weakness. Never listen to someone who tells you to pull yourself together; they are just telling you that the problem is beyond their emotional capacity.

'Life goes on.'

Yes, for those of us here talking about it, it does, but it doesn't for the person I am finding it really hard to no longer have. A mourner isn't worried about their life, they just want the deceased to have theirs. It's slightly more tragic than this throwaway condolence suggests.

'You can always try again' or 'At least you've already got one' or 'At least you know you can conceive.'

In the case of a miscarriage or the loss of a baby, people tend to throw these phrases out without much thought. Maybe the mourning couple don't want to think about trying again or the children they have already got. They want the baby that they were in the process of bringing into the world and they wanted that baby to be healthy and alive. Nothing else exists in the moment.

The religious ones

'They are in heaven now.'

Some people receive this comment with thoughts such as 'Oh, are they? Can you tell that for certain? Do you have any proof of their whereabouts?' The thing with comments stemming from religious belief is that while they would never be meant maliciously, the person listening to you may not feel quite so comforted by you forcing your religious beliefs on them.

'I will pray for them.'

You may mean well by this and to you it might amount to something. Pray if you want, just don't tell them about it, because if a god does exist, that god, depending on the nature and timing of the death, may have been very unfair to the person you're trying to comfort. God, who has just supposedly taken their loved one, is probably not who they want to talk to right now unless, of course, they are religious, and not everyone is.

'God needed him more.'

More than their partner? Their family? Their kids? To someone who is not on best terms with God at this point, that's going to come across a little rich. If they are of a religious background then the above might just appeal to the loved one you're speaking to, but if they're not, prepare to be met with a perplexed look.

And the worst of all?

When people say or do nothing at all or cross the street to avoid talking to you.

So what do I do, then?

You've probably just gathered that 'what to say' and 'what not to say' is a bit of a lottery, especially now we've evaluated that some comments are OK by some but not by others. Here's how we can avoid upsetting people in grief.

1. Just ask them how they feel and LISTEN.
The most invaluable support for someone going through grief is a willing listener to whom they can express the confusion, pain and misery they are going through. If you can provide a pair of ears and understand there is no pressure on you to say something miraculously soothing, you simply can't fail.

2. Don't talk, just hug.
The bereaved want to feel safe and secure and words have the tendency to fall short at times, but when you hug them, while they are being held, if they need it, you are giving them permission to be vulnerable, permission to feel and permission to surrender to the hopelessness of the situation. Doesn't sound like a good thing? But it is. We want that person to be able to confront the reality, not 'keep it together' or to 'be strong' or any of those words and phrases of

suppression. If someone isn't a hugger and the words escape you, revert to step one. Ask and listen. It's better to mis-aim an embrace that someone didn't feel comfortable with than to offer nothing at all, so don't be put off.

3. Replace the words with actions.
Think practicality, overrule the need for instruction or permission, act on that impulse. For example, you might think 'I wonder how they're managing with the school run every day', and then you can turn that thought into action by offering to take the kids to school one day a week. Send shopping; go one step further, make a meal for them! Fix light bulbs, mow the grass, put the rubbish out! Do something so that they don't have to, and that is the key to being of actual practical use to someone you want to help, console and support.

4. The phrases that those participating in my research didn't get upset about.
'I've made a donation to the charity your family or loved one supported, in their memory.'

'My favourite memory of that person is . . .'

'I'm coming round to do your ironing/cooking/cleaning/reading to the kids at bedtime for you.'

'I can't even start to imagine what you're going through, but if you'd like to tell me I'm ready to listen.'

5. Use non-judgmental, open questions that allow the person you're talking to to explore their feelings, such as:
How do you feel?

What's the hardest thing for you right now?

How would you like to be supported?

Some people prefer you to be soft with your words, descriptions and condolences, but our ability to let the grieving individual lead and to activate our listening skills is what sets apart the ones who get it right from the ones who don't. Listen more, speak less. We have two ears and one mouth for a reason! Or even better, just do something helpful or give them a good old-fashioned embrace. I don't see anyone complaining about those.

Remember not to be too harsh on yourself. It's enough that you're there to say the words to them in the first place, and if you say something on this list, let's face it, the potential discomfort it might cause is hardly likely to register for more than a moment given the challenge that they are facing in that present moment.

42

Saying Goodbye: the Funeral

This is the ritual given for the person we have lost, a time when all those who loved and respected them can congregate, pay their respects and say goodbye. A funeral is a pivotal moment of closure, a transitional point between the depths of confusion and despair and a period of reflection and calm. The build-up to a funeral can be chaotic and stressful, but when it's over we often give ourselves permission to 'feel', which takes us into a new state.

It is important to try to have a clear understanding of what the day could and should entail so we can be prepared before the event itself. If we don't take the opportunity to say farewell in a way that is worthy of the individual we leave room for guilt and regret. For example, holding a quiet funeral when they would have loved every-one to sing or dance, or squabbling over petty details that turn the day into a power struggle, are ways we leave ourselves open to this guilt and regret.

There are all kinds of funerals – religious, non-religious, human-ist, spiritual – and while individual cultures and religions do things differently, we all want to do our best on the day, for the person we loved, for our family and for ourselves.

What do we need from a funeral?

There are two sets of factors to consider when planning a funeral: the wishes of the person whose life we are there to mourn and the needs of those closest to them. As mourners we need to pay our respects so that we know that we were there for their send-off and to gain closure, to dispel the disbelief of death and make it real so that the grieving process can venture forwards without our loved one physically present in our life.

For the person we are sending off, we need to do what is befitting of their life and be confident that whatever arrangements and rituals we choose for the day itself will be 'what they would have wanted'. This is obviously much easier when we have received pre-funeral instructions from the departed, who may have asked for one or two particular songs to be played, or may have specified everything, down to what everyone wears – and even how everyone behaves!

If a death has been unexpected or there is an absence of any expressed wishes, then great care needs to be taken over communication – if there are several close mourners, then it is advisable to get together to share thoughts on what the person might have wanted, deciding together how best to achieve that for the funeral itself. Being inclusive and making it a show of love for the person you've lost will make you all feel proud of the final send-off.

Planning the funeral

When arranging a funeral you may still be in shock, so you may find it hard to get out of bed of a morning let alone arrange a big event, so you might need help. That said, you might actually welcome the distraction – a reason to keep busy, to not fall down. There are varying sources of help: your family, friends, other members of your religion, or there may be a community around you that can direct you to a well-trusted funeral director and help with the arrangements.

There are two types of funeral directors: those that are part of a larger corporation and those that are independent, family-owned businesses. Whichever you choose, you absolutely must feel comfortable with the company you select, and it is fine to ask them whatever queries you have, and feel reassured that they have not just answered all of your questions but also given you all of the advice you will need in order to feel confident about the planning of the day. Give yourself some guidelines before you decide – for example, see if the staff make you feel welcome and comfortable. Write out a list of questions and if you can, take someone with you in case you are too upset to take in the answers. Look out for how the people treat you – do they go straight to the paperwork and start quoting costs, or do they want to hear all about the person you will be remembering? The quality of service very much depends on how much time and effort they put into understanding your loss and assessing your very specific needs.

A good company will guide, comfort, counsel and sometimes mediate the family throughout the process, from consultation, to the moment the ceremony ends. One thing I think is important is how they refer to your loved one. If they use the term 'body', you should be out of there. If they use 'Mum' or 'Wife' or better still, the name of the person you have lost, then to me that shows they are going to give your loved one the dignity and respect they deserve.

Establishing your needs

Funerals cost money and it is good to know your budget when discussing options with the funeral director. You should be offered the cheaper options first and you should not be manipulated or pushed into spending more than you can afford. If the person you are talking to makes you feel you aren't 'doing enough' – either in terms of the money you are spending or what you want for the funeral itself – then you should head out the door and go to another firm, as you don't want to be dealing with misplaced feelings of guilt. We only get one chance to send our loved ones off and you need to do what's right for you.

There are many details within the ceremony that you can request from your funeral director, for example, the way your loved one is dressed; the type of service you would like; having things placed in the coffin from photos to the lining of the casket being in their favourite colour. A good funeral director will be expert at asking you the questions you need to be asked in order for you to know what the right choices are for you, so don't feel like you need to walk in knowing exactly what you need. That should be a product of the discussion.

What's the right type of funeral?

There is no 'right' type of funeral. Whatever fulfils the wishes of the departed, or in the absence of direction, whatever feels appropriate to the family, will be the right funeral for you. You may be guided by your religious or cultural beliefs as to what rituals you observe. For some, burial is the way, for others it is cremation.

But what if the person who has died hasn't stipulated burial or cremation? You may have to make that choice. The funeral director can help you make a decision but it's very important you have spoken to your other family members to gauge their opinions too.

If your family members have very strong, opposing views – you think your mother would have wanted to be buried but your sister thinks she would have wanted to be cremated – the way to deal with this ultimately is to communicate clearly with one another about what the deceased would have wanted. In the absence of any clues as to what the person would have wanted, if no agreement can be reached and you're not happy to make an overriding decision, you can ask the family members and their closest friends to vote to decide the outcome diplomatically. This avoids one person being held responsible for any disgruntlement in the future.

Because of the maintenance requirements of a burial I always think it's important that those making the decision are the ones who are going to be at least partly responsible for the upkeep. It's also helpful to determine why someone may have such strong views: do they have beliefs that the rest of the family do not share? It's OK for them to have strong desires for their own burial or cremation, but is this more for them than it is for the person recently departed? I hope you don't find yourself in this position. If more people spoke openly about death we'd all know what to do in the event and the potential for family rifts would be drastically reduced.

If the decision is that your loved one is going to be cremated, you will need to think about what you do with their ashes. Do you want them in a central location or to spread them in different places; do you want them at home with you for a while; do you want the crematorium to hold on to them for you?

Funerals can be sombre but they can also be celebratory and if you want, you can create a service that is as joyous and uplifting as you wish. There is plenty of room for humour in funerals, if that's appropriate for you and your loved ones, and many funerals have moments that make people laugh out loud, for example through music – the Monty Python song, 'Always Look on the Bright Side of Life' always makes people smile; in an address that remembers humorous things about the person's life or in a slide show that captures the person's life. These can bring light relief for a moment or two during the service and if you take both happy and sad emotions from the day then you've cracked it. Humour is a great comfort, carrying an underlying permission to feel whichever emotion we wish and go one step further by expressing it, and funerals that have moments of fun and mischief are an exceptionally healthy catalyst in remembering positively, because it becomes the platform for a strong start to the feelings of grief that are yet to come.

One of my clients told me that at her ex-husband's funeral, his new wife had put up picture boards with photos from all walks and stages of his life, and had thoughtfully included photos from his marriage to her showing how happy he was with their children. Everyone was given a photo to take home and her children have these pictures of their dad by their beds to this day. Having the photos at the funeral helped her children to see how many happy times there had been and how loved their dad was.

The funeral plan – suitable preparation or tempting fate?

In the UK you can take out a funeral plan, which means that when your time comes, however far off, there will be no additional balance to pay even if inflation has made the expense of a funeral ten times the amount. The average cost of a burial funeral was £4,110 in 2015 and only 6% of adults in the UK have a pre-paid funeral plan. You can compare that to the 70% of the Dutch who have prepaid funeral plans, and 20 million Spaniards have funeral insurance. (Reference funeralzone.co.uk)

You can make arrangements for your own or for a loved one's funeral pre-death but of course the specifics can be changed as many times as you want. Paying off your funeral expenses before you die will give your family significant peace of mind. But what about arranging it? It is a pretty selfless act to plan your funeral, as it will help your family avoid making difficult decisions once you are gone or any hassle you might feel they would not be equipped to handle, and when you die there's nothing for them to deal with but the loss itself. If you are a family member who feels put out by not having added anything, there is always room to add a reading in or make a gesture that fulfils your need to express your love at the funeral.

But how many of us really want to face up to the thought of dying? Some people think that planning it might make it more likely to happen. Having a chat with one of your loved ones about what music you would want to be played at your funeral is one thing, but you might like to go a few steps further to avoid any unnecessary arguments at a time when your loss will be hard enough to deal with as it is.

You may feel it comforting for a family to come together and choose what their loved one might have wanted, a last thing they can do for you, an intimacy that they would be denied if you controlled and arranged it all. However, we mustn't presume that all families communicate particularly well without disagreements and that in the shock or pain of death these strains wouldn't become harder. Only you know your family and how they would be likely to react. Even if we provide a base level of instruction and leave some room for our loved ones to personalise, we shouldn't assume that arranging a funeral is always something our families will be able to agree on without contention, so making arrangements eliminates the chances of this.

Realistic expectations

Some of us may set ourselves up for a bit of a fall when we tell ourselves we MUST be OK on the day or that we CAN'T get upset at the funeral. Why not try to leave unrealistic, pressure-inducing, self-imposed demands out of it and feel however you feel? There's nothing more natural and realistic than that, and it's OK to cry, it's OK to yell, it's OK to laugh. There are no rules to limit your emotion unless that emotion causes you to do something that others would find distressing.

You may have dependants present who might find the more extreme reactions hard to witness. I heard about a woman whose ten-year-old son died suddenly in his sleep one perfectly ordinary school night, and at the funeral she threw herself into the grave, much to the distress of her 15-year-old daughter, who became hysterical at seeing her mother do this.

Also, if, for example, you are burying your husband and your children are in their teens and are coming to the funeral, if you know there's a good chance you are going to be inconsolable, then in order to prepare your children for seeing you like that you could simply explain to them beforehand that you have no idea what your emotions are going to do on the day and that if you are really finding it hard you want them to support you with that, and of course vice versa. It pre-empts the question of 'Is my emotion right for others?' Or 'Am I allowed to cry like this without it being frowned upon by members of the family?' It grants permission in a way and takes away the chance of someone's outpouring of emotion coming as a surprise and distressing others.

The balance between personal wishes
and the expectations of others

When instructions for the funeral have been left behind, then it's pretty clear-cut. But when those remaining have to decide upon the order of events and the key details themselves, it can get tricky if others in the family have expectations that, if not met, lead to a trail of complications.

The last thing you need when dealing with a loss is criticism or disapproval from others. The important thing to remember is that you cannot possibly please everyone. There are so many options and details in play that to please everyone would be like ordering everyone's food from a three-course menu and getting everyone's choices exactly right.

Everyone involved is going through something new and difficult and this may make people act and behave in unusual and unnecessary ways. They might create issues that don't really exist in order to find an outlet that doesn't require them to reveal their vulnerabilities. Ideally, you would talk to all the closest mourners and ask for their input, so they feel involved and consulted and part of the process.

If someone makes a request that you don't feel is appropriate or practical, it may be good to look for compromises or at least to discuss with them why there may not be room for it at the chosen service. Is there a way of them getting their wish included at the wake? There may be possibilities for flexibility when we open ourselves up to seeing them.

What to say in an address

There is an element of release in the process of storytelling at a funeral and it's a good opportunity to be honest, to say it as it is. It can upset family members if a person is spoken of as if they were a saint, and while I don't think it a good idea to bad-mouth someone at their own funeral, mentioning the good times and the bad times, forgiving them for things, telling stories that reflect that person's life, is better than sugar-coating and making people think they have turned up to the wrong funeral. A more accurate description of events, spoken in the right tone with the right amount of detail, can leave a greater sense of satisfaction. We don't need to be perfect to be missed; we just need to have been us.

Celebrating a life before it is lost

On being diagnosed with terminal cancer at 69, Mary Turner from Brighton arranged her own wake so that she could say an early goodbye to everyone dear to her before she died. She told everyone that if she was still there in a year she'd have another one and treat the first as a dress rehearsal.

There's nothing I've come across that is anywhere near as forward-thinking as Mary's philosophy to be at her own wake. It gave her the opportunity to show others that she had accepted her death and gave everyone a chance to say what they wanted to say, which will definitely help with their grief when she does die.

How would you feel about celebrating your life with your loved ones before you die?

Should children attend?

I decided to take the boys to the other side of the world rather than attend their mother's funeral. My reasons were very straightforward. I thought that it would be counterproductive for them to be there, that they would become part of the frenetic media circus that surrounded Jade's death. They would also have had to cope with the thousands of well-wishers who wanted to give the boys their condolences, which might have helped them see how highly regarded their mother was (I could show them that later through all the cards and messages they were sent) but at the time, would have been totally overwhelming for them.

The main reason for not taking them was that seeing a box with their mother in it being lowered into the ground didn't run congruently with the story that she and I had been very careful to maintain throughout her illness. Jade had told them that when she went to be with God, who had called for her to do a very important job, she would travel to heaven as the brightest star in the sky. My four- and five-year old boys might well have asked: 'Daddy, how could Mummy be a star in the sky when she is being put into the ground?' I wouldn't have been able to answer that question without totally confusing them. It's one thing Daddy telling you that they can't see their mum any more, but quite another to then add the frustration from not having a plausible explanation as to why.

There is no right or wrong in whether or not you bring your children to the funeral of a close loved one and there may be stories that your religion or beliefs compel you to tell them. But my one recommendation is that whatever you do tell them, do so in a way that's appropriate to their age and try to make sure the story remains consistent throughout.

Not every family has the time to prepare themselves like we did. I wonder, if Jade had died suddenly, if I'd have come up with the star image. I doubt it. I probably would have been too shocked and given the children the cold facts and then caught them when they fell.

If you haven't given your children an explanation at all despite the death being drawn out, then you run the risk of leaving many internalised questions unanswered. We might think the child is dealing with the loss, but the most important question has been left unresolved: 'Where are they now?' They might still be completely stuck believing that their loved one could appear at any moment because their destination hasn't been made final or definite enough.

What if you have a child who doesn't want to attend the funeral but you feel, as a bereaved parent, that they should? It's fair to point out that the funeral can never be repeated and this might lead to regrets later on in life if they didn't, for example, go to their sister or mother's funeral when they were 14. However, there are compromises available. Could they go to part of the funeral so they know in years to come that despite not attending the whole service, they were present for some? Could they at least be nearby so that they can change their mind right at the last minute?

The worrying thing is always that without the confirmation of death and reassurance of love that a funeral provides we are encouraging the possibility of denial and delaying the inevitability of grief and what we need from that process in order to slowly adjust. The child can't be made to feel that they have to go, but you can help them by asking them to imagine how they would feel five years on knowing that they have no memory of the day everyone said goodbye at the funeral. You can also ask how they would feel if, when it was their time many years into the future, their child, niece, daughter didn't attend their send-off. Lastly, while we're trying to give as much perspective as possible, you can also ask what the deceased would want for them to do.

In the absence of any change in that teenager's viewpoint, I would try to identify an agreeable way of saying goodbye instead of just being at home in that moment. Perhaps they can release a balloon at the same time as the service, or be somewhere that was special to them and the person lost? Something that carries meaning so that the risk of regret is reduced, because something was done, just not what everyone else was doing at the funeral.

There are many other ways to honour the person who has passed, both on the day and every day afterwards, but the regret of not doing anything at all is what we must be most mindful to avoid.

Children can play a significant role in a funeral. For example, if a child lets balloons go to symbolise the person ascending to heaven, the very sight of this can resonate with adults on a deeper level, as though the soul or spirit of the person we have lost is somehow ascending with them. If this is something you plan to do, my advice would be to make sure that whatever is released up to the sky runs alongside the explanations that have been given to the children. So, if Mummy becomes a star, maybe release a star-shaped balloon and stick to that theme throughout. Oh, and take it from me, take a spare balloon, because eventually it will get stuck in the tree that you don't think is in the way and cause distress!

How to deal with potentially difficult situations

A client once spoke to me of her intention not to inform her brother about their father's funeral so that she didn't have to deal with his presence given the abusive nature of their past. When we talked about this and put it into a little more context, she realised that no matter how much someone had hurt her in the past, they still had every right to pay their own respects and that denying him that right would bring more harm to her. In the end she invited him through others and he declined to attend anyway.

A funeral belongs to the person whose life you are celebrating and should be accessible to anyone who wishes to attend. However, you don't get a second chance when it comes to funerals and the smooth running of the occasion must be put first. If there is someone whose intention might be to cause disruption or distress to others, then they either need to be spoken to or asked not to attend. You don't want your loved one's memory being forever linked to any chaos or unpleasant behaviour, and it is your duty to protect them from that.

Another client told me that at her ex-husband's funeral, she didn't know where she should sit. He had married again and had had children with his new wife, but my client was still the mother of his other children and they were there, distressed and in need of her presence. In the end she sat at the end of the front row to be close to her children but not quite with his new wife.

After the funeral

In the days between death and the funeral itself, you could quite easily believe that you're operating a hotline. People from all over come out of the proverbial woodwork to call you, and as you are dealing with the arrangements too, the days are full and busy. Even after the funeral itself you may have a gathering for days afterwards when everyone wants to be together.

This can stop suddenly and dramatically once the funeral and the particular traditions that may follow are over, and after days of prolonged company, the peace and quiet can be a relief, but having had so many people around you, buoying you up, comforting you, it can be a little daunting almost from one minute to the next to be given the space you might need, but don't know how to fill. It is advisable to make plans, even just simple lunch or dinner plans, for the days following the funeral to keep yourself occupied; and if you need help with your children, ask for it, even if it means relying on other mourners.

In the pain of your final separation from someone you have shared your life with, the funeral proceedings are a chance to express that love and gratitude for what you had with them and what you lost in them. The funeral brings emotions that have been inaccessible due to the shock, inexpressible due to the rawness and inexplicable due to the years we thought we would have or at least want with them still. Say goodbye to your physical connection and let the day mark the beginning of your spiritual relationship with their very essence and the priceless memories that will comfort you through the adjustments of grief.

43

Special Occasions

It took me the two Christmas Days that followed Jade's death to work out that no matter how many presents were under the tree or treats in the cupboard, it would never be the same for the boys and that after the initial excitement of opening their stockings, I would observe a huge sadness in them. It was then that I appreciated that these special occasions would be the moments when it was most obvious to them that the centre of their world was missing.

I learned to pre-empt these moments of sadness by making plans for us to remember Mummy before the day started. By visiting Jade's 'special place' (the rural church graveyard where she was buried with beautiful, unobstructed views over the countryside and into the city) early on Christmas morning we had paid our respects, eliminating the urge for anyone to feel guilty about enjoying the rest of the day. As simple as it sounds, that is all it took to find a way of approaching Christmas and any other special occasion and while it still feels sad, it also feels constructive and positive, a way that we chose as opposed to sadness dictating to us when it felt like it.

A vital focus for the bereaved is those days when no matter how hard we try we cannot help being overcome with sadness. Maybe it's your loved one's birthday, maybe it's your birthday, a day your loved one always made you feel special.

It's a measure of the sadness of death that the days when you were once happiest become the days when happiness just feels wrong. While taking my boys to Mummy's special place first thing in the morning, after they had opened their stockings and before breakfast, invited the sadness and grief to meet us there, it brought about a calmness that made the rest of the day easier for them. Because we had put Mummy first, they were at peace with themselves for showing their love to their mum before they did anything else that, in comparison, was drastically less significant. The rest of the day was as full of fun and excitement as it used to be and we learned to pre-empt the sadness by putting Mum first and the occasion second.

I have also learned along the way that you can take the weight out of the big days by introducing a monthly day. We have 'Mummy's Day' and on that day, a day we completely dedicate to Jade's memory, the boys decide what we're going to do. Sometimes we do it alone, sometimes we share it with people who mean a lot to us. We have marked Mummy's Day in a variety of ways and our last one saw us release balloons from the Golden Gate Bridge in San Francisco – wherever we go, Mummy comes with us. I like doing something monthly because my biggest fear is not prompting them to talk about Jade enough, so this enables me to rest assured that I'm fulfilling my role.

I was curious as to what other bereaved people's attitudes and experiences of special occasions were. How do others cope? Is it an awful time for everyone or are there clever ways to lighten the weight of these grief-inducing days that I haven't yet encountered?

Martin Hall, widowed father of two, told me:

Special occasions, well, it's a mixed bag for me. I can get quite tense in the build-up to them and regretful about not making the most of my time with Jayne when she was alive. I also start to question my parenting ability because she would have done a better job than me.

All my anniversaries are in a seven-week period. Jayne died on the 5th of November, her funeral was the 18th (exactly two years from her sister's funeral), her birthday is the 23rd December and our anniversary is the 29th December. So that period is a bit of a rollercoaster of emotion.

The anniversary of her death is Bonfire Night so I take the kids to a local firework display, but I find it emotionally complex. Gazing upwards to the heavens is only ever going to remind me of our loss and watching the fireworks illuminate the sky reminds me of how Jayne isn't here illuminating our lives. I also take the kids to Jayne's memorial stone, we group hug and lay some flowers. The kids take it in their stride, I get a bit tearful.

On the anniversary of the funeral, I tend to get a bit tense and snappy with the world. I retreat a little and try to make sense of it. I often have bad dreams of her final days around this time.

I seem to deal with her birthday better, maybe because I remember the good times – the birthday celebrations, her 40th birthday party, her happiness when surprising her with a present that she wasn't expecting. I find myself talking to the kids a little more on her birthday, especially about what their mum liked. We all go to the theatre and watch a musical because Jayne loved them and it's now a tradition for us.

December the 29th is our anniversary, a day where I try to concentrate on the happy times we had together, try to think about the world before she was ill. It's my son's birthday on the same day. I make sure he has a good day but the evening can involve a few tears. I guess I'm reflecting on those plans and dreams we had when we got married fifteen years ago and then had our children, and how fate decided they could never be fulfilled.

Like many people, I go into the New Year looking for change in my life, to transform my world into a better place. But it isn't based on the tradition of New Year resolutions. It is based on a desire to make the most of my life, because Jayne was deprived of hers so young.

I admire Martin's ability to reflect. Such an important trait to those picking up the pieces after a death. I would echo many of his sentiments and I'm pleased for him and his children that his attitude in the wake of such a big loss is to live a full and varied existence in Jayne's memory. It's the perfect positive response and exactly how I'd want my family to react if anything happens to me.

I coached a bereaved friend of mine, Lydia Frempong, who came to me because it was the eve of her late mother's birthday and she was feeling very apprehensive about what lay ahead. Lydia's mother absolutely loved birthdays; she always made them a big celebration of food and she was such a powerful figure within the family and especially on special occasions, but held that importance in a softly spoken, understated refinement.

Lydia has seen her mum's birthday come and go twice already since she lost her. She always goes to the cemetery, she explained, the first year on her own in the snow, placing a red rose on her grave. She was warned by someone, 'The second year is always worse, you know.' So feeling anxious and almost anaesthetised, she retraced her and her mother's favourite things to do, visiting Costa for a blueberry muffin, and then went to the cemetery again like the year before.

Now it's her third year. She feels 'stuck' like she couldn't move and she has nothing planned, which is contrary to the way she lives her life – everything is planned! She was procrastinating about going to the cemetery this time or going to an event (which she later admitted was just as a planned distraction), feeling like as long as she does something on her 'birthday weekend' it will be OK. I always wonder whose standard it is that we spend so much time agonising over trying to please?

While it didn't sound as though Lydia was completely avoiding the situation, just what was it about the occasion, the build-up especially, that was making this day seem so much more complicated for her?

I picked up on a piece of her language as I was listening intently to her story. She said that doing something in particular was 'only going to make me cry'.

I asked what was wrong with crying, to which she responded: 'It would be too painful and I need to be strong.'

'So what does strength look like?'

After a little resistance and a bit of attempted justification – 'I run my own business,' ('Save it for tomorrow, Lydia'), she finally replied: 'OK, I know there is strength in feeling vulnerable and letting yourself express yourself naturally.'

I asked her if something you're feeling on the inside is so painful, does that make crying, expressing that pain, more or less necessary?

She knew that holding that pain in was not being 'strong' and was in fact counterproductive, so she felt relieved that she had given herself permission to cry. I can never allow a client to continue holding on to the misconception that internalising anything that is being felt is in any way constructive because it simply causes harm.

We spoke about the cemetery again and how it 'feels right' for her to be there tomorrow and that she got a sense of peace by being at her mother's graveside. I asked Lydia how she would feel about NOT going to the grave tomorrow.

'No,no, no,' she replied. It was out of the question.

'What is the objective of going to the cemetery?' I asked.

'It feels right. My mum could have been buried in Ghana but she chose to be buried here for the children, that's really important to me.' She spoke about 'responsibility' and how because she signed the bit of paper for the plot her mother is buried in she has this sense of needing to be there for her mum.

'Responsibility to do what?' I wanted to know.

'I signed the paperwork so I have to go.'

Lydia didn't give me an objective, so I circled back round and asked her the same question again.

It turned out that she had two objectives: to remember Mum and to please Mum.

'If you don't go, does that mean you don't remember?'

'I talk about her every day.'

'Do you need to go to please your mum? Would she not be pleased if you were not there?'

Lydia was stuck for an answer because she realised that everything she does personally and professionally brought her mum great pride and satisfaction.

I asked Lydia to imagine herself in that place where she thinks she will be in eighty-odd years' time and ask herself what her expectations would be for how her own child remembers her.

'Imagine your child remembers you every day but doesn't go to your grave on your birthday, how do you feel about that?'

Lydia responded: 'As long as they remember me, I'd be OK with whatever she did!'

So the KEY objective is to remember and that is enough, to remember her and to make her proud?

'Most definitely.'

'Are you doing that on a daily basis anyway?'

'Yes!'

Lydia was sitting a little straighter and was looking like a weight was beginning to lift now that the clarification process she needed was starting to take effect. I continued: 'What's more important, remembering every day or being at the grave and only remembering on that day?'

'As long as I'm remembering and doing her proud I don't need to be at the grave, but I know I can go there because I want to, not because I need to.'

To me the grave sounded very central to validating Lydia's grief or her mother's existence, which is an incredible amount of significance to attach to a piece of stone that marks the final resting place of someone she loves and misses tremendously. It really challenges where we believe our grief or indeed our remembrance should be aimed.

Why is it not always recognised when people spend every day making their loved one proud while thinking beautiful thoughts about them, yet if they don't go to the grave on the special occasion, they're letting them down?

There's so much fluidity and inconsistency to the way we remember someone we love, and to be so unkind and limiting to ourselves doesn't make sense.

Lydia offered that before this, her first experience of bereavement, she was influenced by a friend who had experienced her own loss and because her family visited the grave once a month, laid some flowers and had a coffee, she felt that was what she should do – maybe that was what everyone does?

Lydia once told me that she might move to Ghana, so I asked her what she would do about being at the grave when she's an eight-hour plane journey away. It's not realistic to impose such a rule on ourselves and I've no doubt that some people's lives are greatly affected by self-imposed limitations due to their insistence on stay-ing close to a grave.

The traditional view is often that we can only pay our respects if we physically go to the grave, one central location. Why? It was maybe a convenient arrangement that meant people had the permis-sion to switch off their grief until the following month when they visited again. Grieving remotely is simply remembering wherever you are and whatever you're doing, because as I'm sure you know all too well, that's the reality of grief.

We need to know that we are paying our respects in everything we are and everything we do, so to ignore that fact and place unnecessary guilt on ourselves to be at a specific place makes little sense.

The expectations of others are one of the 'pins' that hold that responsibility in place. Lydia has so many family members who could share the responsibility of tending to the grave, but was there a reason for her not asking for others to help?

Lydia admitted that many of her family members can't get to where their parents are buried so they light candles, read a poem or listen to a song, which is OK for them, so why did she need to be at the grave? It should never be about obligation, which denotes pres-sure that isn't healthy; it should be about wanting to do something, then you can only get the benefits.

Lydia realised the perceived responsibility was a huge pressure: 'I was her carer so you become responsible for everything. Maybe that hasn't ended?' It's like saying your connection is with a bit of marble or a bit of slate when your connection is actually universal – now is that helpful? Not so much.

Lydia also revealed that there is a picture of her mother's face on the grave. I understand very well that from an NLP point of view it's like basically saying that the grave is Mum, like the grave is no longer a resting place but is the actual person herself.

The responsibility of having cared for her mum for those eighteen months before her death had carried over into caring for the grave; the focus that was once her mum's health had been shifted on to her mum's resting place, so no wonder she felt like she could only do right by going there out of responsibility and not desire.

I asked Lydia how she could take some of this unnecessary responsibility away so she could free herself of any self-imposed pressure. Many families have a rota in place between those who are involved in the tending of the grave so the visits can be split between them. Such an arrangement would be beneficial for Lydia's family, since it would maintain the connection of all involved not just to Lydia's mum, but to each other as well, and it would unite everyone in her memory and encourage the communication of memories too.

Lydia was relieved to see that she was putting too much pressure on herself. Now that the grave was a grave again and not her mum, and now she had agreed that she would split the responsibility of tending it between eight relatives and especially now she understood that the objectives of grieving on that or any day were to remember and make her mum 'pleased', she felt lighter and relieved.

So what pressure do you put on yourself around special occasions?

What rule have you imposed on yourself, as Lydia had? Can you identify the statements you make about the beliefs that you hold about yourself or the situation?

Lydia's five main 'pins' that held her sense of pressure and responsibility in place were:

1. 'I signed the bit of paper so it's my responsibility.'
Being the signatory can mean as much or as little as you want it to. The thing that really matters is the invaluable memories that you

own in your mind. Sharing the physical responsibility with other family members will reduce the pressure significantly.

2. 'She could have been buried in Ghana but she chose to be buried here.'
This sounded to me as if her mum had come to visit her and Lydia had left her at the airport. That was her mum's choice to make.

3. 'I'm still being her carer.'
To care in life and to care for someone in death are two very different responsibilities. Lydia realised she was still caring and was dominated by the obligation to be there physically. She just needed to see that she could now be there for her mum in more of a spiritual way, and that she was doing a great job of grieving remotely anyway.

4. 'The picture on the grave – the grave is Mum!'
The indisputable proof of this was when she described her relationship with the grave as feeling tied to it as if there was an umbilical cord! The subconscious mind never fails to deliver the clues.

5. 'What others will say if I don't go.'
The expectations of others, even though they had parents buried in other countries. The pressure wasn't real; it was based on assumption. Being the 'sole carer' for the grave would be a source of worry for fear of family members judging Lydia for how it was being kept.

Everyone grieves differently. There is no right or wrong, but just make sure that the way you remember on those special occasions is something that feels right for you and carries no heightened sense of pressure and is not influenced by the expectations of others.

Be kind to yourself in grief and ask yourself, by your standards, what would be enough for you when one day you're not here and what would be enough for the person you've lost.

The day after her mother's birthday Lydia sent me the following:

First of all, thank you for being part of the journey for me to manage my mum's birthday. The sun shone on her day and it was a beautiful moment visiting the graveside. I definitely felt emotional and I recognise properly now the pressure I was putting on myself in my role as her daughter and carer.

Mum is in God's hands, she is a deeply spiritual person and I truly believe that she's watching over us all and loving us with a passion. I'm going to start living more now as well as recognising that I remember her in all that I do. It's about living life, making myself happy and ultimately she will be happy for me. That's the desire of all parents.

Thank you so much for including my story in your guide. It's raw and real, it's something that establishes where I was in pain and understandably so. I can now leave that behind and begin a new chapter of living and remembering and letting go of guilt.

A sensitive addendum: other family members do visit. I've realised actually it was my perceived idea of bearing the responsibility that I felt I had to shoulder the burden. I feel free and that's my liberation.

Lydia x

44

Widowed and Dating – the Impact on Children

Grief can be a messy business and when someone who has been bereaved finds love again, or even just goes on a date or two to find their feet, it requires a great deal of thought and sensitivity to get it right as far as any children involved are concerned. In fact, it's a process that should be meticulously planned, from telling the person you have children to orchestrating that new partner moving into the family home.

When is appropriate to start looking?

This will be squarely up to you and will depend upon many factors, such as the dying wishes of your partner, the health of the relationship before your partner died, the length of time that feels morally appropriate, the wishes or indeed the expectations of those around you and how your children might feel.

We have different needs to satisfy and we should really define what exactly we are 'looking' for before we, or others, judge its timeliness and suitability. Is it companionship you need? Someone to make you smile or laugh? Physical contact? Simply a friend or a full-blown relationship?

We have to be mindful of our need to allow ourselves the time and space to grieve before allowing the distraction of 'other interests' to interfere too heavily. You may find you know the person already, in which case you have to decide how quickly you share those feelings and how fast you allow it to develop. I think in any separation the longer you give it after the actual split the more solid you'll be in your state of mind and more likely to meet the right person for the right reasons when you do go on that date.

If we're talking about the appropriateness of these situations, a year is deemed a respectful amount of time but that will vary from one person's opinion to another. Will the parents of your deceased partner think a year is enough? In some bereaved families that I've known, the person losing their life has given permission for their partner to seek love in their absence and not to worry about the timing. In other cases, the dying person has requested that their partner leave it for a certain amount of time before they start dating again. In most cases, this is left unsaid and it is then up to the remaining partner to decide when they are ready and what is acceptable to all concerned – you, the children and anyone else whose opinion you value. It's most important to remember, if it's right for you and the children are informed of your intention to look, the rest is secondary.

When do you tell the person you're dating that you have kids and are widowed?

There are two ways of going about this. You can keep it to yourself and after a handful of dates risk the person going cold. Delaying the sharing of facts – which by the way should not be treated like a dirty little secret – just heightens any disappointment you may feel that things were going so well but they were not the person you need them to be.

OR

You can tell them up front. After all, it's an immovable fact, it's what you've been through, and you should be proud to declare yourself a parent because there is no greater job on the planet. Saying you're a widower does not mean people automatically assume you're looking for sympathy either; it's a positive opportunity to see a lot of the other person's character by observing how they deal with that news. If they turn up for the second date you can concentrate on developing or establishing a connection and leave the meeting of the kids for much later, seeing as there are no obvious barriers in the way of that.

Whenever I've dated I've always been up front about having children. Firstly I'm bloody proud of my boys, secondly I knew that if it was an issue for the girl it didn't matter how pretty and funny she was, or how much I wanted to see her again. Let's say it helped me to separate the wheat from the chaff.

How soon is too soon to introduce?

My personal rule has always been six months until the new partner gets to meet the boys. That has been the case since before Bobby and Freddy lost their mum anyway. I just feel it's a respectful amount of time for them. I don't want them to meet someone who just disappears a few weeks later, and it's enough time for the partner to know they like me enough to take the big step of meeting the boys, and of course for me to feel confident that they are going to be around for the foreseeable future based upon how I feel about them at the time.

Do the children know you're dating? Are they happy for you to do so and are they fully aware you plan to introduce them? Let your children know what you're thinking and make them part of the process. If the children understand what is going on and are broadly accepting – even if there is a bit of a bumpy ride ahead – it doesn't matter if anyone else disapproves.

Keep talking to your children, however young they might be, and keep them in the picture. Children are far more perceptive than we think and their sensitivity grows in bereavement, so the chances are they will pick up on the existence of someone else in your life.

What happens when you introduce someone too quickly and it doesn't last? The likelihood is it will confuse the children. It's marginally irresponsible to cause unnecessary confusion in your children just because you can't wait to incorporate someone into your life. They might be absolutely wonderful but the kids' needs should always come before our own romantic requirements. It doesn't hurt for us to stop ourselves from diving in and exercise a little safety first. Mirror, signal, manoeuvre!

When they meet . . .

Give your children some element of choice about when, how and where they meet your new partner for the first time, and then for a few times afterwards. If they like a certain activity, you could ask them if your new partner could come along and then you can all be involved in something practical in a neutral environment so that the children are as comfortable and engaged with as few distractions as possible.

Plan something that will last an appropriate amount of time. If your children are younger, less may be more. You want the meeting to be fun and for all parties to gain a good impression. We know that if you spend a full day with young kids they will show you the full spectrum of their behavioural repertoire. That said, if they do misbehave during the first few meets, they are just acting their age in what might be difficult circumstances for them, and this is the reality, but I guess what we're trying to do is get off to the best possible start.

After the meet ask the children their opinion, ask how they felt it went and they will like the fact that you've taken their feelings into consideration. Let them feel their approval is part of the decision.

What if your new partner has children of their own?

Dependent upon their ages you can view this as an arranged play date. There's nothing more eagerly anticipated than your kids getting off to a good start! Find an activity, again on neutral ground, that interests both and if the age gap is huge, do something that suits the younger child first and then something the older one is into afterwards.

Try to avoid it being the first time that your children are meeting the new partner too, because the two elements, meeting the boyfriend/girlfriend AND the children who might one day share their parent, would be harder to process and more importantly enjoy. You can do a more focused introduction to each other's children on separate occasions first before introducing the children together, just so your partner is not a stranger when you do.

What will people think?

The most common time in life when people will judge if you should be in a relationship is arguably after a loss. This can often create irreparable damage if it offends the moral parameters of those around you. Sometimes there is little you can do to avoid the fall-outs. It will hurt that people put their own evaluations before your personal happiness, but because we don't control their minds or words we should just concentrate on pleasing ourselves and developing the opportunity to allow love back into our lives, and to achieve the understandably alluring prospect of giving our children another role model for the rest of their childhood and beyond, should the person and the timing be right.

Whose business is it really?

If you allow people's opinions to alter your course through life then it isn't necessarily your own any more. While I believe we should be respectful and decent in our behaviour after a loss, I'm also a believer that pleasing others, giving power to the ones who disagree and wish us to conform to their ideals, is to give in to fear: the fear of doing wrong and the guilt that those opposed to your interests could be heaping on your shoulders.

Before you do that to yourself you have to imagine in ten years' time, when these people are possibly far less of a fixture in your life, how much might you look back and regret the pressure and scrutiny that may have influenced your judgment.

We should also recognise that while some may interfere out of what they imagine to be loyalty for the partner you lost, some may actually have your best interests in mind and feel that they are not fully in support for other reasons, ones that you should possibly listen to.

What if your children are older?

If your children are of a teenage or early adult age then they might not be such a pushover and could require a little more patience from both of you because of how little they could possibly give away emotionally or verbally. The overriding factor is hopefully that if the partner makes you happy, the children will always come around. However, if there is ever a problem and things aren't going as well as you'd hoped, you can guarantee that although they may not say anything, they can always sense it, so transparency to the degree that your child's age and maturity will comprehend will help you avoid important feelings going unspoken.

What if your children are totally against?

Maybe one of your children is far from happy with your blossoming relationship. You have to work out whether this is because they don't like the person, in which case you have to decide upon your priorities, or if it's less to do with the suitability of your new partner and everything to do with the fact that you're moving on too soon for their sensitivities towards anyone supposedly replacing the parent they have lost. Communication is vital. You have to try to understand their reservations and help them to feel more comfortable about your relationship plans. Who are they angry with? You? The partner? Themselves? Some children will feel like if they support your new relationship they are betraying their deceased parent. It'll take more than a conversation to make them see that differently, but to change their perspective on guilt they need to hear from those around them, the ones they think will judge, that they don't blame them for feeling this way but that the surviving parent ultimately deserves to be happy and this situation is common for bereaved families. Patience will be key. Not rushing the child sometimes means not rushing the relationship.

What about when they are going to move in?

Children thrive on consistency and in a time of great upheaval you will want to try to make things as steady as possible. If your new partner is soon to be included in your children's home life, don't make immediate changes to your children's environment. If, for example, there are lots of photos of you as a family before their mother or father died, then leave them there. Removing these photos from their vision would be like telling them, right, that's enough of that, we're moving on now. Keep them up, keep their mum or dad in vision, let your children see that they still mean something to you and that you respect that they still mean a lot to them too.

You may want to explain to your new partner that they are staying up, and this is not threatening to them. If your new partner has a problem with this, then they're possibly not the one for you! It's very possible that some partners love and care for you a lot more than they are able to love and care for your children. It's your job to spot that before the children get involved.

Assuming everything is going well with all involved, let the children be a part of the decision to let the partner move in. Ask them if they are ready to share their house with them; maybe have them help you choose a welcoming present. You might be moving into their home, in which case helping your child take ownership of their bedroom is always good to do. Let them choose the bedcovers, curtains and wallpaper and make a big thing of putting a picture of Mum or Dad up in their bedroom in the new house. It signifies an acceptance of the new partner for the child to bring a little piece of their lost parent into their territory.

What if you need to split up?

If things don't go to plan and whether you have moved in or not, you can feel guilty for putting someone in your children's life, letting them get close to them only for it not to work out. These, however, are the risks we take in trying to find love and an adequate role model with all best intentions. I've had three partners since the boys lost their mum and when I split with someone after three years, the first split they experienced after losing Jade, I was really concerned how they would take it.

The girlfriend was everything I could have hoped a female role model for my children to be: attentive, caring, responsible and patient. They really loved her and at seven and eight years old I feared they would link the sudden absence to their mum and go through a sense of abandonment and loss all over again. To my surprise, when I plucked up the courage to tell them she had moved out the first question I remember getting was from Freddy asking, 'Who dumped who?' They actually thought it was hilarious – not in any disrespect to the girlfriend, they thought a lot of her – but what I learned was that, as long as they have you, it's never the end of the world if you split up with someone. Splitting with a good person is a shame for the children but they essentially have everything they want and need in you.

45

The Step-parent or Live-in Partner – Putting the Right Person in Your Children's Life

I have never once introduced new women to my children without feeling like I had qualified our potential, and certainly our exclusivity. The worst thing would have been to introduce them to women who were not guaranteed to be around for the foreseeable future, although of course I could never guarantee after six months that a relationship would blossom into something that lasted years. Fortunately mine did.

My current partner Kate and I had been together for six months when I arranged for us all to go to London to go on the London Eye and visit the Aquarium. They were nine and ten at the time and it was on neutral ground, not at home in their territory. There was a good amount going on so it was guaranteed to be fun, but there was time around eating together when Kate would be able to introduce herself to them and show a keen interest in their likes and dislikes. We didn't all stay together on the same night, though, because that would have represented going from 0–60 mph in too short a time.

While I might have made my mind up about Kate, hence the meeting, it was now over to the boys to decide they liked her enough to ask me if she could stay and it wasn't long before they did. Having their approval was important. Because her staying was their idea, it added value to their relationship with Kate.

It was slightly different when I was with my partner before Kate who also had a beautiful little girl. Having to introduce our children was an additional consideration when integrating our two ready-made families. I remember how we arranged a play date for them to meet at a soft play centre. Again neutral ground, lots of fun and for a relatively short time so that the impression left on each child was that this new relationship could be fun, and as my boys were older it made them feel good when they were given some responsibility to look out for her.

Introducing a new partner can be tricky, whatever the circumstances. When death and grief are involved, the situation can be even more complex. Some children may feel like the new partner is trying to 'replace' Mum or Dad and that, of course, can be difficult for all involved. I was fortunate in that because I wasn't with Jade when she died, no partner that I have been with since has ever had to give my children that reassurance and I too have always reiterated to them that no partner of mine, no matter how committed, will ever take the place of their mum in their life.

You don't need your children's permission to date, but you will save yourself some difficulties if you are honest and open with them about the development of any future relationship, even in its early stages. This will give them time to adjust and eliminates the jolt they might feel when someone suddenly turns up at the door to take Mummy out, or Daddy is away overnight and they hear from Grandma that he has a new girlfriend, or – something I'm sure is on the increase these days – they find out on social media.

You don't just have to look out for your children in this situation. Another layer of complexity can be added when a bereaved parent gives their new partner too much responsibility or expects too much in how they relate to their children, early on. I have seen this happen and that's when children can feel really intruded upon. Again it's not to say they won't grow to like the new partner, but a slower, more gentle approach that gives them time to adapt is key.

I spoke to my children about their experiences and views of step-mums and even the term itself upsets Bobby. You become a stepmum and not a girlfriend when the child personally decides that you are worthy of that role in their life. Children are usually the best judge of when that person is ready to be bestowed with the honour of a title of which half of the name belongs to someone else, although sometimes you can do so much to deserve their recognition but because you're not Mum or Dad, they may not be emotionally able to give you that credit.

As adults we naively think that when a new partner walks down the aisle as our new husband or wife, this is when they get the title, but in an ideal world the children themselves will decide when the time is right, and anyway, what's in a title? Surely the most important thing is that you are happy with the role you're playing? It may not be appreciated for now, but one day the children you helped raise in the confusion of loss will apologise for their barriers and give you all of the credit you deserve. Step-parenting is a thankless task at the best of times but a long-term strategy is vital; if you're wanting to be loved and adored straight away you might have a while to wait. Just remember what you're signing up for: to be with the person you've fallen in love with, you need to build an at least workable, hopefully loving and caring relationship with their children, and that may take time.

Bobby is of the view that as far as he is concerned, until someone marries me, the 'Mum' half of the title is off limits for him. Freddy, on the other hand, doesn't mind. Children have different reactions to such significant things, reminding us that we have to make sure we communicate and listen to them individually and don't assume they all, even siblings, think the same. If your new partner has a child and their other parent is still alive there may be less of an issue surrounding the step title because somehow 'stepdad' isn't so threatening when 'Dad' is still around.

The Don'ts

Here are some insights into the do's and don'ts of being a step-parent/partner. Now if you're not sure which one you are, ask the kids, but please remember this is just a badge pinned to your chest that can be changed for another from one day to the next.

1. Don't break promises.

Step-parent
Whatever you say can and will be used against you! If you set a challenge and the children achieve it, don't then let them down when it comes to giving them the reward you promised. This can be said for parenting generally, but why would they ever make any effort to please you again if they feel you're not going to 'be pleased' regardless of the effort they have made? Stand true to your word no matter how big or small the reward.

Bereaved children and indeed ones who have been through a separation of their parents have experienced trauma that some may process as abandonment, rejection or simply not being good enough or at fault. They need to know that you aren't going anywhere and that they can trust you not to do the same before they let you in.

It's impossible to guarantee your existence from one day to the next, but when you create bonds by sticking to your word and coming through on each and every promise, you not only improve your relationship with them but you also take them further away from the echo of an attachment lost in the past.

Parent

If your word starts on empty then it will remain that way. If someone you're with doesn't value their own words when given to your children, it highlights a desire to just do enough, to say what needs to be said to get what they want from the moment, maybe in a bid to please you without really wanting to carry out the task.

These moments should ring an alarm bell. Don't suppress it. We never need a partner in our lives more than we need a good, honest role model for our children who shows them patience, acceptance and interest. It's not that person's fault if they don't have the tools; it'll always be our fault for putting them there in the first place. Choose wisely and take your time.

Your new partner may already have children. If that's the case, observing how they are with their own children will tell you everything you need to know as to how they may parent your own. Would you be happy with their parenting style? If not, do you think there will be an acceptable compromise between the two?

2. Don't keep us separate from your friends.

Step-parent

There will come a time when you will have been in your new partner and children's lives long enough for them to be introduced to your friends and family. Bereaved children want to feel included, they want you to feel proud of them, as though they are a credit to you, and if they feel that from you, that's exactly what they will give you back in return.

It's commonly misconceived that a child's behaviour comes entirely at its own accord but if you think little of your stepchildren they will give you little; if you anticipate kindness, manners and good behaviour, that's what you'll typically get. If you expect poor behaviour, you're actually asking for it. Understand that children are more perceptive and feeling than adults, so that time when you think, oh, they have no idea what I'm thinking, you've already told them with your body language and tone of voice.

Parent

If your partner leaving your kids out of their plans is still happening after a period of two or more years, what more can this tell you than that your partner doesn't see your children as a credit and potentially sees them as an embarrassment?

Early on in the relationship it can highlight a lack of confidence, but then that's not something to be avoided, because practice makes perfect. In the early stages it's OK for someone to be nervous about the task in hand, especially if they have never been around children. It's also OK for them to not be naturally blessed with a maternal/paternal instinct.

Your new partner's ability to play a healthy role in your children's lives can develop, but it requires a lot of communication between you both to get it right. They also need to have the desire to work on it and that will be testament to their love and optimism for you and the relationship. The partner who is willing to try and fail is the partner who you know will get it right. They need to know from you that it's OK to be upset if your kids embarrass them. Shake their hand and welcome them to parenting! If they have kids already but your kids are older and they aren't yet used to teenagers, give them time and let them get a little sneak preview of what's to come in a few years with their own child, when the tables will be inevitably turned on you. Of course not all teenagers are difficult, well, not all of the time! My partner doesn't have her own children and sometimes my boys' teenage behaviour certainly gives her a look at the bigger picture of parenting. It's not always pretty, but then there are those moments when the sun shines and you realise the best version of your child does exist.

Alternatively, they might have teenagers and have forgotten what it's like to have young children running around. Whatever the case, it will be a stage to parenting that you'll have experienced before or will soon experience, so the motivation to adapt should either be a trip down memory lane or a chance to practise for the future.

3 Don't forget, we come as a three.

Step-parent
You must remember that a child needs to feel especially safe in their own environment, a safeness that existed before you, maybe; therefore respect the fact that you're on their turf. You will not always remain the visitor, you will become a part of the pack, but they need to feel like you're there as much for them as you are for Mum/Dad, or they will fear that you are trying to get between them and Mum/Dad or that you're trying to take Mum/Dad away from them.

Sounds silly, but if you'd lost a parent in childhood you might just be fearing the worst possible outcome, that this new partner might somehow steal your remaining parent away from them. Show acceptance for them by giving your words and efforts to them as well as your partner. They may give you nothing in return at first but they will be storing it all up, evaluating if you're a bad or a good thing. A little effort goes a long way; recognise them whenever you see them.

Parent
Does your partner acknowledge your children when they come into a room? How does your child respond? We are like a middleman in this scenario, helping both parties to be more accepting of one another. You could be feeling more resistance on either side but the key is to keep empowering them to give a little more each time they are in each other's company.

Some partners just get it and they're the real keepers, some need a little more work, which requires patience from all sides, or you might be very happy with someone for your own reasons but they actually give very little of themselves to the children, in which case you have a job on your hands.

A step-parent can only develop a bond and show your child that they are interested if you create the situations for them to do so. If your child goes to bed at 7 p.m. don't ask your partner to come over at 8 p.m. because it's easier; get them round at 6 p.m. so they can put a little development time in the bank. Those savings will only grow!

4. Don't forget to remind me that you care about me as well as my mum/dad.

Step-parent

As you begin to earn trust and acceptance with your partner's children, their barriers will slowly lower, which may in turn reveal their real needs, and as you embed yourself more and more into their lives they will want to see some kind of reassurance that you like them and care for them.

As you would with your partner, tell them they are great, or that you're really impressed with something they did or that you love spending time with them! If you bring your partner a gift, bring them a toy, or a chocolate bar or a magazine and read it with them, and for older children, something that they're into. My kids love it when I buy them scratch-cards from the petrol station! Maybe watch their favourite TV show with them, go for a run with them, ask to look at photos of them as a baby? Reassurance – stability – trust.

Parent

Encourage your partner to be thoughtful and kind, that they don't just need to develop something between you both, but they also need to develop equally with the children so everything grows together. Don't settle for someone who just tolerates your children because to have you they need to have some kind of relationship with them. Praise your partner for every little effort that he or she makes. At first it's for you, then hopefully it becomes something they enjoy and maintain throughout.

5. Don't just save your affection for in front of Mum/Dad.

Step-parent

If you don't have a natural affection for your partner's kids after some time, you can't pretend there isn't an issue. Worse than struggling to get to grips with your partner's kids is struggling but not saying anything about it.

Your partner will know, the kids will know, but if you're honest about things then it's always salvageable. As long as you still want to be with the parent there's always a new approach you haven't tried. Be clear about the issues. Is it the child/ren's attitude towards you? Maybe write a list of the things you can deal with and the things you can't, then you know where you stand.

It may also help to discuss whether the things you can't deal with are down to the child, your partner or are maybe your responsibility too. Now look again at the things that are because of partner and child and ask if they are things that are meant to upset you personally or if you get upset even though it's not aimed at you directly.

Parent

This just reiterates the need for you to keep your eyes open for the suggestion that it's still more about them pleasing you than pleasing all. If it's early days you can afford to be more relaxed about this, but if the relationship is bordering on seriousness, engagement, etc.

then it's a worry if your new partner switches their concern on and off because it's not yet become natural.

Ask yourself, does the social media account tell one story, but the reality feel fairly separate? It's so hard meeting someone you'd happily spend the rest of your life with and you may feel like you have that, but if they can't maintain the level of acceptance for the kids when you're not around there's a good chance they're not the one for you.

6. Don't manage us through our parent!

Step-parent

Are you observing bad behaviour in the children and calling out to their mum or dad, telling them what the child has done instead of actually dealing with it yourself? Kids describe that as snitching. It gives them the impression that you aren't strong enough to communicate with them directly and they do it more as a result.

You may feel like it's too early for you to be stopping the children's indiscretions but there are levels to your reaction; one extent is to run and tell, which they don't like. The other extent is to stand there fully disciplining the kids, which might also be seen as being above your station; somewhere in the middle, however, is the art of communicating in a friendly, reasoning way that doesn't imply that you're personally upset or disapproving but gives the impression that they should stop. All damaging eventualities are halted as a result and when Mum/Dad comes down the stairs they are oblivious to the fact that anything untoward has happened. In my opinion all the children are doing is testing you to see if you're strong enough to keep them safe.

Are you a walkover who needs the parent to do all of the talking or are you adult enough to cope with it yourself? Kids want you to be the latter, but they can't always verbalise that, so you'll just have to try it and see the difference it makes to how much respect they show you. Remember, respect is to be earned.

Parent
Try and avoid the habit of having to listen to your partner's account of what happened and who said what and instead encourage them that if they were on the scene when it happened, they can deal with it instead. Kids need to know their boundaries with your partner and delegating the issue earns them no points with anyone.

Just to make clear, we shouldn't expect our new partners to do all of the discipline because that has to come from us, but the little niggles can be child-concocted tests that, if not dealt with by your partner, are golden opportunities to assert some leadership and in turn give your children the response they were looking for: yep, we can trust this one because we know where we stand with him/her.

The Do's

1. Be Interested in the things that matter to us.

Step-Parent
If you want to build a successful relationship with your partner's kids, whatever really matters to them needs to matter to you. If they play football go and watch! If they love YouTube sit and watch a video with them; if they play computer games sit down and play a game with them. It goes further than you think.

Parent
Don't allow your partner to come and watch something your child does and for them to sit and read a book or disappear off to get a burger at the start of the game only to return with two minutes of

the match left! Your children notice and absorb these things and form damaging opinions that are hard to reverse.

The idea is for the step-parent to prove to the child in small increments that they are interested and looking to get to know them and be a part of their existence. Your job is to provide the levels of acceptable interaction between the two and this increases as the relationship between you both develops, and the time they have been around in each other's lives.

It should be said that if you're on a whirlwind romance the rate at which you fall in love with your partner will most probably not match the rate at which their relationship with your child will blossom. Adults tend to throw themselves into things out of need; children are slightly more cautious and expecting anything more from them will result in them feeling you've tried to replace their mum or dad.

2. Join in!

Step-parent
Sometimes we think taking our step-child somewhere and waiting in the car park constitutes an effort. While you have got them there, which is indeed an effort, why not go one step further and actually go on the trampolines with them or go and meet the parents at the friend's house you just dropped them at. Think: what would I do if this was my child? (It will be your child if you marry their parent.) Start practising for the future.

Parent
In the early stages of introduction create opportunities for the children and your new partner to get to know each other in a fun and neutral environment, without distractions such as phones or TVs if possible. Don't introduce them apologetically, hoping that they can

just 'slip' into the kids' lives. Make an event of it, see the significance in attaching those early intros to things that the kids like already such as ice skating, playing in the park, football, etc. In this way you're making it easier for everyone to get off to the best start.

3. Find something we enjoy together, 'our thing'.

Step-parent

Now you are really investing your time into your relationship with the children, you can absolutely manage to find something that you share a mutual interest in and can do without necessarily involving the parent. My partner recently took Freddy to the zoo. They both had a great time, it strengthened their relationship and took my appreciation to new levels. I'd go so far as to say that I am more impressed by any effort made with my sons than I am by any effort shown to me, although that too is gratefully received. If you're really good with my kids, that's the biggest attraction I can find in a partner.

Parent

You'll get to a point when you feel ready to let them go off and explore something together. If your child has requested this, then grab that opportunity, and if your partner is suggesting this, then you've got a good one.

If, however, you're trying to nudge things forwards you may need to carefully construct a play date between them that doesn't go on for too long and isn't a five-hour drive away, so the awkwardness is minimal. Slowly but surely the step-parent can learn about responsibility in sole care and the child/ren can learn to trust them, especially where letting you out of their sight might be a factor.

4. Trust me!

Step-parent

You may not have been around children before and so have to build up your empathy with your partner's child/ren. Trusting them is a huge step – for you and them – and is the foundation on which your relationship will blossom. You might therefore think of a task that shows them what they can do and when they complete it, tell them: 'I knew you wouldn't let me down', or words to that effect. They will feel trusted and will enjoy giving you many more reasons for that to stay the case.

Parent

Don't allow your new partner to patronise your child/ren. It's OK to ask questions, but follow them with a big dose of praise, otherwise it might feel they are continually suspicious. A child once told me that his stepmother always asked him, an 11-year-old boy, if he had taken his medication for ADHD and it made him feel like she only cared that he wouldn't be a handful for her that day. Needless to say it was detrimental and absorbed by others too.

Our children are blessings to those who are lucky enough to be in their lives, not inconveniences! Do not allow someone to view your child as anything less than a privilege.

5. Remembering the lost parent:
Little gestures go a long way.

Step-parent

Do something with the children for their deceased parent. A caring step-parent will recognise their lost parent respectfully and often. They will initiate conversation about them, think of new ways to remember that person and be there alongside the children to celebrate their life, listen to them when they want to talk and, sorry to say because it's one of the hardest things you'll need to accept, but take the anger and frustration they throw at you when they're expressing their loss.

One day they will thank you for that. It won't necessarily be anytime soon but when they're older they will show that they have a very strong respect for you for the rest of their life. Childhood can seem like such a long and bumpy ride but if all goes to plan any difficulties experienced will be viewed more softly and you'll be forever known as the person who came in and selflessly got them through it.

Parent

It's such a help to the children and the cohesion of the family unit if your partner is able to speak about your loss. It makes things difficult if they can't. You might like to think it better to keep things separate but the message that sends to your children is that you're trying to make out the parent they lost didn't exist, and that will cause untold resentment.

Encourage your partner to join in when you celebrate your loved one's life. Can they show empathy by releasing a balloon for someone they may have lost too? Ask them to ask the kids questions about the parent they are grieving for and be genuinely interested in their answers. That's the way to the kids' hearts as well as your own.

6. Make my mum/dad happy.

Step-parent

The most obvious of the bunch.

The children are not just particularly receptive to how you treat them, they're also very receptive to how you treat their parent!

That's not to say you can't disagree or reason with their parent in front of them – they'll want to see that you're fair but able to vocalise your opinion – but just watch out for being petty or speaking at a volume in front of them that they could misinterpret as anger and aggression, because it'll have a negative impact on all sides.

You're entitled to whatever feelings you go through in the relationship; just be careful what you express, and how, when they're in the house. When your relationship with their parent is going well the children will respond to that by offering far less resistance to you than if they feel things are not going well.

Parent

Don't feel guilty for being happy – that's the reason you got into this relationship in the first place. To deny the children the benefits of seeing and hearing you happy would be to deny them the right to feel good too. They aren't judging you – in fact our kids are the last to judge us; they understand better than we do that what's good for us is good for them.

On the contrary, if the relationship you're in doesn't make you happy and you are only hanging in there because you think the kids will be devastated if another man or woman leaves them (while their loss won't be the same as someone getting up and leaving them out of choice, it's often perceived as that by children) then you must think of the long-term damage you're risking for a short-term comfort.

What example of relationships will this give them, and if you settle for unhappiness in a relationship what might they then do in a relationship of their own in their adult years?

Here are some extra pointers for the new partner who may one day become the step-parent:

1. Reassure them that you're not trying to take Mum/Dad's place.
You will no doubt know this, but for a child to know it – that you know this, through your behaviour towards them – is so soothing for that child, because this fear and insecurity will be flashing in their head from time to time, driven by potential guilt that they are letting someone replace their parent in their own minds.

You can help by just mentioning, 'I know you'll only ever have one Mum/Dad and I totally get that, I'm not trying to be Mum/Dad, I just want to be your friend until you think it's OK for me to be anything else.' You have then made it on their terms and given them control, which they will appreciate.

2. Be patient and understanding.
When times get hard just remind yourself these kids have gone through an unimaginable trauma so early on in life and they should be allowed to make mistakes, to express their grief in a variety of ways, one of which will be bad behaviour that may from time to time be headed in your direction!

You knew all of this when you got involved with their parent, so to expect any less at any point during the relationship is unrealistic and lacking in empathy, albeit human nonetheless. If you find those moments hard, speak to your partner and work through them together. If that doesn't help and you feel that you've given your all, you may need to rethink, because those children aren't going anywhere.

3. Be honest.
You might think parents don't want to hear that you find their children challenging, but we are realists. We know it's not going to be a breeze and we also know that kids have a habit of saving their worst for us at home, especially during those teenage years, but if you put your concerns to us constructively we can work together to find a

solution. I always welcome Kate's insight because she sees when I'm slacking on the rules and she also tells me if I've ever been too harsh, and I appreciate that support.

The truth is, we want to hear it because then we can do something about it. Keeping it to yourself for fear of a negative response only means time goes by and the problems grow needlessly. If you share something and your partner goes mad, they may be in denial and are not ready to hear it, or maybe you didn't communicate it in a constructive enough tone. You have to say it in a way that makes it sound as though you want to work it out, or you might find the parent gets a little defensive – they are his/her babies after all and being a parent is all about protection.

4. Be loving.
It's hard to open your heart to a child who isn't yours, but it will come, and hopefully you will come to see that instead of getting one person to love and be loved by, you get a whole bunch. Give them affection when it feels right to do so and don't worry if the kids run away at first. They'll be battling with the guilt caused by the thought of their deceased parent not being happy with them for allowing that.

Your partner can help by talking to them about how their deceased parent would be happy that they are happy and they shouldn't feel like they are 'not allowed' to get close to you.

5. Help keep their deceased parent's memory alive.
One of the best memories I have from my current relationship was when my girlfriend joined the boys and me in the sea on Christmas Day because the boys wanted to take their traditional balloon release for Jade to new levels by releasing them in the water. Despite the freezing cold, she joined in for the children, and that was something I will be eternally grateful for.

6. Listen.

Children won't be able to talk if you're not willing to listen and they won't waste their time telling you something meaningful if you don't seem interested. When you talk to younger children think about bringing your eye level down to theirs and facing them square on so you're in complete rapport. It makes a big difference when you're not towering above them and facing their direction.

7. Seek the meaning behind the words and not the words themselves.

It will really help if you develop the ability not to react to words that are being spoken in grief, but to see the meaning behind them. What is it the children are really trying to tell you, or in most cases, what is it that they are inadvertently asking you for?

Adults can be rubbish communicators at the best of times, so how we expect children to verbalise their true feelings in loss is quite unrealistic. Disregard the negativity thrown in your direction and ask what they need. Every negative is a chance to show them something positive in return.

8. Be loyal.

When talking about your partner's children in conversation with others, especially when they are in earshot, make sure you speak of them with respect and loyalty. Everything you say is absorbed, and while your actions may say one thing, your words to others can contradict and create doubt and this can get back to them.

9. Show friendship.

Some bereaved children dislike certain titles. Adults have a need to label relationships, so in the early stages just be their friend and keep it as simple as that. Friendship is about caring, paying an interest, taking time, giving space, listening and loving. Each child in your partner's life is a friendship waiting to blossom and if there is more than one, they will be unique, so do remember to notice the subtle differences between them.

10. Routine and consistency.

Kids will find it easier to get to know you and connect if there is a routine and consistency to your presence. Make time for date night with their parent but also factor in time for them, either on the same day before you go out or on a separate occasion. The routine means they can start looking forward to seeing you and most importantly it brings security to a child who had theirs removed through loss.

11. Give me space.

Take the lead from the children and don't force it. If you try too hard you'll be marked down for that; try too little and you'll be marked down for that too. There's a wonderful balance in between and if all of your efforts are genuine they'll feel that you're being natural and start to lower their defences.

I don't want to imply all bereaved children are going to have brick walls up in front of them. I have one who does and I have one who will attach himself to you like it's his responsibility to do the bonding. If a child attaches themselves firmly from the outset and wants you to be part of their family and asks you if you will be staying forever, the way to gently handle over-attachment is to just feel privileged and enjoy the warmth. The child is instinctively getting what they need from you in the absence of not just who, but what they have lost. If you feel it too much, you must remember your obligation to communicate to your partner so they might adjust the time you spend in the child's company. A single parent will be well aware of the balance that must be struck between the needs of their child, your needs and somewhere in all of that their own needs too.

12. Give me time.
When you think things are going great there will inevitably be something that tests you. When you think everything is going wrong, something will restore your faith. Step-parenting a bereaved child can be nothing short of a rollercoaster, but seek solace in the fact that the ultimate responsibility lies with the parent, not you, so relax and have fun with it.

Take the negatives with a pinch of salt and enjoy the good times, for they are the memories you'll look back upon fondly one day. People who step in and make a difference in bereaved children's lives are heroes as far as I'm concerned.

Finally, some perspective

Step-parents
For perspective, imagine these children who you have raised as a step-parent at an adult age. Imagine they are sitting in a coffee shop talking to friends about their experiences of childhood after their loss.

What are they likely to say about you and the role you played? What do you want them to say about you? What do you need to change in order to make that the reality however many years from now?

Parents
The ultimate question is a difficult one but it gives you the answer you need and tells you where you're at with that potential step-parent that you're with.

'If something were ever to happen to you, would you feel safe leaving the rest of your children's childhood in their hands?'

Told you it was a tough one. The ultimate benchmark, the stand-ard we hope our partner will one day achieve, to deem them good enough to be solely responsible for our children should anything happen to us. You might say: 'I'm not ready yet but I might feel differently after more time.' We can't hit our new partner with this question, it's just for you. What do they have to do to earn the level of trust where you might feel them capable of raising your kids? The answer to that is what you need to encourage between your partner and your children from this day forwards. Obviously this is just for perspective; I'm sure many of us would have other family members who we would go to first no matter how wonderful our partner is proving to be.

Do they need to measure up to that? Well, you might have other options, so no, but in terms of standards we set for ourselves, that would be the bar and anything less is a compromise. Do we choose a partner for our own benefit? No. Do we choose a partner just so there is a man or woman in the kids' life? No.

Do we choose a partner so that the kids can have a good example of a male/female role model in their life and so that we too can enjoy love again for now and for the rest of our lives? That sounds a bit more like it. Keep the bar high and settle for nothing less than you and the children deserve, and remember communication is the very foundation of a strong couple.

46

Measurements and Timescales

In grief, we can become preoccupied with how long the bereavement process will go on for, how long we can expect to feel the pain of our loss and how long it will be until we are 'completely over it'.

For starters, we never completely get over the death of a loved one but we do learn to manage and live with our grief. While in the throes of bereavement it may feel as if we don't have a grip on anything but it's important to realise that while there are elements we can't control, there are many that we can.

The following table may help you to identify the areas you do or don't control at any stage during your loss.

Out of our control

The circumstances of the loss

The reaction of family members

The emotions we feel

How our friends react

The judicial system in cases of criminal activity or financial settlements

How sympathetic our employer is to our need for time off

Within our control

Asking for help

Establishing who the people/groups are that are going to be your support

The removal or introduction of visual 'reminders' within our living or work environment

The organisation of the funeral

Our thoughts, or at least the continuation of them (Thoughts are going to come into our heads but we control how long we dwell on those thoughts; we have the ability to make a still picture into a movie and sometimes this is to our detriment.)

The actions we take to remember positively

Who we appoint to look after any legalities

Where we work

How the school adapts to and accommodates the needs of our children

In bereavement, as in many areas of our lives, if we focus on the things we don't control then we are prolonging our pain, 'swimming upstream', battling against a tide that will never turn. However, if we learn to put all of our focus and energy into the things we do have influence over, we can be sure to make the best progress possible. If you want to be as effective as possible in your bereavement, then this is a great mindset to adopt.

We head into grief having absolutely no clue as to what, when and why. What are we meant to do or say? How are we meant to feel or to express our pain? How long will we be at grief's mercy, unable to prepare, to plan or to progress?

I have worked with many bereaved people over the years and I am more often able to help them move forwards when I ask them initially to identify how far they perceive themselves as having come since the loss and how far they think they have yet to travel in their darkness. This exercise can give my client a grounding and positioning in circumstances that have otherwise left them feeling 'stuck'.

All very well, but how do you know where you are with your loss? Consciously you don't, but your subconscious knows better and if you ask yourself the right questions you will get answers that will give you a foothold and something to build on, which in turn will lead you to the first acknowledgement that grief isn't an endless dark tunnel but you are on a progressive journey, and that when you get to the stage when your feet tentatively hit the ground once more, you will realise that an element of control will re-enter your life. It's then, too, that you may come to see with a new clarity that there is no should or shouldn't, no hard-and-fast rules to adhere to, and that the journey into grief is uncharted because it's unique to you, and you are therefore the only person who can decide how you're doing.

As I would in a coaching session, I am going to take you through the process of identification through elimination and scrutiny. Ask yourself the same questions and maybe you'll learn where you stand with grief too.

Cheryle Smith, 37, lost her father Bryan to an ulceration of the legs, a treatable illness that couldn't be cured because of Bryan's battle with schizophrenia, which meant he couldn't accept treatment. Cheryle is a natural born survivor with an incredible ability to look inwardly and self-heal, so I knew she would give an incredibly honest insight into just where she perceived herself to be nine months on after her father's death.

Our conversation went like this:

JB: How many times does your dad pop into your thoughts on a daily/weekly basis at present?

CS: About twenty times per week.

JB: Of those twenty or so thoughts, how many of them are good memories that you enjoy and how many of them are bad memories or thoughts that you find difficult?

CS: About fifty-fifty.

JB: Do you think the ratio should be higher or lower?

CS: No, I think that's exactly where I should be at this point of my loss.

JB: What sort of emotions and difficulties did you experience when you first lost your father?

CS: At first I couldn't say the words, 'My dad's dead', but then I had to when I talked to the funeral directors and when it came to cancelling all of his bills. I was also taken over by a surge of adrenalin that got me through the funeral and the shock of it all. If I had to arrange his funeral now, I don't think I could.

JB: How often were you thinking about him every day back then?

CS: I'd always called him every hour on the hour in the final onset of his illness, so I had this continuous reflex to go to pick up the phone every hour.

JB: Of those hourly thoughts, what percentage of them were positive and what percentage were negative?

CS: A hundred per cent negative. I felt like I was in a state of denial. I was numb and I couldn't deal with it and yet I remember thinking: 'I'm not going to let grief get to me.'

JB: When did the denial stop?

CS: About two months later when everything slowed down and I was no longer distracted by work and travelling. At that point his death became real and it was then that I knew I had to deal with this now and it was then that the pain began. I wanted to call him and thought about calling him on and off all day.

JB: When did that urge to call him start to subside?

CS: Not until the end of August, five months after I lost him. I said to my friend one day: 'I'm sick of this, I can't keep going to call him,' and that's where it stopped.

I now had a good idea about how grief affected Cheryl for the first five months. You could see the stages very clearly: shock, adrenalin, denial, reality, pain; and she had outlined what had caused her to change gear and move from one perceived stage to the next.

How does this compare to your early stages? Draft out a chronological timeline of your transition through the stages and attach the conversations or incidents that took you from one to the next.

I wondered how much, if any, preparation for grief Cheryle had received before her dad had died.

JB: When did you first accept that your dad was going to die?

CS: In early February the doctor said that without hospital treatment my dad would die from his ulcerations. But because of his schizophrenia he refused to leave the residential home he lived in and there wasn't anything that anyone could have done to change that. My mother had tried once and actually got him there but he freaked out and it was particularly stressful for all, especially for Dad.

JB: Did that preparation help you?

CS: Yes, I was able to say all of the things that I wanted to say to him and I was there to care for him to the absolute maximum that I could. We shared some incredible moments that will provide me with so many comforting memories moving forwards.

Cheryl's experiences in her father's last days were far from effortless because she and her father were so close, but there was a clear element of survival mindset about Cheryle's behaviour leading up to his death. She had eliminated the potential for guilt and regret by doing as much as she could when her father was still with her, leaving her less to deal with after he died. Grief in its purest form is quite enough without contributing a few extra ingredients of our own.

JB: What happened after you declared that you couldn't keep going to call him?

CS: I made a conscious decision to make it positive as much as I could because I chose to believe that he was watching me and I had to make him proud and happy. (JB: Positive self-imposed rule.)

JB: How did you go from pain to acceptance? From a hundred per cent negative thoughts to positive memories?

CS: I worked hard at it, I still do every day. I turn my negative thoughts into positive memories by manipulating them consciously. I believe that I can stop a bad thought and turn it into a good memory by talking myself out of one and into the other.

Cheryle had revealed the secret weapon for anyone who is bereaved. In her effort to manage her grief effectively, she had mastered the ability to flick the switch between good and bad, harmful and helpful.

JB: What was grief to you? What does the term actually mean?

CS: I see grief as physical pain.

JB: When you're having a good memory about your dad, is that pain?

CS: No! It's pleasure.

JB: So grief brings you pleasure too?

CS: I hadn't thought of it that way, but indirectly, yes.

JB: What role did grief play in the delivery of that or any reminder?

CS: It put a bad thought in my head and I changed it.

JB: Grief told you what to think?

CS: It reminded me my dad's no longer with me.

JB: So, who decides whether it's a negative or positive thought that follows when grief taps you on the shoulder and says: 'Your dad's dead'?

CS: Maybe me?

JB: So is grief's role negative, positive or neither?

CS: I see it as being neutral.

JB: What would happen if grief didn't exist and there was nothing to remind you of your loss?

CS: We wouldn't think of them anywhere near as much. We would feel the same way about our closest loved ones as we would the friend we haven't seen for a while. It feels like my dad wouldn't be able to be as important to me as he is and that upsets me!

JB: So you can see that grief has some benefits?

CS: It reminds me what I had and with my dad. I had the best possible dad in the world. I don't mind feeling grief for him because it's what our relationship deserves.

What is grief to you?

Cheryl had enlightened me no end. In thinking about grief not existing we had both changed our perception of grief's role in our loss.

Without grief we wouldn't be reminded of what we had, and the more we had, the bigger the sense of grief we would feel. Grief is like a person who is there to provide a service to help us regulate our transition into a new period of time without someone who was always there beforehand. When grief taps us on the shoulder and we return the favour, our relationship with it becomes a two-way thing. We work with grief for our own good. The thought that grief is actually doing us a favour is incredible, but so viable.

This completely changes the idea that grief is a big, scary, monstrous black cloud that hangs over us, casting a miserable shadow everywhere we turn. Maybe that's just an emotion we were already feeling but because grief tapped us on the shoulder, we blame that emotion on grief.

Let's consider grief's characteristics.

- Punctual: it's always on time.
- Dynamic: it doesn't miss a trick.
- Consistent: it doesn't take a day off.
- Loyal: once you've met it never completely leaves you.
- Non-judgmental: it doesn't mind if you turn it into a good or bad thought.
- Thoughtful: it never forgets your birthdays, anniversaries or the big days in the calendar.
- Great listener: it will sit with you in your darkest hours and not leave your side, catching every word.

Imagine you were interviewing grief for a job with lots of responsibility – would you hire it? Maybe we do employ grief to be a full-time job at first, then after a period of time we continue to reduce its hours until we finally retire it and just use it for some consultancy work every now and again.

Back to Cheryle and her measurement and timescale.

JB: What has grief given you?
CS: It's given me strength. Without it I wouldn't have known that I was capable of coping with so much. It's also been a catalyst for

change. Great things are happening to me and this wouldn't
have been the case otherwise.

JB: What percentage of you would you say is managing your grief?

CS: I'm a hundred per cent managing my grief because I'm always
taking action and I give myself targets and goals. I now accept
that responsibility for how I feel is in my hands and I allow myself
to feel sad if that's how I'm feeling because I know I can turn my
thoughts to good memories whenever I choose to.

JB: Of the times you want to cry, what percentage of the time do
you let yourself and how often do you send the tears away?

CS: I let myself cry half the time; sometimes I just don't want to or I
save it for when I'm in private.

JB: What percentage of the time would you say you're dictating yourself to grief? Inviting the emotion, tapping grief on its shoulder?

CS: Actually only about ten per cent. I only seem to set myself up
to think about my dad on the special occasions. I've had his
birthday recently and I went to a restaurant that he would have
loved and I played golf because I know he loved hearing about
how well I was doing in tournaments. So I was dictating that day.
I know I need to do that more.

Some interesting measurements had been brought into question:
how often she allowed herself to cry, how she felt she was doing in
the management of those feelings and how often she felt like she
needed to cry were all revealing.

JB: Talking and thinking are two completely different things, so
how often do you talk about Dad? And how many times a week
would you like to talk about Dad?

CS: I talk about him a couple of times per week but I would really
like to talk about him every day.

JB: What stops you?

CS: I don't want to keep talking about my dad to my friends all of the time. I'm worried they'll get bored of me doing that.

JB: For starters that's what friends are for, but how much do you feel like you need to say about your dad each day for it to count as a good enough expression of the fact you're thinking of him?

CS: I guess even if I say the words, 'my dad loved that' or 'I did that with my dad once' is enough to feel like I've let him out. It probably doesn't need to be a full-blown conversation. A mention will do and now that feels easier, less of a burden on my friends, I can do it in any conversation with anyone.

JB: Do you feel any guilt or regret over anything to do with your relationship with Dad? What percentage would it be?

CS: Yes! I feel guilty about two things in particular so I'd say that's around ten per cent? My dad loved gardening and someone brought me two rose plants as a gift at the funeral. I didn't do anything with them and they died. I feel sad about that because they were his favourite plants. Also he would call me on a Saturday night to talk about *Strictly Come Dancing*. I never watched it but didn't tell him that, so I just pretended to know what he was talking about. I really wish I had watched it so I could have had more of a conversation with him about it. As a result of this I feel negative whenever I hear *Strictly* mentioned. But I don't feel regret. I couldn't have been there any more than I was and I talked to him as much as anyone could.

JB: What guilt might you have had, but avoided?

CS: I would have had so much guilt if I hadn't told him how amazing he was. It always used to make him feel embarrassed; he was shy and bashful and I loved seeing that.

JB: What's coming up that might potentially make you wobble?

CS: It's the anniversary of his death in three months. Oh, and if I were to lose someone else.

JB: How can you prepare yourself for either?

CS: I can do the same for his anniversary as I did for his birthday, plan a day in his memory. When it comes to losing someone else I have to remember that no death in my life will be harder to deal with than that of my dad, so if and when it happens I will know that I've done it already and I will just have to do it again.

JB: In six months, how do you want to be doing on everything we have discussed?

CS: I want to be mentioning him every day. I want to be thinking seventy-five per cent positive thoughts twenty times a week and I want to be dictating myself to grief fifty per cent of the time. I want to feel zero per cent guilt because I don't think I should feel any and I'm going to let myself cry seventy-five per cent of the time by then.

Cheryle was now projecting her desired targets for those measurable areas of grief over the next six months. You might feel it slightly unrealistic to predict how you are coping so far into the future but the big lesson here is that we set the rules for the terms and timescales of our journey through grief. It isn't decided in the stars or set in any stone, and when you feel ready to work with grief instead of trying to fight it, run from it or deny its existence, you are then at the point of being able to plan how your loss affects you from there on.

Here are some questions you can ask yourself to produce your timeline for the effects of grief.

1. What percentage of the way towards managing your grief do you feel you're at?

2. How many times do you get upset per week? What should it be in your opinion? (What do you mean, what *should* it be? Remember we set the rules. It's your interpretation that matters. It's not a test but a measurement, a sense of scale that you will work to.)

3. How many times per hour, day or week do you think of the person you've lost? What do you want that to be?

4 What is the percentage difference between the negative thoughts you have compared to the positive memories you relive?

5. How many physical acts of remembrance do you partake in per month? (Acts such as looking at old photos, reading letters they wrote to you, watching home videos with them in, etc.) How many do you want to?

6. How regular would you describe the waves of grief to be? What is the right amount for where you're at?

7. How many times do you talk about your loved one per week? How many should it be?

8. What triggers or reminders do you expose yourself to that you shouldn't?

9. What reminders or triggers do you not expose yourself to that you should?

10. What do you feel guilty about? Of those guilty feelings, which ones did you actually control?

47

Mindset For the Survival of Grief

I have sought to break down all that is grief in this book for the good of anyone walking along its long and winding path. On interviewing one woman, initially with the intention of learning about losing both parents within five months, I wasn't quite prepared for the impact her story had on me. As I walked from my practice that day it was clear I had just endured a survival master class, not just in grief but in life itself. Louise's story encapsulates everything this book aims to provide – a guide, a model, a template for improvement and understanding ourselves, our innermost feelings and our fate.

At 33, Louise Glover lost her father Louie, not long after his 60th birthday. Years of working in the coal mining industry, battling with chronic obstructive pulmonary disease and a fatal brush with pneumonia ended his life. Just five months later Louise also lost her mother Maria, aged 50, after she suffered a series of heart attacks. While her parents were not together and Louise's mum was in fact in an abusive relationship with a man who took her money and beat her days after she had suffered her first heart attack, she still considered Louie her best friend and Louise believes that his death literally caused her heart to break.

During her childhood Louise's parents had both been in jail, and while living with her now deceased maternal grandmother, Louise experienced abuse at the hands of her grandmother's partner. Louise subsequently found the strength to report this to the police and her grandmother's partner was sent to jail, but sadly Louise's grandmother chose not to believe her granddaughter and when he eventually came out of prison, she took him back.

You'd be forgiven for assuming that on losing her parents Louise would be mentally and physically spent. Where would she begin to unravel such a layered existence in order to have the clarity and presence of mind to begin her journey through grief?

What I witnessed in front of me on the day we talked was the Bear Grylls of life. Louise, just 33 years young, treated me to the most inspirational set of insights into how, regardless of the life you've lived, you can, with the correct mindset, survive anything. In Louise's case grief was just one of the many challenges thrown her way. She shared the ways in which she coped with life – and death – and I was so blown away by her insight and resilience that I am sharing these with you here.

Forgiveness

Louise was able to put the feelings of her mother and the difficult life she had had, before the hostility we might expect her to have had given her mother's absence and the subsequent abuse she suffered by her grandmother's partner. She was able to forgive her mother for not being there to protect her. Louise hadn't spoken to her maternal grandfather for much of her life as he had cut her off due to his differences with Louise's Dad but when he came to her mother's funeral, through forgiveness, Louise was able to be pleased that he had come to pay his respects.

Louise was in control of her pain, well able to deal with negative feelings. When she talked of her maternal grandmother, she told me: 'Some time after her death, I knew that I had to forgive her or I wouldn't be able to move on. I left her a note at her grave years later saying I forgive her, which allowed me to move forward and put the past to rest.'

Self-awareness

Louise also had a remarkable ability to stand still amidst all the chaos and reflect on her state of mind and her needs. She was able to be reasonable with herself and didn't burden herself with labels or accusations. She knew that she had to 'grieve to be stronger' and instead of avoiding the process, she almost invited it.

She told me: 'Whilst dealing with my ongoing grief I found purpose by entering fitness competitions and by climbing Everest, which required a magnitude of training, something that would be tough enough for anyone, let alone someone going through the grieving process.'

Louise's honesty was refreshing. At first, when her mother died she felt 'completely useless, not able to do anything'. People's egos and pride sometimes get in the way of clarity. Who wants to admit helplessness? But to admit helplessness is to completely remove yourself from easily apportioned blame in the direction of others. There's something powerful about surrendering to the mercy of grief as Louise described. There's control in surrender. It represents a stillness, the conviction to stand, but not run.

When Louise told me that she didn't actually feel like she connected to the remaining family any more, I again admired her sensitivity to the bigger picture. I often describe how losing one, or two in Louise's case, is like losing many, because without those two connections, the glue that can hold family members together, it can feel as though we are cast adrift.

I asked Louise what the hardest thing was about her losses and she began to tell me how the loneliness was difficult; however, before she really finished her sentence she proclaimed that she'd prefer that to being surrounded by her complicated family situation.

Both her mother's and father's sides of the family were grieving in different ways, and some people were probably having a harder time than others. Louise's awareness that other people's influence on her emotional state of mind could be very detrimental was key, and she did indeed have a choice as to whether she chose to expose herself to that or keep a measured distance.

Affirmation

Louise made many positive statements during our interview about herself and her ability to cope. These internal commands, such as 'I'm still here', 'I'm stronger than I look' are also known as affirmations and are important as they act like instructions that, when repeated with clarity and conviction, become actual beliefs.

Mine has always been 'I deserve a good life' – what's yours?

Keeping memories alive

Louise understood from early on in the grieving process that you have to remember those you've lost in order to move through the stages of grief. In visiting cousins, aunts and uncles soon after her mother's death, she was able to reminisce about her parents, sharing stories and memories, which made her feel closer to them. Louise had mentioned on numerous occasions that no matter how difficult her upbringing, she never had anything but love for the people who brought her into the world.

It is commendable and positive to allow thoughts and memories of your loved one to enter your mind or to talk about them when this can be painful, but it's those memories that effectively serve as the oil that keeps the engines of grief management running.

Disagreeing with our innate tendency to find guilt

Louise was also able to contemplate some of the choices she had made, about how often she had seen her parents, without retrospectively placing a hefty burden of guilt on herself. She knew she couldn't have been there every minute of the day for them and in talking about her choice to have left her hometown to work in London she told me: 'My dad didn't want me to stay with him and I can't feel guilty that I wasn't there, because he wanted me to be in London pursuing a modelling career and a better life. He was really proud of me for following my dreams.'

In remembering, with clarity and maturity, the reality of her situation, she set herself free from the guilt that could have consumed her. She did what she could; she supported her father in a way that was accepted by all of those involved in his life. Nobody had any complaints at the time, and in being strong enough to do so why would she herself move the goalposts after her father's death?

This is another good example of how being realistic with our expectations allows us to survive grief. She didn't suddenly accuse herself of doing wrong or not doing enough; her actions were as acceptable after they died as they were before.

Finding focus and setting targets

People often describe grief as an upwards spiral. It takes you to places emotionally that you've never been before. Those with a survival mindset put some markers ahead of themselves so that gives them something to aim for, which stops them from involuntarily slipping into bad habits or feeling like they are going round and round a roundabout without ever knowing when to indicate and turn.

Louise got to grips with this by setting herself some fresh and challenging goals. 'I climbed Everest after my dad passed. I wanted to divert all of the negativity by raising money for the British Lung Foundation, a charity that meant so much to me.'

It's no coincidence that Louise gravitated to a challenge that would test her ability to breathe, as a way of showing solidarity and sharing her father's pain. It is very moving to me that she put herself through something that brought her closer to the conditions or difficulties her loved ones experienced before their deaths.

Doing things that 'make them proud'

In grief it makes us feel good if we are in some way carrying out the wishes of our loved ones or repeating the acts that brought them some enjoyment and pride when they were alive. While Louise had always been interested in fitness, competing and pushing herself, something her parents were proud of, wanting to go that step further by training and then climbing Everest, she had that added incentive of not just doing it for herself, but for them too. Grief is a powerful motivation when it's channelled in a positive direction.

There are many things we can do to honour a loved one – raising money for a charity they supported, or which supported them through their illness, will make you feel like someone else might be able to avoid what you've been through. In organising your event you will, like Louise, release positive energy in the process and it's a beautiful way of staying connected to someone in thought and action.

Acceptance

Acceptance is such a big ingredient in the experience of grief and it is far harder to get to the 'other side' of your grief management if you don't have it. A survival mindset looks for acceptance and asks the necessary questions in order to achieve it. You can really either run from it or walk to it. Running from it delays the process, whereas walking to it means you are experiencing grief without adding unwanted complications.

Louise had accepted the choices her parents made, difficult as they were for her. 'I knew growing up that Mum and Dad were not going to last like normal parents because of the lifestyle they chose. Many times I wanted to save them, but I learned that unless they chose to help themselves, then nothing I tried to make them do was going to help. That was their lifestyle and I couldn't change anything about that side of things.'

This situation will apply to few of us, thankfully, but sometimes the outcome of someone's life isn't a huge shock given the lifestyle they lived or habits they suffered from. It doesn't make the result any more welcome but Louise demonstrated that a survival mindset doesn't overlook the breadcrumbs that were dropped leading up to the event and that she had fully accepted that her loss was not her responsibility.

Louise told me, somewhat romantically, that 'My mum died of heartbreak. After Dad died she was just lost within herself. She's with her best friend and that's where she would have wanted to be.'

This sort of idealistic notion isn't for everyone but it helped Louise accept her mother's death and worked for her.

What we do after the event of death depends on expectations. Do we have a survival mindset or do we expect ourselves not to cope, or refuse to cope for that matter? There are so many different ways we can influence our mindset both positively and negatively, and if you are finding it harder to accept your loss than you anticipated, you need to think about your expectations of yourself in grief.

Resilience

'Be strong!' – in my opinion, the most unhelpful and overused phrase that's ever been uttered to those grieving. In the past, when showing emotions was less acceptable, it usually meant 'Don't cry, because we all feel uncomfortable around emotion.' Nowadays, we are less harsh on those who show emotion in public and allowing yourself to cry and express vulnerability is far from being weak, as there is usually progress at the end of your tears.

Louise had signed up to climb Everest after her dad died and it was during her training period that she lost her mum. Far from giving in, she saw the opportunity to take steps towards recognising both losses by taking her mother's ashes with her on the trip.

A little resilience and strength go a long way in grief. Looking at ways we can face our loss with resolve and fortitude helps with the grieving process.

Knowing your comforts

Louise identified and held on to the invaluable comforts she collected and cherished both leading up to and after her dad's death. In the final days of her dad's life, he leaned on her as they listened to his favourite albums by Pink Floyd. She also held on to the memory of the crowd of people outside the church gathered for his funeral. She felt – and to this day still feels – proud that so many people turned up. These are the memories that you realise become more and more priceless as time goes by and we can all, while there is time, go and make some more with those we love.

Louise painfully recalled how 'after three days of being back home from the hospital' after one of her mum's strokes, her mother's partner sickeningly beat her up. 'I was miles away in London so I called my aunty who went to get her and took her to my brother's house. It brought me enormous comfort to know that when she suffered the heart attack that killed her, she died in my brother's arms, away from her abusive partner.'

Comforts are the fuel that will help you to remember positively. We can so easily dwell on what didn't happen, what could have been, why we didn't do this, why they didn't do that, but those regrets will never change the past, least of all bring anyone back.

Visualising happiness

Louise used her imagination to create a wonderful visual image of what her parents might be doing while at rest. 'They're in heaven together,' she said dreamily, 'riding their motorbikes and having fun like they did when they were young and in love.' This is a great survival tactic, allowing ourselves comfort by dreaming of people we love being happy and in Louise's parents' case, reunited.

Communication and permission

Louise told me: 'I often felt so selfish and guilty for not being there to take care of Dad when his COPD worsened. I would wake up in the middle of the night consumed with guilt, but most of the time when I called my dad and aunty, they reassured me that he was comfortable and how proud of me he was for all I was doing in my career. I felt so much better for that and I took their reassurances as permission to carry on.'

By communicating her constant desire to travel back up north and put her life on hold, her family could see that she was thinking about them and was willing to return home and help care for her dad. Knowing this, I am sure, contributed to the fact that, despite the pressures they must have been under, they were able to reassure her that they had everything under control and that it was very much her father's wishes that he wanted her to stay in London pursuing her dream.

Simply put, if you or others give permission to know you're doing or have done enough, then you are less likely to experience guilt at any stage. If you can't give yourself that permission, then you're potentially imprisoning yourself in a self-made cell with walls made of the blame you've put on yourself. If you visualise that image for a moment, you can ask yourself if you put yourself inside that cell and then ask who has the key, or if the door is even locked, and most importantly, what stops you from walking out and being blameless or guilt-free?

Responsibility

A common way of getting through grief is the ability to keep going in spite of your loss. Those of us with children will recognise the great motivation they give us to make life as normal as possible, to help us find an extra gear that we may not have known we even had.

It was the same for Louise, who told me: 'After the man who abused me was sent to jail, I was put in care until my aunt on my dad's side came and got me. My brother stayed with Mum's side of the family and I don't think they should have ever split us siblings up. I was also disconnected from my twin sisters, who were my mum's with another man, and they went straight to his side of the family, but I wrote to them every year on their birthday and was reunited with them when they turned eighteen.'

It was apparent throughout the chat I had with Louise that she took responsibility for those affected by the mistakes of others, when many would just have been concerned with their own grievances.

Taking charge like that can also be a coping mechanism and in some cases can be adopted to distract yourself from what you are going through. It's fine to be the captain leading everyone on, taking responsibility for those around you, as long as you make sure you allow yourself moments of emotional clarity, while being true to your loss.

Respect

Louise had a difficult and at times troubling childhood and maybe someone who had had her experiences would be better equipped to deal with the challenge of grief when it happens. But Louise was still able to show respect to her parents, which helped her connect to her losses.

She told me a little about a memory of her mum's funeral: 'My brother, twin sisters and I brought my mum a hundred red roses and laid fifty of them on top of the casket and I can't even describe just how beautiful it looked.' The emotional freedom and relief this allowed Louise to feel stayed with her long after the funeral and the respect shown to her mother's memory will always be with her.

Summary

A survival mindset doesn't make you impervious to grief. It's not a shield or impenetrable force field. It simply means that if grief were a person, you would accept their arrival and work on your relationship with them, learning to co-exist and not allowing yourself to be intimidated as you swung from being passive, equal or dominant in that relationship.

While Louise may appear to be top of the class as far as bereavement is concerned, her mindset and ability to overcome the details surrounding the loss of both her parents, particularly given the hardships of her life, is an inspiration to us all. Don't for one second think that she hasn't had her struggles, just like all of us. But she has thought about things, faced up to the reality of her situation and past and done things to face and embrace grief.

To encourage a survival mindset takes time, patience and a whole lot of mistakes along the way, because there is no such thing as failure in grief, just tools you can use to bring about a more desired outcome next time a wave of grief hits your shores.

Acknowledgements

A big thank you to Briony Gowlett at Hodder for seeing the profound need for the bookstore shelves to feature an accessible guide to bereavement, written by a normal person, for normal people.

To Carolyn Mays and everyone at Hodder for backing the acquisition and publication of the book. They have worked tirelessly with me on this project.

To Gillian Stern for keeping my work to the highest possible standard even if at times I felt the editing process was the worst experience of my life!

To Louise Swannell for creating so many opportunities for me to talk about grief and encourage others to think of their own.

To Sarah Christie for helping me to create a front cover that I am exceptionally proud of.

To my beautiful partner Kate for living and breathing this project with me for 4 very solid months.

To my children Bobby and Freddy for keeping my motivation up by reminding me how proud they are of me for writing this book.

To my agent Nick Canham for believing in the premise of the book and getting me in front of the right people to carry this project over the line.

To those that have selflessly contributed to this book by sharing their own personal stories:

To the memory of Mary Turner, a courageous woman who shared her final months with me before her life sadly ended on the 12th of April 2017.

To Shelly Gilbert for her expertise and knowledge on all things child bereavement related. The person I always turn to for answers and a constant support for myself and my children.

To a young mother Heidi McLoughlin who shared the despair caused by her life-limiting prognosis.

To Dawn Sharpe, the miracle worker who has turned a 2 year prognosis into 7 . . . and counting.

To Aundrea Bannatyne for letting me in to how she cannot and will not accept that cancer will take her life irrespective of what the doctors say.

To Amy Scrivener who taught me what it was like to lose a partner that you didn't get to say goodbye to and be left with two children coping with the worst news imaginable.

To Vikki Bussell for showing me what death denial looks like and the effects it inevitably has on one's life and those around us.

To my Grandmother Molly Faldo for sharing her feelings of blame for those responsible for my father's death and her thoughts on why she can't let go of it nearly 30 years on.

To Stephanie Orange for sharing her incredible story of how she managed to finally start the grieving process around 10 years after she lost her father.

To Jo Coare for allowing me to help her to unravel the heightened complications in grief caused when you lose more than one person in a short space of time.

To Michelle Maher for teaching me what it felt like to be an adult orphan in her early 40's and allowing me to help her understand some of the effects that was having on the way she was bringing up her own child.

To Ragan Montgomery and Liz Henry of LCF Law for giving me

the legal insight and professional angle on family disputes and employment issues surrounding grief.

To Zoe Clark-Coates for sharing her story of multiple child loss. The feelings that it generates and the loneliness caused by grieving a loss that few people want to acknowledge or understand.

To John Frangiamore at Albert English Funeral Directors in Harlow for letting me in to the world of funerals and those that facilitate our most feared occasions on almost a daily basis.

To James Mace for sharing the details of the untimely deaths of his Mum and Nephew so we could identify the rules of grief he was placing upon himself as we all so very often do.

To Natasha for sharing the unimaginable loss of her daughter to suicide and the guilt that it has created causing such a lack of motivation in her life.

To Beverley Warner, bereavement counsellor from St Clare's Hospice who gave me an insight into the end of life stages and the small but vital details that families should know about if that is where they sadly find themselves.

To Nikki Truman for the intriguing insight into anticipatory grief caused by the dementia currently being suffered by her father.

To Conor Sharpe for breaking his silence, sharing his feelings about his Mother Dawn living with a terminal prognosis and discussing how he has come to believe that he is keeping his Mum alive.

To Charlie Donovan who at just 12 years of age bravely shared with me the fears he has for losing his father who only has a short time left to live.

To Louise Glover for sharing one of the strongest insights of a survival mindset in her account of not just the loss of both of her parents but a life spent surviving, which has given her the tools to cope with grief in the most constructive of ways.

To Samantha Martin for sharing her honest and insightful perspective on the unique effects grief has when it is combined with pre-existing family issues.

To the incredible Dad that is Martin Hall for sharing the difficulties he has faced in losing his wife and bringing up two bereaved children and for always contributing when I needed other people's views.

To Lydia Frempong for giving me great insight into why we place so much pressure on ourselves to visit the grave and answer many questions I had about the locations we like to remember our loved ones from.

To Cheryle Smith for sharing the pain caused by the recent loss of her father and helping me to challenge a template for all bereaved individuals to be able to establish exactly where they are at with their grief through measurement and timescale.

To my next door neighbour Dan Thurgood for sharing the transition from the 'typical bloke' dealing with bereavement in a less constructive way to what he would now describe as being a parent who, through the love of his children, has learned to express his emotions far more freely.

To Jenny Swift for sharing her concerns relating to the changes at work that would affect her employment status and financial stability whilst anticipating grief.

To my old school friend Rob Tadman who let me in beautifully to the male perspective and a wonderful reflection of what he would have done differently following the loss of his wife.

To Mrs Haswell for her care and attention and for being the teacher in Freddy's junior school who wanted to know more about how grief will affect a child in the classroom.

To Saying Goodbye, the leading division of the Mariposa Trust, for all the work they are doing. If you need support following the loss of a baby during pregnancy, at birth or in early years, contact them via their website – www.sayinggoodbye.org, or on Twitter: @sayinggoodbyeUK and on Facebook at: /SayinggoodbyeUK

To those that have contributed to my Facebook group for all things relevant to this book. your help was invaluable in allowing me to form a balance within each chapter so thank you Moira, Angela, Lisa, Catherine, Victoria, Ryan, Linda and Charlotte for those insights.